PENGUIN ENGLISH LIBRARY

# CONFESSIONS OF AN ENGLISH OPIUM EATER

## THOMAS DE QUINCEY

Alethea Hayter has written *Opium and the Romantic Imagination*, *Mrs Browning: a Poet's Work and its Setting*, *A Sultry Month*, *Horatio's Version* and *A Voyage in Vain: Coleridge's Journey to Malta in 1804*. She has also edited *Melmoth the Wanderer* by Charles Maturin for the Penguin English Library.

THOMAS DE QUINCEY

*Confessions of an
English Opium Eater*

EDITED WITH AN
INTRODUCTION BY
ALETHEA HAYTER

PENGUIN BOOKS

Penguin Books Ltd, Harmondsworth, Middlesex, England
Penguin Books, 625 Madison Avenue, New York, New York 10022, U.S.A.
Penguin Books Australia Ltd, Ringwood, Victoria, Australia
Penguin Books Canada Ltd, 2801 John Street, Markham, Ontario, Canada L3R 1B4
Penguin Books (N.Z.) Ltd, 182–190 Wairau Road, Auckland 10, New Zealand

—

First published in the *London Magazine* 1821
Published in Penguin Books 1971
Reprinted 1973, 1975, 1976, 1978, 1979, 1981, 1982

—

Introduction and notes copyright © Alethea Hayter, 1971
All rights reserved

—

Made and printed in Great Britain by
Hazell Watson & Viney Ltd,
Aylesbury, Bucks
Set in Linotype Juliana

# Contents

Introduction 7

Note on the Text 25

Suggested Further Reading 26

CONFESSIONS OF AN ENGLISH OPIUM EATER 29

Appendix: De Quincey's Second Thoughts about the
*Confessions*
    A. Notes, Letters and Articles Commenting on the
       *Confessions*, 1821–55 117
    B. Selected Passages from the 1856 Revision 135

Notes 216

# Introduction

A TRUTHFUL *Confessions of an English Heroin Addict*, written today by a typical user of the drug, would present a world of pallid queues at all-night chemists, of weary doctors arguing with lying persistent junkies, of pushers slipping packets into waiting hands in amusement arcades and public lavatories. It would be a scene of squalor and procrastination, of infected syringes, of dishevelled bivouacs in derelict houses, of the restlessness and dirt of withdrawal symptoms; a scene of complacent apathy, of capricious unfocused protest, and the hard hands of policemen.

A century and a half ago, when Thomas de Quincey wrote his *Confessions*, the situation of an opium addict was very different. He was breaking no law, public opinion was not against him or focused on him, supplies of the drug were cheap and easy to buy, and its dangers – though nearly as great then as now – were not understood. Anyone who expects to find in De Quincey's account of his experiences a parallel with the kind of evidence given in police-courts and medical case-histories today will not only get some surprises, but will miss the main drift of De Quincey's book.

He did indeed share with other addicts of his own and our times the pariah temperament which makes such a life supportable, even preferable. He led a pariah life of this kind during the months of his truancy in London, years before he started taking opium, and later he experienced much of the squalor and degradation of addiction, more so after he wrote the *Confessions of an English Opium Eater* than before. He felt the indolence and despair, the detested craving, the reproach of vital tasks unperformed, the disgusts and indignities of withdrawal periods; he lived with chaotic rooms, disordered clothes, hunger, homelessness and dirt.

But very little of this appears in the *Confessions*. It is not what they were about. They are a meditation on the mechanism of the imagination, an exploration of the interior life of an altogether exceptional being who happened also to be an opium eater, but from whose experience no valid conclusions can be drawn about

7

what will happen to the ordinary opium addict. 'Was it opium, or was it opium in combination with something else, that raised these storms?' he asked himself many years later, and concluded that it was the 'something else' – a natural dreaming faculty enhanced by deeply felt griefs in childhood – that accounted for his extraordinary visions under the influence of opium.

De Quincey included some of the events of his early life in the *Confessions*, to explain why he became an opium eater, what sort of personality the opium worked on, and whence came the beings and landscapes that were transmuted into his dreams. Later in his life he came to see more clearly, and to relate in a series of autobiographical revelations, the full connection between his youthful experiences and his later visions: how childhood events and emotions, adolescent encounters, things read and things seen, combined into new imaginative patterns which dominated his dreams. This was to have been the theme of his *Suspiria de Profundis*, the never-completed sequel to the *Confessions of an English Opium Eater*. The picture of his own early history which he later unveiled helps to explain the psychological background to his first work, the *Confessions*.

Thomas de Quincey was born in 1785. He was the second son of a Manchester merchant who died of tuberculosis when Thomas was seven. The return of the dying man, in a carriage whose slow approach through dark lanes was heard from far away by his waiting family, became a component of many of De Quincey's subsequent dreams of solemn processions of doom. After his father's death, De Quincey's upbringing was in the hands of his mother and his guardians, who were just but unimaginative. For a time he was bullied by his wildly inventive and aggressive elder brother William. His real allies and sympathizers in his family were his sisters. Two of them, one especially beloved, died as children. The death of the nine-year-old Elizabeth, in the height of summer, and a trance which the six-year-old Thomas experienced as he stood beside her body, were among the strongest themes of his adult dreams, to which all his later experiences of girl children suffering, betrayed, dying, attached themselves in his imagination.

De Quincey thus had early experiences of sorrow from losing those of his family who loved him best, and from a failure in sympathy by those who survived. But his was not really an oppressed or deprived childhood. His family life was stable and prosperous, if not congenial; he was neither neglected nor ill-treated. But he was under psychological pressure. His mother's stern sense of duty, the exacting tasks of memorizing which his tutor-guardian imposed, his elder brother's contempt for his dreaminess and inadequacy, all made him feel that much was expected of him. Lessons were easy to him, but he could not fit into the strait-jacket of normal regularity into which his family and friends wanted to insert him.

There was in fact no need for him to be afraid of inadequacy. He was outstandingly clever and gifted; though very small in stature, he had a fine elegant face and much charm of manner; and almost everyone he ever met took to him instantly. Crusty old schoolmasters, mill-girls, rascally attorneys, saintly recluses, prostitutes, Irish noblemen, Scottish professors, everyone from George III to a half-starved kitchen-maid succumbed to his charm. He was an especial favourite with charming and clever young women, from the sophisticated Lady Carbery to the shy and visionary Dorothy Wordsworth. Children trusted him at once; total strangers did him services. Few men have had less need to fear social or intellectual failure. But the 'chronic passion of anxiety', as he himself put it, from which he suffered is not a rational calculation of the probabilities of failure or success; it is a disease, unaffected by the lessons of experience. He recognized in himself a 'craze for being despised', a 'perpetual sense of desertion'. In after-life he established a kind of equilibrium – an invulnerable secret life of the mind, behind a psychological wall of glass through which he looked out with affectionate sympathy towards others, but through which no demands, no sympathies, no approaches, could reach back to him. But in his early days he was still vulnerable.

He was sent to three schools, in Bath, Wiltshire and Manchester, and at all of them he was brilliantly successful in his work, got on well with the other boys, and found some of the masters congenial. His last school was the famous Manchester

Grammar School, and there he enjoyed the stimulus of working with other brilliant minds; a discipline preserved by the boys themselves, without bullying or beating; the indulgence of a room to himself, with a piano and all the books he wanted. Yet he felt that he must escape. The reasons that he gave – that lack of opportunities for exercise gave him a depressing liver complaint, aggravated by the mistaken treatment which a local apothecary administered; and that he wanted to go immediately to a university, instead of staying on at school for another year, but his guardian would not agree to this – hardly seem enough to explain his overmastering impulse to get away, to cut himself off from everyone that he knew, from all the planned security of home and school. It was the working-out of the sense of inadequacy imposed on him by his upbringing, which made him feel himself a pariah, a drop-out. But he was not the kind of drop-out who feels that the world owes him a living but that he owes no obligations to anyone or anything. He was always able to see other people's points of view, and to recognize his own mistakes.

His flight from school, his wanderings on foot through Wales, his desperate journey to London to raise money on his expectations, his months of near-starvation there in the winter of 1802–3 while he waited for the money-lenders' advances, his friendship with the fifteen-year-old prostitute Ann, are vividly described in the *Confessions*. His mother had given him a meagre allowance of a guinea a week while he was in Wales, but when he went to London he cut himself off from all supplies from his family, who did not know what had happened to him. In the months of 1802 and 1803 which he spent in Wales and London, he had not yet tasted opium, and he was not to become a regular addict for another ten years; but these months were crucial for his opium experience. The privations he then suffered were the cause of the painful gastric disease for which he began to take opium as a regular anodyne ten years later; and the emotions of anxiety, of fear over wrong choices, of partings and exclusions and resentments, the visions of endless crowds of faces, of great cavernous buildings, and of a betrayed and lost girl, became the master themes of the terrific dreams which he experienced under opium.

In the spring of 1804 his family discovered his whereabouts and there was a reconciliation. In the winter he became an undergraduate at Worcester College, Oxford, where he remained till 1808, leading a solitary life and studying hard, but he left the University without taking a degree. His father had left him enough money to live on, and for the next few years he wandered between London, Westmorland and the West Country, spending much of his time in the study of the German philosophers Kant, Schelling and Fichte. He hoped eventually to write a great work of philosophy himself; the name, taken from Spinoza, was to be *De emendatione humani intellectus*. But in fact he never published any book before the *Confessions*.

In 1807, on a visit to Somerset, he met Coleridge. The relationship between the two men was never an easy or relaxed friendship; each knew or suspected the other's addiction to opium, and a fog of unacknowledged guilt and disingenuous excuses obscured their view of each other. But De Quincey deeply admired the older writer's genius, and soon after their meeting he generously and anonymously lent Coleridge £300. When De Quincey settled in Westmorland, he saw a good deal of Coleridge at Keswick and Allan Bank, and they also met in London, where De Quincey often listened to the great glittering monologues which were Coleridge's conception of conversation. At this period, Coleridge's addiction to opium was far more advanced than De Quincey's.

In the original version of the *Confessions*, De Quincey referred to Coleridge's addiction only twice, in passing, and not by name. But after Coleridge's death in 1834, one of his biographers published a letter from him about De Quincey's *Confessions* in which he blamed De Quincey for taking opium to obtain pleasurable sensations, although Coleridge had warned him against it; in the same letter Coleridge claimed that he himself had taken opium only as an anodyne against pain. De Quincey was not unnaturally cut to the quick by this stab from a man whom he revered and had helped; and thereafter his published references to Coleridge were indiscreet and sometimes spiteful. His *Reminiscences of the Lake Poets* contained passages which Coleridge's friends much resented; and when he revised the *Confessions* in 1856 he inserted several passages maintaining that he and

Coleridge were alike driven to opium as an anodyne for acute pain, and that both of them could have renounced it sooner if they had not both come to relish the pleasurable sensations which it brought. He also mocked Coleridge for his overpowering monologues, the lugubrious wail in which he read aloud his own poetry, the sweaty shine of his face when an exceptionally large opium dose incapacitated him from writing.

These passages show the least attractive side of De Quincey's character, his resentful malice when he thought that he or those whom he loved had been unjustly treated. But they are valuable as lively if slightly caricatured sketches of Coleridge and, as he said in defence of Coleridge against a charge of having unfairly attacked Pitt, 'Malice is not always of the heart; there is a malice of the understanding and the fancy.' His own malice was more fanciful than heartfelt.

De Quincey's reverence for Wordsworth was a much deeper and more lasting sentiment than his feeling for Coleridge. He boldly claimed to be 'the very earliest (without one exception) of all who came forward, in the beginning of his career, to honour and welcome him'. When De Quincey ran away from Manchester Grammar School, he thought of making for Westmorland to see Wordsworth, but was deterred by the shame which his escapade would cast over a first meeting with the object of his veneration. In the following year he sent a fan letter to Wordsworth, and received a kind reply encouraging him to visit Westmorland; but diffidence prevented him from doing so till, in 1807, he volunteered to escort Mrs Coleridge back to Westmorland, and at last met the Wordsworths under these auspices. He became a friend of the whole family, specially of Dorothy, and an affectionate playfellow of the Wordsworth children. He was particularly fond of little Kate Wordsworth, and her death in 1812 caused him to have something like a nervous breakdown, perhaps the origin of the revived gastric complaint which in 1813 finally drove him to daily opium-taking.

For Wordsworth's sake De Quincey spent many months of 1809 in London, seeing the poet's pamphlet, *The Convention of Cintra*, through the press, harassed by and harassing both poet and printers. When the Wordsworth family outgrew their Grasmere cottage and moved to a larger house, he took over the cottage, which remained his home for many years. It has been conjectured that the Wordsworths expected, or at least hoped, that De Quincey would marry Dorothy Wordsworth, and that this explains their hostility when De Quincey began a liaison with a local farmer's daughter, Margaret Simpson, by whom he had a son in 1816 and whom he married the following spring. In these years the Wordsworths broke off almost all connection with De Quincey, near neighbours though they still were. De Quincey felt that his wife had been ostracized, unjustly insulted; and her image coalesced with those other betrayed and suffering girls who already haunted his imagination. The working-out of this complex of feeling is shown in the beautiful Easter dream recorded under the 'Pains of Opium' section in the *Confessions*, in which De Quincey wanders out at dawn into the valley of Grasmere, grown huge with the magic expansion of dreams, and sees the grave of the child Kate Wordsworth, and promises himself that 'old griefs shall be forgotten today', and then sees a vision of Ann of Oxford Street, the archetype of the wronged girl with whom his wife and her griefs had become identified – her griefs at the Wordsworths' hands which had darkened for him the valley where once he was so happy with their dead child, whose memory now called on him to wash away resentment with Easter dew.

For the rest of his life De Quincey continued to admire and constantly quote Wordsworth's poetry, but neither side any longer felt the warm affection that once had made him almost a part of the Wordsworth family. The only relics of that were the all too intimate descriptions of their appearance and habits which De Quincey was able to give when he wrote his *Reminiscences of the Lake Poets*. Their estrangement after the publication of these articles was scarcely surprising, but their original turning against him was very possibly due not so much to his irregular union with Margaret Simpson as to his increasing opium addiction, so miserably reminiscent of what the Wordworths had suffered with Coleridge.

De Quincey describes in the *Confessions* how he first tasted opium in 1804, when an undergraduate friend of his recommended

13

it as a remedy for the violent neuralgia from which De Quincey was then suffering. In the next few years he used it partly as an anodyne for gastric pain, and to ward off the incipient tuberculosis to which he was believed to be succumbing. He also took it as a tranquillizer in moments of anxiety, as when he was taking his final examinations at Oxford, which he abandoned halfway through. But above all, he took it in search of pleasurable sensations, for the sake of euphoria, freedom from worry and from inadequacy. At first he took it only about once every three weeks; by 1812 he was taking it once a week; in 1813, after a painful gastric disorder, he started taking it daily. By 1816 his dosage was 320 grains, or 8,000 drops, a day. Strictly speaking, De Quincey was an opium drinker, not an opium eater; he generally took the drug in the form of laudanum, that is, of alcoholic tincture of opium. 320 grains a day, and still more the 480 grains a day which De Quincey's addiction reached at its extreme heights in 1817–18 and in 1843, have been considered an impossibility by some modern experts. Twenty grains of heroin a day is regarded as a fairly advanced addict's dose now. De Quincey may have exaggerated, as addicts commonly do about the extent of their dosage. In any case his opium was diluted by alcohol in the laudanum which he took.

He had no trouble in procuring it; it could then be bought over the counter without prescription in any chemist's shop for a very low price – De Quincey's original purchase in 1804, which was enough for several doses, cost less than a shilling. Opium-taking, even regular opium addiction, were commonplaces in the early nineteenth century, though few men indulged in the enormous quantities that De Quincey and Coleridge took. Its perils were little understood; the very possibility of becoming addicted to it was not generally recognized. It was the pain-killer most often prescribed by doctors for maladies of all kinds, and every household had a supply of it. Many respected public figures took it daily without concealment or shame. Besides the ones whom De Quincey mentions in the *Confessions* – William Wilberforce the Emancipator of the Slaves, Dean Milner, Lord Erskine, Henry Addington, Coleridge – there were the poet George Crabbe, the Baptist preacher Robert Hall, the lawyer and writer Sir James

Mackintosh. A whole host of industrial workers in the North of England, both men and women, took it weekly, as a cheaper escape from their miseries than either beer or gin. Mothers and nurses gave it to fretful children. Writers, painters, doctors, used it to tranquillize their nerves. De Quincey's *Confessions* were the first indication to the general public that opium was special in any way, either as an inspiration or as a danger.

By 1818 De Quincey's increasing family and vanishing income made it imperative for him to do something to earn his livelihood. He managed during the next three years to get his opium dosage down to 300 drops a day, and reluctantly he turned to journalism to earn bread for his family. For sixteen months he edited a local newspaper, the *Westmorland Gazette*, but his esoteric intellectual tastes and dilatory business methods were most unsuited to such a task, and he had to give it up. Other journalistic openings were available. His old friend John Wilson, once a neighbour in the Lake District and now a principal contributor to the Edinburgh magazine *Blackwood's*, had long been trying to induce De Quincey to contribute articles or reviews to the magazine, and in December 1820 De Quincey finally went to Edinburgh with a view to becoming a regular contributor. His only published work so far had been a Postscript to Wordworth's *Convention of Cintra* pamphlet, and the anonymous editorials and other articles which he had written for the *Westmorland Gazette*. But his friends, who had perhaps seen unpublished drafts of his, and who knew how prodigiously stocked with learning his memory was and had heard his absorbing conversation, were convinced that he could be a brilliant writer if he would only apply himself to it.

Arrived in Edinburgh, he started work on half a dozen articles for *Blackwood's*, among them one which he referred to as 'the Opium article'. Searching for subjects which he could turn into money, he had the inspiration of making use of the strange experiences through which he had passed. 'Opium has reduced me for the last six years to one general discourtesy of utter silence. But this I shall think of with not so much pain, if this same opium enables me (as I think it will) to send you an article not unserviceable to your magazine,' he wrote to Blackwood. He may already have written the passages on his dreams in the 'Pains of

Opium' section of the *Confessions*, which he afterwards said was the only part of the work not written in a hurry. They had, he said, been 'composed slowly, and by separate efforts of thought, at wide intervals of time, according to the actual prevalence, at any particular time, of the separate elements of such dream in my own real dream-experience'. While he was in Edinburgh he arranged these and other 'notes and memoranda' on his opium experiences with a view to the article for *Blackwood's*. But early in January 1821 he quarrelled with Blackwood, who took too seriously a rather heavy-footed joke of De Quincey's and was irritated by his endless delays. The connection was broken off, and *Blackwood's* lost the chance of publishing the narrative which was to make such an immense sensation a few months later.

De Quincey went back to Grasmere, but four months later his desperate need to earn some money sent him to London, armed with a letter from Wordsworth to the barrister and writer Thomas Noon Talfourd, who in turn introduced him to Taylor and Hessey, proprietors and joint editors of the *London Magazine*. Taylor and Hessey were interested by De Quincey's offer of an article on his opium experiences, the project which he had begun in Edinburgh the previous winter, and he set to work to finish it. He found lodgings at 4 York Street, Covent Garden, and there in a small back room, during the late summer of 1821, he completed the *Confessions of an English Opium Eater*.

It was a rushed job, giving him no time for revision, barely for proof-reading, since the narrative was to appear in the September and October issues of the *London Magazine*. Moreover he was writing without the help of his wife, who usually acted as his amanuensis and kept his papers in order. He had the passages on the dreams, and the notes which he had prepared the previous Christmas; writing from memory, he hastily composed the narrative leading up to the climax of the dreams. The effort needed for this strenuous job was only summoned up by renewed recourse to opium. He found that by suddenly increasing his doses for a few days running, he enjoyed a glow of mental energy, 'preter-natural paroxysms of intermitting power' in which he could write brilliantly; but he paid for it by heavy suffering when the paroxysm was over.

*Introduction*

It is not surprising that a work written in these circumstances has no firm logical structure, and that De Quincey's theories and deductions on opium addiction are scattered here and there in the narrative of his life. As he himself said, his way of writing was like thinking aloud, it followed the movements of his own mind. But the sweep of his narrative, and the sustained interest of what he has to tell, carry the work along with such impetus that it is only afterwards, when one analyses or summarizes it, that the lack of logical sequence becomes apparent.

The title which De Quincey chose for his narrative has inevitably provoked comparisons with the *Confessions* of Rousseau; and perhaps De Quincey's claim to be unique, an unparalleled special case, and to strict frankness, do owe something to Rousseau's example. But he disavowed the connection; he made this clear on the first page of his work by referring scornfully to 'the spectacle of a human being obtruding on our notice his moral ulcers or scars' with 'the spurious and defective sensibility of the French'. There was in fact an essential difference between his approach and Rousseau's; he undertook to tell the truth, but not the whole truth; in everything that concerned his relationships with other people, on every fact whose revelation might embarrass or hurt the living or their families, he kept a decent reticence. His revelations were confined to his own interior life. In this aspect, the nearest parallel to De Quincey's *Confessions* was the Methodist or Evangelical narratives of religious conversion, in which men who, after a wandering and dissatisfied youth, had found salvation, told of their personal experience in the hope of helping others. De Quincey spoke of his discovery of opium as though it were a revelation of divine truth : 'This is the doctrine of the true church on the subject of opium, of which I acknowledge myself to be the only member.' That, with a suspicion of mocking parody, is the language of the tracts of 'witness' handed round among Evangelical and dissenting sects such as the Clapham Saints by whom De Quincey's mother was converted.

De Quincey's disclosures about the effects of opium were so novel and fascinating that they have preoccupied the attention of readers of the *Confessions* ever since, but they are not the most important part of the work. Opium, not the opium eater, was the 'true hero of the tale', he said; not in itself, but because of its 'marvellous agency' on the human mind. Twenty-four years later he wrote that 'the object of that work was to reveal something of the grandeur which belongs *potentially* to human dreams ... The *Opium Confessions* were written with some slight secondary purpose of exposing this specific power of opium upon the faculty of dreaming, but much more with the purpose of displaying the faculty itself.' The real originality of the *Confessions* is not their record of a case of opium addiction, but their pioneering study of the operation of the subconscious mind in dreams. In them De Quincey began the exploration, which he carried much further in his later work *Suspiria de Profundis*, of how the mind, especially in childhood, registers experience in the shape of concrete objects which become linked together in subconscious patterns, 'involutes' as he called them. These involutes, which are ever afterwards associated with particular events and emotions, are crystallized by the dreaming mind. The symbolic patterns of dreams reveal the formative influences of childhood and youth. Everyone knows this now, but De Quincey revealed it twenty-five years before Freud was born.

He included the narrative of his childhood and youth, the 'Preliminary Confessions', in the plan of his work because, as he said, it furnished 'a key to some parts of that tremendous scenery which afterwards peopled the dreams of the opium eater'. The tragedy of the fifteen-year-old prostitute Ann of Oxford Street, blending with the ill-treated child servant in the attorney's house (and, as he later revealed, with memories of his own sisters and of Wordsworth's daughter Kate, who all died as children, and with his own suffering young wife), produced the ever-recurring dream pattern of a lost betrayed girl-child, an innocent pariah. The slow approach at night of the carriage bringing home his dying father, joined with organ music heard at funerals and with cathedral processions, became what he called 'an ineffaceable agency among my dreams', a vision of vast marches and cavalcades and reverberating anthems. The severe faces of his mother, his guardians, his schoolmasters, the curious gaze of London passers-by, all watching him, all expecting him to conform to some impossible norm of behaviour, became the innumerable faces which surged up through the sea-waves of his nightmares. Lines of poetry, anecdotes from history, visual impressions of his surroundings, casual encounters with strangers, twined themselves into his involutes and floated up with them to the surface of his dreams. His visual reactions to the taste of his day in architecture, sculpture and interior decoration, to Neo-Classic friezes and medallions, to Chinoiserie screens covered with pagodas and dragons, to chairs in the Egyptian taste with sphinx-head arm-rests and gryphon-clawed feet, proliferated into his nightmares. The Neo-Classic friezes became vast Roman processions of Consuls carried in triumph and of marching shouting legions. The pagodas on the Chinoiserie screens engulfed him in their narrow secret rooms. The claw feet of the chairs writhed and swelled into crocodiles.

Descriptions of even the wildest dreams can be very boring. De Quincey's dreams are unforgettably vivid and fascinating because of the wizardry of his style. The word 'wizardry' is used advisedly; De Quincey's prose works like a spell, powerfully moving even apart from the meaning of the words. His style is so distinctive that it seems unprecedented, but in fact it had identifiable models. De Quincey's reading was enormously wide, and echoes from many recondite sources might be traced in his work, but one influence is particularly strong. In English history and literature the period which interested De Quincey most was the first half of the seventeenth century. He was a great admirer of the prose works of Walter Ralegh and Donne and Milton, of Sir Thomas Browne and Jeremy Taylor, and their influence is audible in the style of the *Confessions*, whose language is intricate, sonorous, Latinate, but never impersonal or mechanical; rhetorical, perhaps, but it is a real rhetoric, individual to the speaker, not a set of clichés or abstractions. A strong idiosyncrasy breaks through in sudden colloquialisms, in questions and addresses to the reader, in eccentric humour. The structure of the sentence is stretched and manipulated; there are nouns without verbs, there are sentences of three words and of nearly two hundred. Words, phrases and quotations are repeated like refrains. The pace is always changing – now it is a solemn *largo*, now a brisk *allegretto*. Digressions unfold from the theme like variations, intricately developing and diverging, but always returning to the original subject. These musical terms seem natural in describing De Quincey's style. He was himself a connoisseur of music, and his prose was consciously modelled on musical forms; sometimes he actually used the sonata framework of first and second subject, development, return to the tonic key, coda.

Both De Quincey's debt to seventeenth-century prose and his preoccupation with musical equivalents in language are illustrated by his rapturous comment on a passage in Sir Thomas Browne's *Urn-Burial*. 'What a melodious ascent as of a prelude to some impassioned requiem breathing from the pomps of earth, and from the sanctities of the grave! What a *fluctus decumanus* of rhetoric! Time expounded, not by generations or centuries, but by the vast periods of conquests and dynasties; by cycles of Pharaohs and Ptolemies, Antiochi and Arsacides! And these vast successions of time distinguished and figured by the uproars which revolve at their inaugurations; by the drums and trumpets rolling overhead upon the chambers of forgotten dead – the trepidations of time and mortality vexing, at secular intervals, the everlasting sabbaths of the grave.' The play of assonance in this passage – in melodious, ascent, prelude, requiem, rhetoric, generations, centuries; and then again in dead, trepidations, vexing, secular, everlasting – has the effect of a recurring note in music, such as the A flat in the opening of the second movement of Beethoven's *Appassionata* Sonata.

De Quincey's own favourite word for prose of this kind, both his own and that of the seventeenth-century writers whom he followed, was 'impassioned'. It was a key word with him. He did not use it to mean passionate, impulsively emotional, ardent, uncontrolled, but something very different: highly charged, close-textured, every word and syllable choice and enriched with music and imagery. It is the language itself which is impassioned, not the man who uses it.

Such was the extraordinary work that emerged from the back room in York Street at the end of August 1821. The first part was published anonymously in the September issue of the *London Magazine*, the second part in the following month, with an excited editorial note by Taylor and Hessey – 'We are not often in the habit of eulogizing our own work, – but we cannot neglect the opportunity which the following explanatory note gives us of calling the attention of our readers to the deep, eloquent and masterly paper which stands first in our present Number. Such Confessions, so powerfully uttered, cannot fail to do more than interest the reader.'

This prediction immediately came true. The *Confessions* aroused intense interest. They were commented on at length in other journals and magazines, discussed in letters and at dinner-parties, their veracity questioned and defended, their originality and superb language widely praised. Everyone wanted to meet the Opium Eater, whose identity was not long a secret, though some people continued to believe that the work was by Coleridge, and its authorship was claimed by an occasional impostor such as the painter, journalist and murderer Thomas Griffiths Wainewright.

With every decade the influence of the book grew wider. The tragedy is that it was not the aspects of the book that mattered most to De Quincey – his theory of dream mechanism, his use of language – which were influential. Very many readers of the *Confessions* – ignoring the point which De Quincey made on the very first page of the 'Preliminary Confessions', that opium cannot give you interesting dreams unless you already have the power to dream interestingly – were tempted into experimenting with opium by De Quincey's account of his own magnificent dreams. As the articles and autobiographies and medical studies of opium addiction mounted up through the nineteenth century, the name of De Quincey was sure to be found in the early pages of every addict's narrative. Among his more famous disciples were Branwell Brontë and Francis Thompson. Edgar Allan Poe's *Tales* are steeped in De Quincey's influence, and much of the second half of Baudelaire's *Paradis Artificiels* is a verbatim translation of passages from De Quincey's *Confessions* and *Suspiria de Profundis*.

The *Confessions*, which first appeared in book form in 1822, were constantly reprinted. Replying in November 1821 to some of the comments and criticisms on the work, De Quincey promised to write a third part, which would meet some of the objections made. This third part was never written, but throughout the next thirty years, in private letters and published articles, De Quincey constantly harked back to his methods and motives in writing the *Confessions*, and defended himself against the accusation that he had influenced others to become addicts. (Selections from these letters and articles are given in Appendix A to this volume.)

At last in 1856, when an edition of his Collected Works was being produced, he decided that the *Confessions* must be revised before they were reprinted in the Collected Works. What began as a revision became a re-shaping, a vast expansion. Its length was nearly tripled. An extra 'Prefatory Notice' was added. The 'Preliminary Confessions' describing his experiences in childhood and youth was filled out with a quantity of detail and digression. An extra dream, in the form of a story called 'The Daughter of Lebanon', was added at the end.

This revised version of the *Confessions* is the one which is most often reprinted and most widely known, and the reputation of the work has suffered accordingly, for De Quincey undoubtedly spoiled his masterpiece by revising it. He claimed that he had added nothing which did not belong to the original outline of the work, and that in the hurry of publication in 1821 much had been left out that he had meant to include, and which should have led up to the Second Part. But he himself had doubts, which he expressed in a letter to his daughter, whether the new version had not lost the spontaneous charm of the original during the process of revision. Although there are some splendid additional passages in the 1856 version, anyone who compares the two will prefer the unflagging vigour and tension of the original version to the tired prosiness of much of the revised one.

In the present edition, therefore, the original 1821 version of the *Confessions* has been printed, but those passages from the 1856 version which are interesting and beautiful as well as new have also been printed in Appendix B. These include further information on the effects of opium, and attempted justification of its use; an increased emphasis on the influence of early experiences in forming dreams and imaginative patterns; details of his relationships with his family and guardians, with Coleridge and with Wordsworth; and many more incidents of his schooldays, his walking-tour in Wales and his miseries in London.

The new passages in the revised version of the *Confessions* which have not been included in the Appendix are some tedious digressions on guardianship, on Greek studies, on travel in Wales, on the incidence of tuberculosis, and on insurance; a long story of a letter and cheque intended for a French refugee which reached De Quincey by mistake just as he was about to run away from Manchester, and about whose restoration he worried interminably; figures and explanations about his financial position; excessive detail about conversations at his school and its buildings and curriculum, of which he himself said, 'These explanations are too long'; and the short story 'The Daughter of Lebanon', which he arbitrarily attached to the end of the revised *Confessions* but which properly belongs to *Suspiria de Profundis*.

The seventy-year-old man who revised the *Confessions of an English Opium Eater* had changed a good deal from the thirty-six-year-old man who wrote the first version of them. He had endured many years of great poverty and hardship, a desperate struggle to earn a living for himself and his family. His wife and two of his sons had died. He had been an opium eater for more than half a century, and though for most of those years his dosage had been controlled at a fairly low level, there had been another period, lasting some years, of relapse into deep addiction. But in spite of this he was now a celebrated author, whose articles appeared in many of the leading journals of the day and were widely read in England and America and France; though he had still not produced a real book, apart from one inconsiderable Gothick novel, since the original *Confessions*.

He was celebrated also as a confirmed eccentric, a shabby skinny figure who lived on tea and grains of rice and scraps of meat, in dusty rooms piled high with papers, who often walked all night and slept all day. He was entirely incapable of dealing with money, of observing times and dates, of tidiness, because he was not prepared to waste thought on matters such as those, which did not touch his inner life. An affectionate father and friend, a wonderful talker when you could capture him, he nevertheless eluded all penetration into his labyrinthine personality, so that his contemporaries found him full of contradictions – tender-hearted but fascinated by horrors, by murders and conspiracies; courteous in speech but sometimes malicious, even impertinent, on paper; touchy on the surface, but unreachable in the recesses of his mind.

Those labyrinths he explored with tireless self-scrutiny. Perhaps no other writer has combined such vivid and intense subconscious activity with such acute observation of it and such a command of language to describe it. Virginia Woolf said that he was 'capable of being transfixed by the mysterious solemnity of certain emotions; of realizing how one moment may transcend in value fifty years'. By his recognition of these transcendent moments he brought to the art of prose autobiography something entirely new, and his influence has been felt by every self-conscious English writer, whether of reminiscences or of autobiographical novels, ever since.

ALETHEA HAYTER

# Note on the Text

The text is that of *Confessions of an English Opium Eater* as it first appeared, anonymously and in two parts, in the September and October 1821 issues of the *London Magazine* (Vol. IV, nos. xxi, pp. 293–312, and xxii, pp. 353–79).

*Text references*
Asterisks, etc., refer to De Quincey's own notes, reprinted at the foot of the page in question.

Arabic numerals, 1–169, refer to the editor's notes printed at the end of the volume, pp. 216–227.

Roman numerals, I–XXV, refer to passages from the revised *Confessions* reprinted in Appendix B, and show where De Quincey inserted these passages into the original version of the *Confessions* when he made his revision.

# Suggested Further Reading

The most complete edition of De Quincey's works is *Collected Writings* of Thomas de Quincey, edited by David Masson (14 vols., 1889–90). Modern editions and selections include:

*The Opium Eater, and Selections from the Autobiography*, edited and with an introduction by Edward Sackville-West (1950)

*Confessions of an English Opium Eater in both the Revised and the Original Texts, with its Sequels Suspiria de Profundis and The English Mail Coach*, with an introduction and life by Malcolm Elwin (1956)

*Reminiscences of the English Lake Poets*, with an introduction and notes by J. E. Jordan (1961)

The first full biography was *Thomas de Quincey: His Life and Writings* by H. A. Page (A. H. Japp) (1877).

Recent biographies include:

*Thomas de Quincey*, H. A. Eaton (1936)

*A Flame in Sunlight; The Life and Works of Thomas de Quincey*, Edward Sackville-West (1936)

Critical studies include:

*The Common Reader, Second Series*, Virginia Woolf (1948)

*Thomas de Quincey, Literary Critic: His Method and Achievement*, J. E. Jordan (1952)

*Thomas de Quincey*, Hugh Sykes Davies (1964)

*Opium and the Romantic Imagination*, Alethea Hayter (1968)

# CONFESSIONS

OF AN

# ENGLISH OPIUM-EATER.

———

LONDON:

PRINTED FOR TAYLOR AND HESSEY, FLEET STREET.

——

1822.

*Facsimile of the title page of the first edition (1822)*

# PART I

## *To the Reader*

I HERE present you, courteous reader, with the record of a remarkable period in my life: according to my application of it, I trust that it will prove, not merely an interesting record, but, in a considerable degree, useful and instructive. In *that* hope it is, that I have drawn it up: and *that* must be my apology for breaking through that delicate and honourable reserve, which, for the most part, restrains us from the public exposure of our own errors and infirmities. Nothing, indeed, is more revolting to English feelings, than the spectacle of a human being obtruding on our notice his moral ulcers or scars, and tearing away that 'decent drapery', which time, or indulgence to human frailty, may have drawn over them: accordingly, the greater part of *our* confessions (that is spontaneous and extra-judicial confessions) proceed from demireps,[1] adventurers, or swindlers: and for any such acts of gratuitous self-humiliation from those who can be supposed in sympathy with the decent and self-respecting part of society, we must look to French literature,[2] or to that part of the German, which is tainted with the spurious and defective sensibility of the French. All this I feel so forcibly, and so nervously am I alive to reproach of this tendency, that I have for many months hesitated about the propriety of allowing this, or any part of my narrative, to come before the public eye, until after my death (when, for many reasons, the whole will be published): and it is not without an anxious review of the reasons for and against this step, that I have, at last, concluded on taking it.

Guilt and misery shrink, by a natural instinct, from public notice: they court privacy and solitude: and, even in their choice of a grave, will sometimes sequester themselves from the general population of the churchyard, as if declining to claim fellowship with the great family of man, and wishing (in the affecting language of Mr Wordsworth)

– humbly to express
A penitential loneliness.

It is well, upon the whole, and for the interest of us all, that it should be so : nor would I willingly, in my own person, manifest a disregard of such salutary feelings; nor in act or word do any thing to weaken them. But, on the one hand, as my self-accusation does not amount to a confession of guilt, so, on the other, it is possible that, if it *did*, the benefit resulting to others, from the record of an experience purchased at so heavy a price, might compensate, by a vast overbalance, for any violence done to the feelings I have noticed, and justify a breach of the general rule. Infirmity and misery do not, of necessity, imply guilt. They approach, or recede from, the shades of that dark alliance, in proportion to the probable motives and prospects of the offender, and the palliations, known or secret, of the offence : in proportion as the temptations to it were potent from the first, and the resistance to it, in act or in effect, was earnest to the last. For my own part, without breach of truth or modesty, I may affirm, that my life has been, on the whole, the life of a philosopher : from my birth I was made an intellectual creature : and intellectual in the highest sense my pursuits and pleasures have been, even from my school-boy days. If opium-eating be a sensual pleasure, and if I am bound to confess that I have indulged in it to an excess, not yet *recorded* * of any other man, it is no less true, that I have struggled against this fascinating enthralment with a religious zeal, and have, at length, accomplished what I never yet heard attributed to any other man – have untwisted, almost to its final links, the accursed chain which fettered me. Such a self-conquest may reasonably be set off in counterbalance to any kind or degree of self-indulgence. Not to insist, that in my case, the self-conquest was unquestionable, the self-indulgence open to doubts of casuistry, according as that name shall be extended to acts aiming at the bare relief of pain, or shall be restricted to such as aim at the excitement of positive pleasure.

---

* 'Not yet *recorded*,' I say : for there is one celebrated man[3] of the present day who, if all be true which is reported of him, has greatly exceeded me in quantity.

Guilt, therefore, I do not acknowledge: and, if I did, it is possible that I might still resolve on the present act of confession, in consideration of the service which I may thereby render to the whole class of opium-eaters. But who are they? Reader, I am sorry to say, a very numerous class indeed. Of this I became convinced some years ago, by computing, at that time, the number of those in one small class of English society (the class of men distinguished for talents, or of eminent station), who were known to me, directly or indirectly, as opium-eaters: such, for instance, as the eloquent and benevolent ——, the late dean of——; Lord ——; Mr ——, the philosopher; a late under-secretary of state (who described to me the sensation which first drove him to the use of opium, in the very same words as the dean of ——, viz. 'that he felt as though rats were gnawing and abrading the coats of his stomach'); Mr ——; and many others, hardly less known, whom it would be tedious to mention.[4] Now, if one class, comparatively so limited, could furnish so many scores of cases (and *that* within the knowledge of one single inquirer), it was a natural inference, that the entire population of England would furnish a proportionable number. The soundness of this inference, however, I doubted, until some facts became known to me, which satisfied me that it was not incorrect. I will mention two: 1. Three respectable London druggists, in widely remote quarters of London, from whom I happened lately to be purchasing small quantities of opium, assured me, that the number of *amateur* opium-eaters (as I may term them) was, at this time, immense; and that the difficulty of distinguishing these persons, to whom habit had rendered opium necessary, from such as were purchasing it with a view to suicide, occasioned them daily trouble and disputes. This evidence respected London only. But, 2. (which will possibly surprise the reader more,) some years ago, on passing through Manchester, I was informed by several cotton-manufacturers, that their work-people were rapidly getting into the practice of opium-eating; so much so, that on a Saturday afternoon the counters of the druggists were strewed with pills of one, two, or three grains,[5] in preparation for the known demand of the evening. The immediate occasion of this practice was the lowness of wages, which, at that time, would not allow them to indulge in ale or spirits: and, wages rising, it may be thought that this practice would cease: but, as I do not readily believe that any man, having once tasted the divine luxuries of opium, will afterwards descend to the gross and mortal enjoyments of alcohol, I take it for granted,

> That those eat now, who never ate before;
> And those who always ate, now eat the more.

Indeed the fascinating powers of opium are admitted, even by medical writers, who are its greatest enemies: thus, for instance, Awsiter, apothecary to Greenwich-hospital, in his 'Essay on the Effects of Opium' (published in the year 1763), when attempting to explain why Mead[6] had not been sufficiently explicit on the properties, counteragents, &c. of this drug, expresses himself in the following mysterious terms, ($\varphi\omega\nu\acute{\alpha}\nu\tau\alpha\ \sigma\nu\nu\varepsilon\tau\omicron\iota\sigma\iota$):[7] 'perhaps he thought the subject of too delicate a nature to be made common; and as many people might then indiscriminately use it, it would take from that necessary fear and caution, which should prevent their experiencing the extensive power of this drug: *for there are many properties in it, if universally known, that would habituate the use, and make it more in request with us than the Turks themselves*:[8] the result of which knowledge,' he adds, 'must prove a general misfortune.' In the necessity of this conclusion I do not altogether concur:[9] but upon that point I shall have occasion to speak at the close of my confessions, where I shall present the reader with the *moral* of my narrative. [I, II]

# Preliminary Confessions

THESE preliminary confessions, or introductory narrative of the youthful adventures which laid the foundation of the writer's habit of opium-eating in after-life, it has been judged proper to premise, for three several reasons:

1. As forestalling that question, and giving it a satisfactory answer, which else would painfully obtrude itself in the course of the Opium-Confessions – 'How came any reasonable being to subject himself to such a yoke of misery, voluntarily to incur a captivity so servile, and knowingly to fetter himself with such a sevenfold chain?' – a question, which, if not somewhere plausibly resolved, could hardly fail, by the indignation which it would be apt to raise as against an act of wanton folly, to interfere with that degree of sympathy which is necessary in any case to an author's purposes.

2. As furnishing a key to some parts of that tremendous scenery which afterwards peopled the dreams of the opium-eater.

3. As creating some previous interest of a personal sort in the confessing subject, apart from the matter of the confessions, which cannot fail to render the confessions themselves more interesting. If a man 'whose talk is of oxen', should become an opium-eater, the probability is, that (if he is not too dull to dream at all) – he will dream about oxen: whereas, in the case before him, the reader will find that the opium-eater boasteth himself to be a philosopher; and accordingly, that the phantasmagoria of *his* dreams (waking or sleeping, day-dreams, or night-dreams)[10] is suitable to one who in that character,

*Humani nihil à se alienum putat.*[11]

For amongst the conditions which he deems indispensable to the sustaining of any claim to the title of philosopher, is not merely the possession of a superb intellect in its *analytic* functions (in which part of the pretension, however, England can for some generations show but few claimants; at least, he is not aware of

33

any known candidate for this honour, who can be styled emphatically *a subtle thinker*, with the exception of *Samuel Taylor Coleridge*, and in a narrower department of thought, with the recent illustrious exception* of *David Ricardo*[12]) – but also such a constitution of the *moral* faculties, as shall give him an inner eye and power of intuition for the vision and the mysteries of our human nature : *that* constitution of faculties, in short, which (amongst all the generations of men that from the beginning of time have deployed into life, as it were, upon this planet) our English poets have possessed in the highest degree, – and Scottish† professors in the lowest.

I have often been asked, how I first came to be a regular opium-eater; [111] and have suffered, very unjustly, in the opinion of my acquaintance, from being reputed to have brought upon myself all the sufferings which I shall have to record, by a long course of indulgence in this practice purely for the sake of creating an artificial state of pleasurable excitement. This, however, is a misrepresentation of my case. True it is, that for nearly ten years I did occasionally take opium, for the sake of the exquisite pleasure it gave me : but so long as I took it with this view, I was effectually protected from all material bad consequences, by the necessity of interposing long intervals between the several

---

*A third exception[13] might have been added : and my reason for not adding that exception is chiefly because it was only in his juvenile efforts that the writer whom I allude to expressly addressed himself to philosophical themes; his riper powers having been all dedicated (on very excusable and very intelligible ground, under the present direction of the popular mind in England) to criticism and the fine arts. This reason apart, however, I doubt whether he is not rather to be considered an acute thinker than a subtle one. It is, besides, a great drawback on his mastery over philosophical subjects, that he has obviously not had the advantage of a regular scholastic education : he has not read Plato in his youth (which most likely was only his misfortune); but neither has he read Kant in his manhood (which is his fault).

†I disclaim any allusion to *existing* professors, of whom indeed I know only one.[14]

34

acts of indulgence, in order to renew the pleasurable sensations. It was not for the purpose of creating pleasure, but of mitigating pain in the severest degree, that I first began to use opium as an article of daily diet. In the twenty-eighth year of my age, a most painful affection of the stomach, which I had first experienced about ten years before, attacked me in great strength. This affection had originally been caused by extremities of hunger, suffered in my boyish days. During the season of hope and redundant happiness which succeeded (that is, from eighteen to twenty-four) it had slumbered: for the three following years it had revived at intervals: and now, under unfavourable circumstances, from depression of spirits, it attacked me with a violence that yielded to no remedies but opium. As the youthful sufferings which first produced this derangement of the stomach, were interesting in themselves, and in the circumstances that attended them, I shall here briefly retrace them.

My father died when I was about seven years old, and left me to the care of four guardians. [IV] I was sent to various schools, great and small; and was very early distinguished for my classical attainments, especially for my knowledge of Greek. At thirteen, I wrote Greek with ease; and at fifteen my command of that language was so great, that I not only composed Greek verses in lyric metres, but could converse in Greek fluently, and without embarrassment – an accomplishment which I have not since met with in any scholar of my times, and which, in my case, was owing to the practice of daily reading off the newspapers into the best Greek I could furnish *extempore*: for the necessity of ransacking my memory and invention, for all sorts and combinations of periphrastic expressions, as equivalents for modern ideas, images, relations of things, &c. gave me a compass of diction which would never have been called out by a dull translation of moral essays, &c. 'That boy,' said one of my masters,[15] pointing the attention of a stranger to me, 'that boy could harangue an Athenian mob, better than you or I could address an English one.' He who honoured me with this eulogy, was a scholar, 'and a ripe and good one': and, of all my tutors, was the only one whom I loved or reverenced. Unfortunately for me (and, as I afterwards learned, to this worthy man's great indignation),

I was transferred to the care, first of a blockhead,[16] who was in a perpetual panic, lest I should expose his ignorance; and finally, to that of a respectable scholar,[17] at the head of a great school on an ancient foundation. This man had been appointed to his situation by —— College, Oxford; and was a sound, well-built scholar, but (like most men, whom I have known from that college) coarse, clumsy, and inelegant. [V] A miserable contrast he presented, in my eyes, to the Etonian brilliancy of my favourite master: and, besides, he could not disguise from my hourly notice, the poverty and meagreness of his understanding. It is a bad thing for a boy to be, and to know himself, far beyond his tutors, whether in knowledge or in power of mind. This was the case, so far as regarded knowledge at least, not with myself only: for the two boys, who jointly with myself composed the first form, were better Grecians than the head-master, though not more elegant scholars, nor at all more accustomed to sacrifice to the graces. [VI] When I first entered, I remember that we read Sophocles; and it was a constant matter of triumph to us, the learned triumvirate of the first form, to see our 'Archididascalus'[18] (as he loved to be called) conning our lesson before he went up, and laying a regular train, with lexicon and grammar, for blowing up and blasting (as it were) any difficulties he found in the choruses; whilst *we* never condescended to open our books until the moment of going up, and were generally employed in writing epigrams upon his wig, or some such important matter. My two class-fellows were poor, and dependent for their future prospects at the university, on the recommendation of the head-master: but I, who had a small patrimonial property, the income of which was sufficient to support me at college, wished to be sent thither immediately. I made earnest representations on the subject to my guardians, but all to no purpose. One, who was more reasonable, and had more knowledge of the world than the rest, lived at a distance: two of the other three resigned all their authority into the hands of the fourth; and this fourth with whom I had to negotiate, was a worthy man, in his way, but haughty, obstinate, and intolerant of all opposition to his will. After a certain number of letters and personal interviews, I found that I had nothing to hope for, not even a compromise of the matter, from my guardian: unconditional submission was what he demanded: and I prepared myself, therefore, for other measures. [VII] Summer was now coming on with hasty steps, and my seventeenth birthday was fast approaching; after which day I had sworn within myself, that I would no longer be numbered amongst school-boys. Money being what I chiefly wanted, I wrote to a woman of high rank,[19] who, though young herself, had known me from a child, and had latterly treated me with great distinction, requesting that she would 'lend' me five guineas. For upwards of a week no answer came; and I was beginning to despond, when, at length, a servant put into my hands a double letter, with a coronet on the seal. The letter was kind and obliging: the fair writer was on the sea-coast, and in that way the delay had arisen: she enclosed double of what I had asked, and good-naturedly hinted, that if I should *never* repay her, it would not absolutely ruin her. Now then, I was prepared for my scheme: ten guineas, added to about two which I had remaining from my pocket money, seemed to me sufficient for an indefinite length of time: and at that happy age, if no *definite* boundary can be assigned to one's power, the spirit of hope and pleasure makes it virtually infinite. [VIII]

It is just a remark of Dr Johnson's (and what cannot often be said of his remarks, it is a very feeling one,) that we never do any thing consciously for the last time (of things, that is, which we have long been in the habit of doing) without sadness of heart. [IX] This truth I felt deeply, when I came to leave ——,[20] a place which I did not love, and where I had not been happy. On the evening before I left —— for ever, I grieved when the ancient and lofty school-room resounded with the evening service, performed for the last time in my hearing; and at night, when the muster-roll of names was called over, and mine (as usual) was called first, I stepped forward, and passing the head master, who was standing by, I bowed to him, and looked earnestly in his face, thinking to myself, 'He is old and infirm, and in this world I shall not see him again.' I was right: I never *did* see him again, nor ever shall. He looked at me complacently, smiled good-naturedly, returned my salutation (or rather, my valediction), and we parted (though he knew it not) for ever. I could not reverence him intellectually : but he had been uniformly kind to me, and had allowed me many indulgences : and I grieved at the thought of the mortification I should inflict upon him.

The morning came, which was to launch me into the world, and from which my whole succeeding life has, in many important points, taken its colouring. I lodged in the head master's house, and had been allowed, from my first entrance, the indulgence of a private room, which I used both as a sleeping-room and as a study. At half after three I rose, and gazed with deep emotion at the ancient towers of ——,[21] 'drest in earliest light,' and beginning to crimson with the radiant lustre of a cloudless July morning. I was firm and immovable in my purpose : but yet agitated by anticipation of uncertain danger and troubles; and, if I could have foreseen the hurricane, and perfect hail-storm of affliction which soon fell upon me, well might I have been agitated. To this agitation the deep peace of the morning presented an affecting contrast, and in some degree a medicine. The silence was more profound than that of midnight : and to me the silence of a summer morning is more touching than all other silence, because, the light being broad and strong, as that of noon-day at other seasons of the year, it seems to differ from perfect day, chiefly because man is not yet abroad; and thus, the peace of nature, and of the innocent creatures of God, seems to be secure and deep, only so long as the presence of man, and his restless and unquiet spirit, are not there to trouble its sanctity. I dressed myself, took my hat and gloves, and lingered a little in the room. For the last year and a half this room had been my 'pensive citadel' : here I had read and studied through all the hours of night : and, though true it was, that for the latter part of this time I, who was framed for love and gentle affections, had lost my gaiety and happiness, during the strife and fever of contention with my guardian; yet, on the other hand, as a boy, so passionately fond of books, and dedicated to intellectual pursuits, I could not fail to have enjoyed many happy hours in the midst of general dejection. [x] I wept as I looked round on the chair, hearth, writing-table, and other familiar objects, knowing too certainly, that I looked upon them for the last time. Whilst I write this, it is eighteen years ago : and yet, at this moment, I see distinctly as if it were yesterday, the lineaments and expression of the object on which I fixed my parting gaze: it was a picture of the lovely ——,[22] which hung over the mantle-piece; the eyes and mouth of which were so beautiful, and the whole countenance so radiant with benignity, and divine tranquillity, that I had a thousand times laid down my pen, or my book, to gather consolation from it, as a devotee from his patron saint. Whilst I was yet gazing upon it, the deep tones of —— clock proclaimed that it was four o'clock. I went up to the picture, kissed it, and then gently walked out, and closed the door for ever!

*

So blended and intertwisted in this life are occasions of laughter and of tears, that I cannot yet recall, without smiling, an incident which occurred at that time, and which had nearly put a stop to the immediate execution of my plan. I had a trunk of immense weight; for, besides my clothes, it contained nearly all my library. The difficulty was to get this removed to a carrier's: my room was at an aerial elevation in the house, and (what was worse) the staircase, which communicated with this angle of the building, was accessible only by a gallery, which passed the head master's chamber-door. I was a favourite with all the servants; and, knowing that any of them would screen me, and act confidentially, I communicated my embarrassment to a groom of the head master's. The groom swore he would do anything I wished; and, when the time arrived, went up stairs to bring the trunk down. This I feared was beyond the strength of any one man: however, the groom was a man –

> Of Atlantean shoulders, fit to bear
> The weight of mightiest monarchies;

and had a back as spacious as Salisbury plain. Accordingly he persisted in bringing down the trunk alone, whilst I stood waiting at the foot of the last flight, in anxiety for the event. For some time I heard him descending with slow and firm steps; but unfortunately, from his trepidation as he drew near the dangerous quarter, within a few steps of the gallery, his foot slipped; and the mighty burden falling from his shoulders, gained such increase of impetus at each step of the descent, that, on reaching the bottom, it tumbled, or rather leaped, right across, with the noise of twenty devils, against the very bed-room door of the Archididascalus. My first thought was, that all was lost; and that my only chance for executing a retreat was to sacrifice my baggage. However, on reflection, I determined to abide the issue. The groom was in the utmost alarm, both on his own account and on mine: but, in spite of this, so irresistibly had the sense of the ludicrous, in this unhappy *contretems*,[23] taken possession of his fancy, that he sang out a long, loud, and canorous peal of laughter, that might have wakened the Seven Sleepers.[24] At the sound of this resonant merriment, within the very ears of insulted authority, I could not myself forbear joining in it: subdued to this, not so much by the unhappy *étourderie*[25] of the trunk, as by the effect it had upon the groom. We both expected, as a matter of course, that Dr —— would sally out of his room: for, in general, if but a mouse stirred, he sprang out like a mastiff from his kennel. Strange to say, however, on this occasion, when the noise of laughter had ceased, no sound, or rustling even, was to be heard in the bed-room. Dr —— had a painful complaint, which, sometimes keeping him awake, made his sleep, perhaps, when it *did* come, the deeper. Gathering courage from the silence, the groom hoisted his burden again, and accomplished the remainder of his descent without accident. I waited until I saw the trunk placed on a wheel-barrow, and on its road to the carrier's: then, 'with Providence my guide,' I set off on foot, – carrying a small parcel, with some articles of dress, under my arm; a favourite English poet in one pocket; and a small 12mo. volume, containing about nine plays of Euripides, in the other.

It had been my intention originally to proceed to Westmorland, both from the love I bore to that country, and on other personal accounts.[26] Accident, however, gave a different direction to my wanderings, and I bent my steps towards North Wales. [XI, XII, XIII]

After wandering about for some time in Denbighshire, Merionethshire, and Caernarvonshire, I took lodgings in a small neat house in B——.[27] Here I might have staid with great comfort for many weeks; for provisions were cheap at B——, from the scarcity of other markets for the surplus produce of a wide agricultural district. An accident, however, in which, perhaps, no offence was designed, drove me out to wander again. I know not whether my reader may have remarked, but I have often remarked, that the proudest class of people in England (or at any rate, the class whose pride is most apparent) are the families of bishops. Noblemen, and their children, carry about with them, in their very titles, a sufficient notification of their rank. Nay, their very names (and this applies also to the children of many untitled houses) are often, to the English ear, adequate exponents of high birth, or descent. Sackville, Manners, Fitzroy, Paulet, Cavendish, and scores of others, tell their own tale. Such persons, therefore, find every where a due sense of their claims already established, except among those who are ignorant of the world by virtue of their own obscurity : 'Not to know *them*, argues one's self unknown.' Their manners take a suitable tone and colouring; and, for once that they find it necessary to impress a sense of their consequence upon others, they meet with a thousand occasions for moderating and tempering this sense by acts of courteous condescension. With the families of bishops it is otherwise : with them it is all up-hill work, to make known their pretensions : for the proportion of the episcopal bench, taken from noble families, is not at any time very large; and the succession to these dignities is so rapid, that the public ear seldom has time to become familiar with them, unless where they are connected with some literary reputation. Hence it is, that the children of bishops carry about with them an austere and repulsive air, indicative of claims not generally acknowledged, a sort of *noli me tangere* manner, nervously apprehensive of too familiar approach, and shrinking with the sensitiveness of a gouty man, from all contact with the οἱ πολλοί. [28] Doubtless, a powerful understanding, or unusual goodness of nature, will preserve a man from such weakness, but, in general, the truth of my representation will be acknowledged : pride, if not of deeper root in such families, appears, at least, more upon the surface of their manners. This spirit of manners naturally communicates itself to their domestics, and other dependents. Now, my landlady had been a lady's maid, or a nurse, in the family of the Bishop of ——;[29] and had but lately married

41

away and 'settled' (as such people express it) for life. In a little town like B—, merely to have lived in the bishop's family, conferred some distinction: and my good landlady had rather more than her share of the pride I have noticed on that score. What 'my lord' said, and what 'my lord' did, how useful he was in parliament, and how indispensable at Oxford, formed the daily burden of her talk. All this I bore very well: for I was too good-natured to laugh in any body's face, and I could make an ample allowance for the garrulity of an old servant. Of necessity, however, I must have appeared in her eyes very inadequately impressed with the bishop's importance: and, perhaps, to punish me for my indifference, or possibly by accident, she one day repeated to me a conversation in which I was indirectly a party concerned. She had been to the palace to pay her respects to the family; and, dinner being over, was summoned into the dining-room. In giving an account of her household economy, she happened to mention that she had let her apartments. Thereupon the good bishop (it seemed) had taken occasion to caution her as to her selection of inmates: 'for,' said he, 'you must recollect, Betty, that this place is in the high road to the Head; so that multitudes of Irish swindlers, running away from their debts into England – and of English swindlers running away from their debts to the Isle of Man, are likely to take this place in their route.' This advice was certainly not without reasonable grounds: but rather fitted to be stored up for Mrs Betty's private meditations, than specially reported to me. What followed, however, was somewhat worse: – 'Oh, my lord,' answered my land-lady (according to her own representation of the matter), 'I really don't think this young gentleman is a swindler; because – :' 'You don't *think* me a swindler?' said I, interrupting her, in a tumult of indignation: 'for the future I shall spare you the trouble of thinking about it.' And without delay I prepared for my departure. Some concessions the good woman seemed disposed to make: but a harsh and contemptuous expression, which I fear that I applied to the learned dignitary himself, roused *her* indignation in turn: and reconciliation then became impossible. I was, indeed, greatly irritated at the bishop's having suggested any grounds of suspicion, however remotely, against a person whom he had never seen: and I thought of letting him know my mind in Greek: which, at the same time that it would furnish some presumption that I was no swindler, would also (I hoped) compel the bishop to reply in the same language; in which case, I doubted not to make it appear, that, if I was not so rich as his lordship, I was a better Grecian. Calmer thoughts, however, drove this boyish design out of my mind: for I considered that the bishop was in the right to counsel an old servant; that he could not have designed that his advice should be reported to me; and that the same coarseness of mind which led Mrs Betty to repeat the advice at all, might have coloured it in a way more agreeable to her own style of thinking, than to the actual expressions of the worthy bishop.

I left the lodgings the same hour; and this turned out a very unfortunate occurrence for me: because, living henceforward at inns, I was drained of my money very rapidly. [XIV] In a fortnight I was reduced to short allowance; that is, I could allow myself only one meal a day. From the keen appetite produced by constant exercise, and mountain air, acting on a youthful stomach, I soon began to suffer greatly on this slender regimen; for the single meal, which I could venture to order, was coffee or tea. Even this, however, was at length withdrawn: and afterwards, so long as I remained in Wales, I subsisted either on blackberries, hips, haws, &c., or on the casual hospitalities which I now and then received, in return for such little services as I had an opportunity of rendering. Sometimes I wrote letters of business for cottagers, who happened to have relatives in Liverpool, or in London: more often I wrote love-letters to their sweethearts for young women who had lived as servants in Shrewsbury, or other towns on the English border. On all such occasions I gave great satisfaction to my humble friends, and was generally treated with hospitality: and once, in particular, near the village of Llan-y-styndw (or some such name), in a sequestered part of Merionethshire, I was entertained for upwards of three days by a family of young people, with an affectionate and fraternal kindness that left an impression upon my heart not yet impaired. The family consisted, at that time, of four sisters, and three brothers, all grown up, and all remarkable for elegance and delicacy of manners. So much beauty, and so much native good-breeding and refinement, I do not remember to have seen before or since in any cottage, except once or twice in Westmorland and Devonshire. They spoke English : an accomplishment not often met with in so many members of one family, especially in villages remote from the high road. Here I wrote, on my first introduction, a letter about prize-money,[30] for one of the brothers, who had served on board an English man of war; and more privately, two love-letters for two of the sisters. They were both interesting looking girls, and one of uncommon loveliness. In the midst of their confusion and blushes, whilst dictating, or rather giving me general instructions, it did not require any great penetration to discover that what they wished was, that their letters should be as kind as was consistent with proper maidenly pride. I contrived so to temper my expressions, as to reconcile the gratification of both feelings : and they were as much pleased with the way in which I had expressed their thoughts, as (in their simplicity) they were astonished at my having so readily discovered them.[31] The reception one meets with from the women of a family, generally determines the tenour of one's whole entertainment. In this case, I had discharged my confidential duties as secretary, so much to the general satisfaction, perhaps also amusing them with my conversation, that I was pressed to stay with a cordiality which I had little inclination to resist. I slept with the brothers, the only unoccupied bed standing in the apartment of the young women : but in all other points, they treated me with a respect not usually paid to purses as light as mine; as if my scholarship were sufficient evidence, that I was of 'gentle blood'. Thus I lived with them for three days, and great part of a fourth : and, from the undiminished kindness which they continued to show me, I believe I might have staid with them up to this time, if their power had corresponded with their wishes. On the last morning, however, I perceived upon their countenances, as they sat at breakfast, the expression of some unpleasant communication which was at hand; and soon after one of the brothers explained to me, that their parents had gone, the day before my arrival, to an annual meeting of Methodists, held at Caernarvon, and were that day expected to return : 'and if they should not be so civil as they ought to be,' he begged, on the part of all the young people, that

I would not take it amiss. The parents returned, with churlish faces, and 'Dym Sassenach' (no English), in answer to all my addresses. I saw how matters stood; and so, taking an affectionate leave of my kind and interesting young hosts, I went my way. For, though they spoke warmly to their parents in my behalf, and often excused the manner of the old people, by saying, that it was 'only their way', yet I easily understood that my talent for writing love-letters would do as little to recommend me, with two grave sexagenarian Welsh Methodists, as my Greek Sapphics or Alcaics: [32] and what had been hospitality, when offered to me with the gracious courtesy of my young friends, would become charity, when connected with the harsh demeanour of these old people. Certainly, Mr Shelley [33] is right in his notions about old age: unless powerfully counteracted by all sorts of opposite agencies, it is a miserable corrupter and blighter to the genial charities of the human heart.

Soon after this, I contrived, by means which I must omit for want of room, to transfer myself to London. [XV, XVI, XVII] And now began the latter and fiercer stage of my long sufferings; without using a disproportionate expression I might say, of my agony. For I now suffered, for upwards of sixteen weeks, the physical anguish of hunger in various degrees of intensity; but as bitter, perhaps, as ever any human being can have suffered who has survived it. I would not needlessly harass my reader's feelings by a detail of all that I endured: for extremities such as these, under any circumstances of heaviest misconduct or guilt, cannot be contemplated, even in description, without a rueful pity that is painful to the natural goodness of the human heart. Let it suffice, at least on this occasion, to say, that a few fragments of bread from the breakfast-table of one individual (who supposed me to be ill, but did not know of my being in utter want), and these at uncertain intervals, constituted my whole support. During the former part of my sufferings (that is, generally in Wales, and always for the first two months in London) I was houseless, and very seldom slept under a roof. To this constant exposure to the open air I ascribe it mainly that I did not sink under my torments. Latterly, however, when colder and more inclement weather came on, and when, from the length of my sufferings, I had begun to sink into a more languishing condition, it was, no doubt, fortunate for me, that the same person to whose breakfast-table I had access, allowed me to sleep in a large unoccupied house, of which he was tenant. Unoccupied, I call it, for there was no household or establishment in it; nor any furniture, indeed, except a table, and a few chairs. But I found, on taking possession of my new quarters, that the house already contained one single inmate, a poor, friendless child, apparently ten years old; but she seemed hunger bitten; and sufferings of that sort often make children look older than they are. From this forlorn child I learned, that she had slept and lived there alone for some time before I came: and great joy the poor creature expressed, when she found that I was, in future, to be her companion through the hours of darkness. The house was large; and, from the want of furniture, the noise of the rats made a prodigious echoing on the spacious staircase and hall; and, amidst the real fleshly ills of cold, and, I fear, hunger, the forsaken child had found leisure to suffer still more (it appeared) from the self-created one of ghosts. I promised her protection against all ghosts whatsoever! but, alas! I could offer her no other assistance. We lay upon the floor, with a bundle of cursed law papers for a pillow: but with no other covering than a sort of large horseman's cloak: afterwards, however, we discovered, in a garret, an old sofa-cover, a small piece of rug, and some fragments of other articles, which added a little to our warmth. The poor child crept close to me for warmth, and for security against her ghostly enemies. When I was not more than usually ill, I took her in my arms, so that, in general, she was tolerably warm, and often slept when I could not: for, during the last two months of my sufferings, I slept much in the day-time, and was apt to fall into transient dozings at all hours. But my sleep distressed me more than my watching: for, besides the tumultuousness of my dreams (which were only not so awful as those which I shall have to describe hereafter as produced by opium), my sleep was never more than what is called *dog-sleep*; so that I could hear myself moaning, and was often, as it seemed to me, wakened suddenly by my own voice; and, about this time, a hideous sensation began to haunt me as soon as I fell into a slumber, which has since returned upon me, at different periods of my life, viz. a sort of twitching (I know not where, but apparently about the region of my stomach), which compelled me violently to throw out my feet for the sake of relieving it. This sensation coming on as soon as I began to sleep, and the effort to relieve it constantly awaking me, at length I slept only from exhaustion; and from increasing weakness (as I said before) I was constantly falling asleep, and constantly awaking. [XVIII] Meantime, the master of the house sometimes came in upon us suddenly, and very early, sometimes not till ten o'clock, sometimes not at all. He was in constant fear of bailiffs: improving on the plan of Cromwell, every night he slept in a different quarter of London; and I observed that he never failed to examine, through a private window, the appearance of those who knocked at the door, before he would allow it to be opened. He breakfasted alone: indeed, his tea equipage would hardly have admitted of his hazarding an invitation to a second person – any more than the quantity of esculent *matériel*, which, for the most part, was little more than a roll, or a few biscuits, which he had bought on his road from the place where he had slept. Or, if he *had* asked a party, as I once learnedly and facetiously observed to him – the several members of it must have *stood* in the relation to each other (not *sat* in any relation whatever) of succession, as the metaphysicians have it, and not of co-existence; in the relation of the parts of time, and not of the parts of space. During his breakfast, I generally contrived a reason for lounging in; and, with an air of as much indifference as I could assume, took up such fragments as he had left – sometimes, indeed, there were none at all. In doing this, I committed no robbery except upon the man himself, who was thus obliged (I believe) now and then to send out at noon for an extra biscuit; for, as to the poor child, *she* was never admitted into his study (if I may give that name to his chief depository of parchments, law writings, &c.); that room was to her the Blue-beard room of the house, being regularly locked on his departure to dinner, about six o'clock, which usually was his final departure for the night. Whether this child were an illegitimate daughter of Mr ——,[34] or only a servant, I could not ascertain; she did not herself know; but certainly she was treated altogether as a menial servant. No sooner did Mr —— make his appearance, than she went below stairs, brushed his shoes, coat, &c.; and, except when she was summoned to run an errand, she never emerged from the dismal Tartarus of the kitchens, &c. to the upper air, until my welcome knock at night called up her little trembling footsteps to the front door. Of her life during the day-time, however, I knew little but what I gathered from her own account at night; for, as soon as the hours of business commenced, I saw that my absence would be acceptable; and, in general, therefore, I went off, and sat in the parks, or elsewhere, until night-fall.

But who, and what, meantime, was the master of the house himself? Reader, he was one of those anomalous practitioners in lower departments of the law, who – what shall I say? – who, on prudential reasons, or from necessity, deny themselves all indulgence in the luxury of too delicate a conscience: (a periphrasis which might be abridged considerably, but *that* I leave to the reader's taste:) in many walks of life, a conscience is a more expensive encumbrance, than a wife or a carriage; and just as people talk of 'laying down' their carriages, so I suppose my friend, Mr —— had 'laid down' his conscience for a time; meaning, doubtless, to resume it as soon as he could afford it. The inner economy of such a man's daily life would present a most strange picture, if I could allow myself to amuse the reader at his expense. Even with my limited opportunities for observing what went on, I saw many scenes of London intrigues, and complex chicanery, 'cycle and epicycle, orb in orb,' at which I sometimes smile to this day – and at which I smiled then, in spite of my misery. My situation, however, at that time, gave me little experience, in my own person, of any qualities in Mr ——'s character but such as did him honour; and of his whole strange composition, I must forget every thing but that towards me he was obliging, and, to the extent of his power, generous.

That power was not, indeed, very extensive; however, in common with the rats, I sat rent free; and, as Dr Johnson has recorded, that he never but once in his life had as much wall-fruit as he could eat, so let me be grateful, that on that single occasion I had as large a choice of apartments in a London mansion as I could possibly desire. Except the Blue-beard room, which the poor child believed to be haunted, all others, from the attics to the cellars, were at our service; 'the world was all before us'; and we pitched our tent for the night in any spot we chose. This house I have already described as a large one; it stands in a conspicuous situation, and in a well-known part of London. Many of my readers will have passed it, I doubt not, within a few hours of reading this. For myself, I never fail to visit it when business draws me to London; about ten o'clock, this very night, August 15, 1821, being my birth-day – I turned aside from my evening walk, down Oxford-street, purposely to take a glance at it: it is now occupied by a respectable family; and, by the lights in the front drawing-room, I observed a domestic party, assembled perhaps at tea, and apparently cheerful and gay. Marvellous contrast in my eyes to the darkness – cold – silence – and desolation of that same house eighteen years ago, when its nightly occupants were one famishing scholar, and a neglected child ! – Her, by the by, in after years, I vainly endeavoured to trace. Apart from her situation, she was not what would be called an interesting child : she was neither pretty, nor quick in understanding, nor remarkably pleasing in manners. But, thank God ! even in those years I needed not the embellishments of novel-accessaries to conciliate my affections; plain human nature, in its humblest and most homely apparel, was enough for me: and I loved the child because she was my partner in wretchedness.[35] If she is now living, she is probably a mother, with children of her own; but, as I have said, I could never trace her.

This I regret, but another person there was at that time, whom I have since sought to trace with far deeper earnestness, and with far deeper sorrow at my failure. This person was a young woman, and one of that unhappy class who subsist upon the wages of prostitution. I feel no shame, nor have any reason to feel it, in avowing that I was then on familiar and friendly terms with many women in that unfortunate condition. The reader needs neither smile at this avowal, nor frown. For, not to remind my classical readers of the old Latin proverb – '*Sine Cerere*',[36] &c., it may well be supposed that in the existing state of my purse, my connexion with such women could not have been an impure one. But the truth is, that at no time of my life have I been a person.

to hold myself polluted by the touch or approach of any creature that wore a human shape: on the contrary, from my very earliest youth it has been my pride to converse familiarly, *more Socratico*,[37] with all human beings, man, woman, and child, that chance might fling in my way: a practice which is friendly to the knowledge of human nature, to good feelings, and to that frankness of address which becomes a man who would be thought a philosopher. For a philosopher should not see with the eyes of the poor limitary creature, calling himself a man of the world, and filled with narrow and self-regarding prejudices of birth and education, but should look upon himself as a Catholic creature, and as standing in an equal relation to high and low – to educated and uneducated, to the guilty and the innocent. Being myself at that time of necessity a peripatetic, or a walker of the streets, I naturally fell in more frequently with those female peripatetics who are technically called street-walkers. Many of these women had occasionally taken my part against watchmen who wished to drive me off the steps of houses where I was sitting. But one amongst them, the one on whose account I have at all introduced this subject – yet no! let me not class thee, oh noble-minded Ann ——, with that order of women; let me find, if it be possible, some gentler name to designate the condition of her to whose bounty and compassion, ministering to my necessities when all the world had forsaken me, I owe it that I am at this time alive. – For many weeks I had walked at nights with this poor friendless girl up and down Oxford-street, or had rested with her on steps and under the shelter of porticos. She could not be so old as myself: she told me, indeed, that she had not completed her sixteenth year. By such questions as my interest about her prompted, I had gradually drawn forth her simple history. Hers was a case of ordinary occurrence (as I have since had reason to think), and one in which, if London beneficence had better adapted its arrangements to meet it, the power of the law might oftener be interposed to protect, and to avenge. But the stream of London charity flows in a channel which, though deep and mighty, is yet noiseless and underground; not obvious or readily accessible to poor houseless wanderers: and it cannot be denied that the outside air and frame-work of London society is harsh, cruel, and repulsive. In any case, however, I saw that part of her injuries might easily have been redressed; and I urged her often and earnestly to lay her complaint before a magistrate: friendless as she was, I assured her that she would meet with immediate attention; and that English justice, which was no respecter of persons, would speedily and amply avenge her on the brutal ruffian who had plundered her little property. She promised me often that she would; but she delayed taking the steps I pointed out from time to time; for she was timid and dejected to a degree which showed how deeply sorrow had taken hold of her young heart: and perhaps she thought justly that the most upright judge, and the most righteous tribunals, could do nothing to repair her heaviest wrongs. Something, however, would perhaps have been done: for it had been settled between us at length, but unhappily on the very last time but one that I was ever to see her, that in a day or two we should go together before a magistrate, and that I should speak on her behalf. This little service it was destined, however, that I should never realize. Meantime, that which she rendered to me, and which was greater than I could ever have repaid her, was this: – One night, when we were pacing slowly along Oxford-street, and after a day when I had felt more than usually ill and faint, I requested her to turn off with me into Soho-square: thither we went; and we sat down on the steps of a house, which, to this hour, I never pass without a pang of grief, and an inner act of homage to the spirit of that unhappy girl, in memory of the noble action which she there performed. Suddenly, as we sat, I grew much worse: I had been leaning my head against her bosom; and all at once I sank from her arms and fell backwards on the steps. From the sensations I then had, I felt an inner conviction of the liveliest kind that without some powerful and reviving stimulus, I should either have died on the spot – or should at least have sunk to a point of exhaustion from which all re-ascent under my friendless circumstances would soon have become hopeless. Then it was, at this crisis of my fate, that my poor orphan companion – who had herself met with little but injuries in this world – stretched out a saving hand to me. Uttering a cry of terror, but without a moment's delay, she ran off into Oxford-street, and in less time than could be imagined, returned to me with a glass of port wine and spices, that acted upon my empty stomach, (which at that time would have rejected all solid food) with an instantaneous power of restoration: and for this glass the generous girl without a murmur paid out of her own humble purse at a time – be it remembered! – when she had scarcely wherewithal to purchase the bare necessaries of life, and when she could have no reason to expect that I should ever be able to reimburse her. – Oh! youthful benefactress! how often in succeeding years, standing in solitary places, and thinking of thee with grief of heart and perfect love, how often have I wished that, as in ancient times the curse of a father was believed to have a supernatural power, and to pursue its object with a fatal necessity of self-fulfilment, – even so the benediction of a heart oppressed with gratitude, might have a like prerogative; might have power given to it from above to chase – to haunt – to way-lay – to overtake – to pursue thee into the central darkness of a London brothel, or (if it were possible) into the darkness of the grave – there to awaken thee with an authentic message of peace and forgiveness, and of final reconciliation!

I do not often weep: for not only do my thoughts on subjects connected with the chief interests of man daily, nay hourly, descend a thousand fathoms 'too deep for tears'; not only does the sternness of my habits of thought present an antagonism to the feelings which prompt tears – wanting of necessity to those who, being protected usually by their levity from any tendency to meditative sorrow, would by that same levity be made incapable of resisting it on any casual access of such feelings: – but also, I believe that all minds which have contemplated such objects as deeply as I have done, must, for their own protection from utter despondency, have early encouraged and cherished some tranquillizing belief as to the future balances and the hieroglyphic meanings of human sufferings. On these accounts, I am cheerful to this hour; and, as I have said, I do not often weep. Yet some feelings, though not deeper or more passionate, are more tender than others; and often, when I walk at this time in Oxford-street by dreamy lamp-light, and hear those airs played on a barrel-organ which years ago solaced me and my dear companion (as I must always call her), I shed tears, and muse with myself at the mysterious dispensation which so suddenly and so critically separated us for ever. How it happened, the reader will understand from what remains of this introductory narration.

Soon after the period of the last incident I have recorded, I met, in Albemarle-street, a gentlemen of his late majesty's household. This gentleman had received hospitalities, on different occasions, from my family: and he challenged me upon the strength of my family likeness. I did not attempt any disguise: I answered his questions ingenuously – and, on his pledging his word of honour that he would not betray me to my guardians, I gave him an address to my friend the attorney's. The next day I received from him a 10*l*. Bank-note. The letter enclosing it was delivered with other letters of business to the attorney; but, though his look and manner informed me that he suspected its contents, he gave it up to me honourably and without demur.

This present, from the particular service to which it was applied, leads me naturally to speak of the purpose which had allured me up to London, and which I had been (to use a forensic word) *soliciting* from the first day of my arrival in London, to that of my final departure.

In so mighty a world as London, it will surprise my readers that I should not have found some means of staving off the last extremities of penury: and it will strike them that two resources at least must have been open to me, – viz. either to seek assistance from the friends of my family, or to turn my youthful talents and attainments into some channel of pecuniary emolument. As to the first course, I may observe, generally, that what I dreaded beyond all other evils was the chance of being reclaimed by my guardians; not doubting that whatever power the law gave them would have been enforced against me to the utmost; that is, to the extremity of forcibly restoring me to the school which I had quitted: a restoration which as it would in my eyes have been a dishonour, even if submitted to voluntarily, could not fail, when extorted from me in contempt and defiance of my known wishes and efforts, to have been a humiliation worse to me than death, and which would, indeed, have terminated in death. I was, therefore, shy enough of applying for assistance even in those quarters where I was sure of receiving it – at the risk of furnishing my guardians with any clue for recovering me. But, as to London in particular, though, doubtless, my father had in his life-time had many friends there, yet (as ten years had passed since his death) I remembered few of them even by name: and never having seen London before, except once for a few hours, I knew not the address of even those few. To this mode of gaining help, therefore, in part the difficulty, but much more the paramount fear which I have mentioned, habitually indisposed me. In regard to the other mode, I now feel half inclined to join my reader in wondering that I should have overlooked it. As a corrector of Greek proofs (if in no other way), I might doubtless have gained enough for my slender wants. Such an office as this I could have discharged with an exemplary and punctual accuracy that would soon have gained me the confidence of my employers. But it must not be forgotten that, even for such an office as this, it was necessary that I should first of all have an introduction to some respectable publisher : and this I had no means of obtaining. To say the truth, however, it had never once occurred to me to think of literary labours as a source of profit. No mode sufficiently speedy of obtaining money had ever occurred to me, but that of borrowing it on the strength of my future claims and expectations. This mode I sought by every avenue to compass, and amongst other persons I applied to a Jew named D—.[38]*

---

*To this same Jew, by the way, some eighteen months afterwards, I applied again on the same business; and, dating at that time from a respectable college, I was fortunate enough to gain his serious attention to my proposals. My necessities had not arisen from any extravagance, or youthful levities (these my habits and the nature of my pleasures raised me far above), but simply from the vindictive malice of my guardian, who, when he found himself no longer able to prevent me from going to the university, had, as a parting token of his good nature, refused to sign an order for granting me a shilling beyond the allowance made to me at school – viz. 100l. per annum. Upon this sum it was, in my time, barely possible to have lived in college; and not possible to a man who, though above the paltry affectation of ostentatious disregard for money, and without any expensive tastes, confided, nevertheless, rather too much in servants,

To this Jew, and to other advertising money-lenders (some of whom were, I believe, also Jews), I had introduced myself with an account of my expectations; which account, on examining my father's will, at Doctor's Commons, they had ascertained to be correct. The person there mentioned as the second son of ——,[39] was found to have all the claims (or more than all) that I had stated: but one question still remained, which the faces of the Jews pretty significantly suggested, – was I that person? This doubt had never occurred to me as a possible one: I had rather feared, whenever my Jewish friends scrutinized me keenly, that I might be too well known to be that person – and that some scheme might be passing in their minds for entrapping me, and selling me to my guardians. It was strange to me to find my own self, *materialiter* considered (so I expressed it, for I doted on logical accuracy of distinctions), accused, or at least suspected, of counterfeiting my own self, *formaliter* considered. However, to satisfy their scruples, I took the only course in my power. Whilst I was in Wales, I had received various letters from young friends: these I produced: for I carried them constantly in my pocket – being, indeed, by this time, almost the only relics of my personal encumbrances (excepting the clothes I wore) which I had not in one way or other disposed of. Most of these letters were from the Earl of ——,[40] who was at that time my chief (or rather only) confidential friend. These letters were dated

---

and did not delight in the petty details of minute economy. I soon, therefore, became embarrassed: and at length, after a most voluminous negotiation with the Jew (some parts of which, if I had leisure to rehearse them, would greatly amuse my readers), I was put in possession of the sum I asked for – on the 'regular' terms of paying the Jew seventeen and a half per cent, by way of annuity, on all the money furnished; Israel, on his part, graciously resuming no more than about ninety guineas of the said money, on account of an attorney's bill (for what services, to whom rendered, and when, whether at the siege of Jerusalem – at the building of the Second Temple – or on some earlier occasion, I have not yet been able to discover). How many perches this bill measured I really forget: but I still keep it in a cabinet of natural curiosities; and sometimes or other, I believe, I shall present it to the British Museum.

from Eton. I had also some from the Marquess of ——, his father, who, though absorbed in agricultural pursuits, yet having been an Etonian himself, and as good a scholar as a nobleman needs to be – still retained an affection for classical studies, and for youthful scholars. He had, accordingly, from the time that I was fifteen, corresponded with me; sometimes upon the great improvements which he had made, or was meditating, in the counties of M— and S— since I had been there; sometimes upon the merits of a Latin poet; at other times suggesting subjects to me, on which he wished me to write verses.

On reading the letters, one of my Jewish friends agreed to furnish two or three hundred pounds on my personal security – provided I could persuade the young Earl, who was, by the way, not older than myself, to guarantee the payment on our coming of age: the Jew's final object being, as I now suppose, not the trifling profit he could expect to make by me, but the prospect of establishing a connexion with my noble friend, whose immense expectations were well known to him. In pursuance of this proposal on the part of the Jew, about eight or nine days after I had received the 10l., I prepared to go down to Eton. Nearly 3l. of the money I had given to my money-lending friend, on his alleging that the stamps must be bought, in order that the writings might be preparing whilst I was away from London. I thought in my heart that he was lying; but I did not wish to give him any excuse for charging his own delays upon me. A smaller sum I had given to my friend the attorney (who was connected with the money-lenders as their lawyer), to which, indeed, he was entitled for his unfurnished lodgings. About fifteen shillings I had employed in re-establishing (though in a very humble way) my dress. Of the remainder I gave one quarter to Ann, meaning on my return to have divided with her whatever might remain. These arrangements made, – soon after six o'clock, on a dark winter evening, I set off, accompanied by Ann, towards Piccadilly; for it was my intention to go down as far as Salt-hill on the Bath or Bristol mail. Our course lay through a part of the town which has now all disappeared, so that I can no longer retrace its ancient boundaries: Swallow-street, I think it was called. Having time enough before us, however, we bore away to the left until we came into Golden-square: there, near the corner of Sherrard-street, we sat down; not wishing to part in the tumult and blaze of Piccadilly. I had told her of my plans some time before; and I now assured her again that she should share in my good fortune, if I met with any; and that I would never forsake her, as soon as I had power to protect her. This I fully intended, as much from inclination as from a sense of duty: for, setting aside gratitude, which in any case must have made me her debtor for life, I loved her as affectionately as if she had been my sister: and at this moment, with sevenfold tenderness, from pity at witnessing her extreme dejection. I had, apparently, most reason for dejection, because I was leaving the saviour of my life: yet I, considering the shock my health had received, was cheerful and full of hope. She on the contrary, who was parting with one who had little means of serving her, except by kindness and brotherly treatment, was overcome by sorrow; so that, when I kissed her at our final farewell, she put her arms about my neck, and wept without speaking a word. I hoped to return in a week at farthest, and I agreed with her that on the fifth night from that, and every night afterwards, she should wait for me at six o'clock, near the bottom of Great Titchfield-street, which had been our customary haven, as it were, of rendezvous, to prevent our missing each other in the great Mediterranean of Oxford-street. This, and other measures of precaution, I took: one only I forgot. She had either never told me, (or as a matter of no great interest) I had forgotten, her surname. It is a general practice, indeed, with girls of humble rank in her unhappy condition, not (as novel-reading women of higher pretentions) to style themselves – *Miss Douglass, Miss Montague*, &c. but simply by their Christian names, *Mary, Jane, Frances*, &c. Her surname, as the surest means of tracing her hereafter, I ought now to have inquired: but the truth is, having no reason to think that our meeting could, in consequence of a short interruption, be more difficult or uncertain than it had been for so many weeks, I had scarcely for a moment adverted to it as necessary, or placed it amongst my memoranda against this parting interview: and, my final anxieties being spent in comforting her with hopes, and in pressing upon her the necessity of getting some medicines for a violent cough and hoarseness with which she was troubled, I wholly forgot it until it was too late to recall her.

It was past eight o'clock when I reached the Gloucester coffee-house[41]: and, the Bristol mail being on the point of going off, I mounted on the outside. The fine fluent motion* of this mail soon laid me asleep: it is somewhat remarkable, that the first easy or refreshing sleep which I had enjoyed for some months, was on the outside of a mail-coach – a bed which, at this day, I find rather an uneasy one. Connected with this sleep was a little incident, which served, as hundreds of others did at that time, to convince me how easily a man who has never been in any great distress, may pass through life without knowing, in his own person at least, any thing of the possible goodness of the human heart – or, as I must add with a sigh, of its possible vileness. So thick a curtain of *manners* is drawn over the features and expression of men's *natures*, that to the ordinary observer, the two extremities, and the infinite field of varieties which lie between them, are all confounded – the vast and multitudinous compass of their several harmonies reduced to the meagre outline of differences expressed in the gamut or alphabet of elementary sounds. The case was this: for the first four or five miles from London, I annoyed my fellow-passenger on the roof by occasionally falling against him when the coach gave a lurch to his side; and indeed, if the road had been less smooth and level than it is, I should have fallen off from weakness. Of this annoyance he complained heavily, as perhaps in the same circumstances most people would; he expressed his complaint, however, more morosely than the occasion seemed to warrant; and, if I had parted with him at that moment, I should have thought of him (if I had considered it worth while to think of him at all) as a surly and almost brutal fellow. However, I was conscious that I had given him some cause for complaint: and, therefore, I apologized to him, and assured him I would do what I could to avoid falling asleep for

---

*The Bristol mail is the best appointed in the kingdom – owing to the double advantage of an unusually good road, and of an extra sum for expenses subscribed by the Bristol merchants.

the future; and, at the same time, in as few words as possible, I explained to him that I was ill and in a weak state from long suffering; and that I could not afford at that time to take an inside place. The man's manner changed, upon hearing this explanation, in an instant: and when I next woke for a minute from the noise and lights of Hounslow (for in spite of my wishes and efforts I had fallen asleep again within two minutes from the time I had spoken to him), I found that he had put his arm round me to protect me from falling off: and for the rest of my journey he behaved to me with the gentleness of a woman, so that, at length, I almost lay in his arms: and this was the more kind, as he could not have known that I was not going the whole way to Bath or Bristol. Unfortunately, indeed, I *did* go rather farther than I intended: for so genial and refreshing was my sleep, that the next time after leaving Hounslow that I fully awoke, was upon the sudden pulling up of the mail (possibly at a post office); and, on inquiry, I found that we had reached Maidenhead – six or seven miles, I think, a-head of Salt-hill. Here I alighted: and for the half minute that the mail stopped, I was entreated by my friendly companion (who, from the transient glimpse I had had of him in Piccadilly, seemed to me to be a gentleman's butler – or person of that rank) to go to bed without delay. This I promised, though with no intention of doing so: and in fact, I immediately set forward, or rather backward, on foot. It must then have been nearly midnight: but so slowly did I creep along, that I heard a clock in a cottage strike four before I turned down the lane from Slough to Eton. The air and the sleep had both refreshed me; but I was weary nevertheless. I remember a thought (obvious enough, and which has been prettily expressed by a Roman poet) which gave me some consolation at that moment under my poverty. There had been some time before a murder committed on or near Hounslow-heath. I think I cannot be mistaken when I say that the name of the murdered person was *Steele*, and that he was the owner of a lavender plantation in that neighbourhood. Every step of my progress was bringing me nearer to the heath: and it naturally occurred to me that I and the accursed murderer, if he were that night abroad, might at every instant be unconsciously approaching each other through the darkness: in which case, said I, – supposing that I, instead of being (as indeed I am) little better than an outcast, –

Lord of my learning and no land beside,

were, like my friend, Lord ——,[42] heir by general repute to 70,000l. per ann., what a panic should I be under at this moment about my throat! – indeed, it was not likely that Lord —— should ever be in my situation. But nevertheless, the spirit of the remark remains true – that vast power and possessions make a man shamefully afraid of dying: and I am convinced that many of the most intrepid adventurers, who, by fortunately being poor, enjoy the full use of their natural courage, would, if at the very instant of going into action news were brought to them that they had unexpectedly succeeded to an estate in England of 50,000l. a year, feel their dislike to bullets considerably sharpened* – and their efforts at perfect equanimity and self-possession proportionately difficult. So true it is, in the language of a wise man whose own experience had made him acquainted with both fortunes, that riches are better fitted –

> To slacken virtue, and abate her edge,
> Than tempt her to do aught may merit praise.
> *Paradise Regained.*

I dally with my subject because, to myself, the remembrance of these times is profoundly interesting. But my reader shall not have any further cause to complain: for I now hasten to its close. – In the road between Slough and Eton, I fell asleep: and, just as the morning began to dawn, I was awakened by the voice of a man standing over me and surveying me. I know not what he was: he was an ill-looking fellow – but not therefore of necessity an ill-meaning fellow: or, if he were, I suppose he thought that no person sleeping out-of-doors in winter could be worth robbing. In which conclusion, however, as it regarded myself,

---

*It will be objected that many men, of the highest rank and wealth, have in our own day, as well as throughout our history, been amongst the foremost in courting danger in battle. True: but this is not the case supposed: long familiarity with power has to them deadened its effect and its attractions.

I beg to assure him, if he should be among my readers, that he was mistaken. After a slight remark he passed on: and I was not sorry at his disturbance, as it enabled me to pass through Eton before people were generally up. The night had been heavy and lowering: but towards the morning it had changed to a slight frost: and the ground and the trees were now covered with rime. I slipped through Eton unobserved; washed myself, and, as far as possible, adjusted my dress at a little public-house in Windsor; and about eight o'clock went down towards Pote's.[43] On my road I met some junior boys of whom I made inquiries: an Etonian is always a gentleman; and, in spite of my shabby habiliments, they answered me civilly. My friend, Lord ——, was gone to the University of ——[44]. 'Ibi omnis effusus labor!'[45] I had, however, other friends at Eton: but it is not to all who wear that name in prosperity that a man is willing to present himself in distress. On recollecting myself, however, I asked for the Earl of D—,[46] to whom, (though my acquaintance with him was not so intimate as with some others) I should not have shrunk from presenting myself under any circumstances. He was still at Eton, though I believe on the wing for Cambridge. I called, was received kindly, and asked to breakfast.

Here let me stop for a moment to check my reader from any erroneous conclusions: because I have had occasion incidentally to speak of various patrician friends, it must not be supposed that I have myself any pretensions to rank or high blood. I thank God that I have not: – I am the son of a plain English merchant, esteemed during his life for his great integrity, and strongly attached to literary pursuits (indeed, he was himself, anonymously, an author): if he had lived, it was expected that he would have been very rich; but, dying prematurely, he left no more than about 30,000l. amongst seven different claimants. My mother I may mention with honour, as still more highly gifted. For though unpretending to the name and honours of a *literary* woman, I shall presume to call her (what many literary women are not) an *intellectual* woman: and I believe that if ever her letters should be collected and published, they would be thought generally to exhibit as much strong and masculine sense, delivered in as pure 'mother English', racy and fresh with idiomatic graces, as any in our language – hardly excepting those of Lady M. W. Montagu. – These are my honours of descent: I have no others: and I have thanked God sincerely that I have not, because, in my judgment, a station which raises a man too eminently above the level of his fellow-creatures is not the most favourable to moral, or to intellectual qualities.

Lord D— placed before me a most magnificent breakfast. It was really so; but in my eyes it seemed trebly magnificent – from being the first regular meal, the first 'good man's table', that I had sat down to for months. Strange to say, however, I could scarcely eat any thing. On the day when I first received my 10l. Bank-note, I had gone to a baker's shop and bought a couple of rolls: this very shop I had two months or six weeks before surveyed with an eagerness of desire which it was almost humiliating to me to recollect. I remembered the story about Otway[47]; and feared that there might be danger in eating too rapidly. But I had no need for alarm, my appetite was quite sunk, and I became sick before I had eaten half of what I had bought. This effect from eating what approached to a meal, I continued to feel for weeks: or, when I did not experience any nausea, part of what I ate was rejected, sometimes with acidity, sometimes immediately, and without any acidity. On the present occasion, at Lord D—'s table, I found myself not at all better than usual: and, in the midst of luxuries, I had no appetite. I had, however, unfortunately, at all times a craving for wine: I explained my situation, therefore, to Lord D—, and gave him a short account of my late sufferings, at which he expressed great compassion, and called for wine. This gave me a momentary relief and pleasure; and on all occasions when I had an opportunity, I never failed to drink wine – which I worshipped then as I have since worshipped opium. I am convinced, however, that this indulgence in wine contributed to strengthen my malady; for the tone of my stomach was apparently quite sunk; but by a better regimen it might sooner, and perhaps effectually, have been revived. I hope that it was not from this love of wine that I lingered in the neighbourhood of my Eton friends: I persuaded myself *then* that it was from reluctance to ask of Lord D—, on whom I was conscious I had not sufficient claims, the particular service in quest of which I had come down to Eton. I was, however, unwilling to lose my journey, and – I asked it. Lord D—, whose good nature was unbounded, and which, in regard to myself, had been measured rather by his compassion perhaps for my condition, and his knowledge of my intimacy with some of his relatives, than by an over rigorous inquiry into the extent of my own direct claims, faltered, nevertheless, at this request. He acknowledged that he did not like to have any dealings with money-lenders, and feared lest such a transaction might come to the ears of his connexions. Moreover, he doubted whether *his* signature, whose expectations were so much more bounded than those of Lord ——,[48] would avail with my unchristian friends. However, he did not wish, as it seemed, to mortify me by an absolute refusal : for after a little consideration, he promised, under certain conditions which he pointed out, to give his security. Lord D— was at this time not eighteen years of age : but I have often doubted, on recollecting since the good sense and prudence which on this occasion he mingled with so much urbanity of manner (an urbanity which in him wore the grace of youthful sincerity), whether any statesman – the oldest and the most accomplished in diplomacy – could have acquitted himself better under the same circumstances. Most people, indeed, cannot be addressed on such a business, without surveying you with looks as austere and unpropitious as those of a Saracen's head.

Recomforted by this promise, which was not quite equal to the best, but far above the worst that I had pictured to myself as possible, I returned in a Windsor coach to London three days after I had quitted it. And now I come to the end of my story : – the Jews did not approve of Lord D—'s terms; whether they would in the end have acceded to them, and were only seeking time for making due inquiries, I know not; but many delays were made – time passed on – the small fragment of my Bank-note had just melted away; and before any conclusion could have been put to the business, I must have relapsed into my former state of wretchedness. Suddenly, however, at this crisis, an opening was made, almost by accident, for reconciliation with my friends. I quitted London, in haste, for a remote part of England : after some time, I proceeded to the university; and it was not until many months had passed away, that I had it in my power again to revisit the ground which had become so interesting to me, and to this day remains so, as the chief scene of my youthful sufferings.

Meantime, what had become of poor Ann? For her I have reserved my concluding words: according to our agreement, I sought her daily, and waited for her every night, so long as I staid in London, at the corner of Titchfield-street. I inquired for her of every one who was likely to know her; and, during the last hours of my stay in London, I put into activity every means of tracing her that my knowledge of London suggested, and the limited extent of my power made possible. The street where she had lodged I knew, but not the house; and I remembered at last some account which she had given me of ill treatment from her landlord, which made it probable that she had quitted those lodgings before we parted. She had few acquaintances; most people, besides, thought that the earnestness of my inquiries arose from motives which moved their laughter, or their slight regard; and others, thinking I was in chase of a girl who had robbed me of some trifles, were naturally and excusably indisposed to give me any clue of her, if, indeed, they had any to give. Finally, as my despairing resource, on the day I left London I put into the hands of the only person who (I was sure) must know Ann by sight, from having been in company with us once or twice, an address to —— in —shire, at that time the residence of my family. But, to this hour, I have never heard a syllable about her. This, amongst such troubles as most men meet with in this life, has been my heaviest affliction. – If she lived, doubtless we must have been sometimes in search of each other, at the very same moment, through the mighty labyrinths of London; perhaps even within a few feet of each other – a barrier no wider in a London street, often amounting in the end to a separation for eternity! During some years, I hoped that she *did* live; and I suppose that, in the literal and unrhetorical use of the word *myriad*, I may say that on my different visits to London, I have looked into many, many myriads of female faces, in the hope of meeting her. I should know her again amongst a thousand, if

I saw her for a moment; for, though not handsome, she had a sweet expression of countenance, and a peculiar and graceful carriage of the head. – I sought her, I have said, in hope. So it was for years; but now I should fear to see her: and her cough, which grieved me when I parted with her, is now my consolation. I now wish to see her no longer; but think of her, more gladly, as one long since laid in the grave; in the grave, I would hope, of a Magdalen taken away, before injuries and cruelty had blotted out and transfigured her ingenuous nature, or the brutalities of ruffians had completed the ruin they had begun.

# PART II

So then, Oxford-street, stony-hearted stepmother! thou that listenest to the sighs of orphans, and drinkest the tears of children, at length I was dismissed from thee: the time was come at last that I no more should pace in anguish thy never-ending terraces; no more should dream, and wake in captivity to the pangs of hunger. Successors, too many, to myself and Ann, have, doubtless, since trodden in our footsteps, – inheritors of our calamities: other orphans than Ann have sighed: tears have been shed by other children: and thou, Oxford-street, hast since, doubtless, echoed to the groans of innumerable hearts. For myself, however, the storm which I had outlived seemed to have been the pledge of a long fair-weather; the premature sufferings which I had paid down, to have been accepted as a ransom for many years to come, as a price of long immunity from sorrow: and if again I walked in London, a solitary and contemplative man (as oftentimes I did), I walked for the most part in serenity and peace of mind. And, although it is true that the calamities of my noviciate in London had struck root so deeply in my bodily constitution that afterwards they shot up and flourished afresh, and grew into a noxious umbrage that has overshadowed and darkened my latter years, yet these second assaults of suffering were met with a fortitude more confirmed, with the resources of a maturer intellect, and with alleviations from sympathising affection – how deep and tender!

Thus, however, with whatsoever alleviations, years that were far asunder were bound together by subtle links of suffering derived from a common root. And herein I notice an instance of the short-sightedness of human desires, that oftentimes on moonlight nights, during my first mournful abode in London, my consolation was (if such it could be thought) to gaze from Oxford-street up every avenue in succession which pierces through the heart of Marylebone to the fields and the woods; and *that*, said I, travelling with my eyes up the long vistas which lay part in light and part in shade, '*that* is the road to the north, and therefore to ——,[49] and if I had the wings of a dove, *that* way I would fly for comfort.' Thus I said, and thus I wished, in my blindness; yet, even in that very northern region it was, even in that very valley, nay, in that very house to which my erroneous wishes pointed, that this second birth of my sufferings began; and that they again threatened to besiege the citadel of life and hope. There it was, that for years I was persecuted by visions as ugly, and as ghastly phantoms as ever haunted the couch of an Orestes: and in this unhappier than he, that sleep, which comes to all as a respite and a restoration, and to him especially, as a blessed* balm for his wounded heart and his haunted brain, visited me as my bitterest scourge. Thus blind was I in my desires; yet, if a veil interposes between the dim-sightedness of man and his future calamities, the same veil hides from him their alleviations; and a grief which had not been feared is met by consolations which had not been hoped. I, therefore, who participated, as it were, in the troubles of Orestes (excepting only in his agitated conscience), participated no less in all his supports: my Eumenides, like his, were at my bed-feet, and stared in upon me through the curtains: but, watching by my pillow, or defrauding herself of sleep to bear me company through the heavy watches of the night, sat my Electra: for thou, beloved M.,[50] dear companion of my later years, thou wast my Electra! and neither in nobility of mind nor in long-suffering affection, wouldst permit that a Grecian sister should excel an English wife. For thou thoughtest not much to stoop to humble offices of kindness, and to servile† ministrations of tenderest affection; – to wipe away for years the unwholesome dews upon the fore-head, or to refresh the lips when parched and baked with fever; nor, even when thy own peaceful slumbers had by long sym-pathy become infected with the spectacle of my dread contest with phantoms and shadowy enemies that oftentimes bade me 'sleep no more!' – not even then, didst thou utter a complaint or any murmur, nor withdraw thy angelic smiles, nor shrink from thy service of love more than Electra did of old. For she

---

* φιλον ἱπνου θελγητρον ἐπικουζον νοσον.

† ἡδυ δουλευμα. Eurip. *Orest.*

68

too, though she were a Grecian woman, and the daughter of the king* of men, yet wept sometimes, and hid her face† in her robe.

But these troubles are past: and thou wilt read these records of a period so dolorous to us both as the legend of some hideous dream that can return no more. Meantime, I am again in London[51]: and again I pace the terraces of Oxford-street by night: and oftentimes, when I am oppressed by anxieties that demand all my philosophy and the comfort of thy presence to support, and yet remember that I am separated from thee by three hundred miles, and the length of three dreary months, – I look up the streets that run northwards from Oxford-street, upon moonlight nights, and recollect my youthful ejaculation of anguish; – and remembering that thou art sitting alone in that same valley, and mistress of that very house[52] to which my heart turned in its blindness, nineteen years ago, I think that, though blind indeed, and scattered to the winds of late, the promptings of my heart may yet have had reference to a remoter time, and may be justified if read in another meaning: – and, if I could allow myself to descend again to the impotent wishes of childhood, I should again say to myself, as I look to the north, 'Oh, that I had the wings of a dove –' and with how just a confidence in thy good and gracious nature might I add the other half of my early ejaculation – 'And *that* way I would fly for comfort.'

---

\* ἄναξ ἀνδρῶν Ἀγαμεμνων.

† ὄμμα θεισ᾽ ἐιοω πεπλων. The scholar will know that throughout this passage I refer to the early scenes of the *Orestes;* one of the most beautiful exhibitions of the domestic affections which even the dramas of Euripides can furnish. To the English reader, it may be necessary to say, that the situation at the opening of the drama is that of a brother attended only by his sister during the demoniacal possession of a suffering conscience (or, in the mythology of the play, haunted by the furies), and in circumstances of immediate danger from enemies, and of desertion or cold regard from nominal friends.

# The Pleasures of Opium

IT is so long since I first took opium, that if it had been a trifling incident in my life, I might have forgotten its date: but cardinal events are not to be forgotten; and from circumstances connected with it, I remember that it must be referred to the autumn of 1804. During that season I was in London, having come thither for the first time since my entrance at college. And my introduction to opium arose in the following way. From an early age I had been accustomed to wash my head in cold water at least once a day: being suddenly seized with toothache, I attributed it to some relaxation caused by an accidental intermission of that practice; jumped out of bed: plunged my head into a basin of cold water; and with hair thus wetted went to sleep. The next morning, as I need hardly say, I awoke with excruciating rheumatic pains of the head and face, from which I had hardly any respite for about twenty days. On the twenty-first day, I think it was, and on a Sunday, that I went out into the streets; rather to run away, if possible, from my torments, than with any distinct purpose. By accident I met a college acquaintance who recommended opium. Opium! dread agent of unimaginable pleasure and pain! I had heard of it as I had of manna or of ambrosia, but no further: how unmeaning a sound was it at that time! what solemn chords does it now strike upon my heart! what heart-quaking vibrations of sad and happy remembrances! Reverting for a moment to these, I feel a mystic importance attached to the minutest circumstances connected with the place and the time, and the man (if man he was) that first laid open to me the Paradise of Opium-eaters. It was a Sunday afternoon, wet and cheerless: and a duller spectacle this earth of ours has not to show than a rainy Sunday in London. My road homewards lay through Oxford-street; and near 'the *stately* Pantheon'[53] (as Mr Wordsworth has obligingly called it) I saw a druggist's shop. The druggist, unconscious minister of celestial pleasures! – as if in sympathy with the rainy Sunday, looked dull and stupid, just as any mortal druggist might be expected to look on a Sunday: and, when I asked for the tincture of opium,[54] he gave it to me as any other man might do: and furthermore, out of my shilling, returned to me what seemed to be real copper halfpence, taken out of a real wooden drawer. Nevertheless, in spite of such indications of humanity, he has ever since existed in my mind as the beatific vision of an immortal druggist, sent down to earth on a special mission to myself. And it confirms me in this way of considering him, that, when I next came up to London, I sought him near the stately Pantheon, and found him not: and thus to me, who knew not his name (if indeed he had one) he seemed rather to have vanished from Oxford-street than to have removed in any bodily fashion. The reader may choose to think of him as, possibly, no more than a sublunary druggist: it may be so: but my faith is better: I believe him to have evanesced,* or evaporated. So unwillingly would I connect any mortal remembrances with that hour, and place, and creature, that first brought me acquainted with the celestial drug.

Arrived at my lodgings, it may be supposed that I lost not a moment in taking the quantity prescribed. I was necessarily ignorant of the whole art and mystery of opium-taking: and, what I took, I took under every disadvantage. But I took it: – and in an hour, oh! heavens! what a revulsion! what an upheaving, from its lowest depths, of the inner spirit! what an apocalypse of the world within me! That my pains had vanished, was now a trifle in my eyes: – this negative effect was swallowed up in the immensity of those positive effects which had opened before me – in the abyss of divine enjoyment thus suddenly revealed. Here

---

*Evanesced:* – this way of going off the stage of life appears to have been well known in the 17th century, but at that time to have been considered a peculiar privilege of blood-royal, and by no means to be allowed to druggists. For about the year 1686, a poet of rather ominous name (and who, by the by, did ample justice to his name), viz. Mr Flat-man, in speaking of the death of Charles II expresses his surprise that any prince should commit so absurd an act as dying; because, says he,

*Kings should disdain to die, and only* disappear.
They should *abscond*, that is, into the other world.

was a panacea – a φαρμακον νήωενθες[55] for all human woes:
here was the secret of happiness, about which philosophers had
disputed for so many ages, at once discovered: happiness might
now be bought for a penny, and carried in the waistcoat pocket:
portable ecstasies might be had corked up in a pint bottle: and
peace of mind could be sent down in gallons by the mail coach.
But, if I talk in this way, the reader will think I am laughing:
and I can assure him, that nobody will laugh long who deals
much with opium: its pleasures even are of a grave and solemn
complexion; and in his happiest state, the opium-eater cannot
present himself in the character of *l'Allegro:* even then, he speaks
and thinks as becomes *Il Penseroso.* Nevertheless, I have a very
reprehensible way of jesting at times in the midst of my own
misery: and, unless when I am checked by some more powerful
feelings, I am afraid I shall be guilty of this indecent practice
even in these annals of suffering or enjoyment. The reader must
allow a little to my infirm nature in this respect: and with a few
indulgences of that sort, I shall endeavour to be as grave, if not
drowsy, as fits a theme like opium, so antimercurial[56] as it really
is, and so drowsy as it is falsely reputed.

And, first, one word with respect to its bodily effects: for upon
all that has been hitherto written on the subject of opium,
whether by travellers in Turkey (who may plead their privilege of
lying as an old immemorial right), or by professors of medicine,
writing *ex cathedrá,* – I have but one emphatic criticism to pro-
nounce – Lies! lies! lies! I remember once, in passing a book-
stall, to have caught these words from a page of some satiric
author: – "By this time I became convinced that the London
newspapers spoke truth at least twice a week, viz., on Tuesday
and Saturday,[57] and might safely be depended upon for — the
list of bankrupts." In like manner, I do by no means deny that
some truths have been delivered to the world in regard to opium:
thus it has been repeatedly affirmed by the learned, that opium
is a dusky brown in colour; and this, take notice, I grant:
secondly, that it is rather dear; which also I grant: for in my
time, East-India opium has been three guineas a pound, and
Turkey eight: and, thirdly, that if you eat a good deal of it, most
probably you must do – what is particularly disagreeable to any

man of regular habits, viz. die.* These weighty propositions are, all and singular, true: I cannot gainsay them: and truth ever was, and will be, commendable. But in these three theorems, I believe we have exhausted the stock of knowledge as yet accumulated by man on the subject of opium. And therefore, worthy doctors, as there seems to be room for further discoveries, stand aside, and allow me to come forward and lecture on this matter.

First, then, it is not so much affirmed as taken for granted, by all who ever mention opium, formally or incidentally, that it does, or can produce intoxication. Now, reader, assure yourself, *meo periculo*,[58] that no quantity of opium ever did, or could intoxicate. As to the tincture of opium (commonly called laudanum) *that* might certainly intoxicate if a man could bear to take enough of it; but why? because it contains so much proof spirit, and not because it contains so much opium. But crude opium, I affirm peremptorily, is incapable of producing any state of body at all resembling that which is produced by alcohol: and not in *degree* only incapable, but even in *kind*: it is not in the quantity of its effects merely, but in the quality, that it differs altogether. The pleasure given by wine is always mounting, and tending to a crisis, after which it declines: that from opium, when once generated, is stationary for eight or ten hours: the first, to borrow a technical distinction from medicine, is a case of acute – the second, of chronic pleasure: the one is a flame, the other a steady and equable glow. But the main distinction lies in this, that whereas wine disorders the mental faculties, opium, on the contrary (if taken in a proper manner), introduces amongst them the most exquisite order, legislation, and harmony. Wine robs a man of his self-possession: opium greatly invigorates it. Wine unsettles and clouds the judgment, and gives a preternatural brightness, and a vivid exaltation to the contempts and the admirations, the

---

*Of this, however, the learned appear latterly to have doubted: for in a pirated edition of Buchan's *Domestic Medicine*, which I once saw in the hands of a farmer's wife who was studying it for the benefit of her health, the doctor was made to say – 'Be particularly careful never to take above five-and-twenty *ounces* of laudanum at once'; the true reading being probably five-and-twenty *drops*, which are held equal to about one grain of crude opium.

loves and the hatreds, of the drinker: opium, on the contrary, communicates serenity and equipoise to all the faculties, active or passive: and with respect to the temper and moral feelings in general, it gives simply that sort of vital warmth which is approved by the judgment, and which would probably always accompany a bodily constitution of primeval or antediluvian health. Thus, for instance, opium, like wine, gives an expansion to the heart and the benevolent affections: but then, with this remarkable difference, that in the sudden development of kind-heartedness which accompanies inebriation, there is always more or less of a maudlin character, which exposes it to the contempt of the bystander. Men shake hands, swear eternal friendship, and shed tears – no mortal knows why: and the sensual creature is clearly uppermost. But the expansion of the beniger feelings, incident to opium, is no febrile access, but a healthy restoration to that state which the mind would naturally recover upon the removal of any deep-seated irritation of pain that had disturbed and quarrelled with the impulses of a heart originally just and good. True it is, that even wine, up to a certain point, and with certain men, rather tends to exalt and to steady the intellect: I myself, who have never been a great wine-drinker, used to find that half a dozen glasses of wine advantageously affected the faculties – brightened and intensified the consciousness – and gave to the mind a feeling of being 'ponderibus librata suis':[59] and certainly it is most absurdly said, in popular language, of any man, that he is *disguised* in liquor: for, on the contrary, most men are disguised by sobriety; and it is when they are drinking (as some old gentleman says in Athenæus), that men ἑαυτοὺς ἐμφανίζουσιν οἵτινες εἰσίν – display themselves in their true complexion of character; which surely is not disguising themselves. But still, wine constantly leads a man to the brink of absurdity and extravagance; and, beyond a certain point, it is sure to volatilize and to disperse the intellectual energies: whereas opium always seems to compose what had been agitated, and to concentrate what had been distracted. In short, to sum up all in one word, a man who is inebriated, or tending to inebriation, is, and feels that he is, in a condition which calls up into supremacy the merely human, too often the brutal, part of his nature: but the opium-eater (I speak of him who is not suffering from any disease, or other remote effects of opium,) feels that the diviner part of his nature is paramount; that is, the moral affections are in a state of cloudless serenity; and over all is the great light of the majestic intellect.

This is the doctrine of the true church on the subject of opium: of which church I acknowledge myself to be the only member[60] – the alpha and the omega: but then it is to be recollected, that I speak from the ground of a large and profound personal experience: whereas most of the unscientific* authors who have at all treated of opium, and even of those who have written expressly on the materia medica, make it evident, from the horror they express of it, that their experimental knowledge of its action is none at all. I will, however, candidly acknowledge that I have met with one person who bore evidence to its intoxicating power, such as staggered my own incredulity: for he was a surgeon,[61]

---

*Amongst the great herd of travellers, &c. who show sufficiently by their stupidity that they never held any intercourse with opium, I must caution my readers specially against the brilliant author of *Anastasius*. This gentleman, whose wit would lead one to presume him an opium-eater, has made it impossible to consider him in that character from the grievous misrepresentation which he gives of its effects, at p. 215–17, of vol. i. – Upon consideration, it must appear such to the author himself: for, waiving the errors I have insisted on in the text, which (and others) are adopted in the fullest manner, he will himself admit, that an old gentleman 'with a snow-white beard', who eats 'ample doses of opium', and is yet able to deliver what is meant and received as very weighty counsel on the bad effects of that practice, is but an indifferent evidence that opium either kills people prematurely, or sends them into a mad-house. But, for my part, I see into this old gentleman and his motives: the fact is, he was enamoured of 'the little golden receptacle of the pernicious drug' which Anastasius carried about him; and no way of obtaining it so safe and so feasible occurred, as that of frightening its owner out of his wits (which, by the by, are none of the strongest). This commentary throws a new light upon the case, and greatly improves it as a story: for the old gentleman's speech, considered as a lecture on pharmacy, is highly absurd: but, considered as a hoax on Anastasius, it reads excellently.

and had himself taken opium largely. [XIX] I happened to say to him, that his enemies (as I had heard) charged him with talking nonsense on politics, and that his friends apologized for him, by suggesting that he was constantly in a state of intoxication from opium. Now the accusation, said I, is not *primâ facie*, and of necessity, an absurd one: but the defence *is*. To my surprise, however, he insisted that both his enemies and his friends were in the right: 'I will maintain,' said he, 'that I *do* talk nonsense; and secondly, I will maintain that I do not talk nonsense upon principle, or with any view to profit, but solely and simply, said he, solely and simply, – solely and simply, (repeating it three times over), because I am drunk with opium; and *that* daily.' I replied that, as to the allegation of his enemies, as it seemed to be established upon such respectable testimony, seeing that the three parties concerned all agreed in it, it did not become me to question it; but the defence set up I must demur to. He proceeded to discuss the matter, and to lay down his reasons; but it seemed to me so impolite to pursue an argument which must have presumed a man mistaken in a point belonging to his own profession, that I did not press him even when his course of argument seemed open to objection: not to mention that a man who talks nonsense, even though 'with no view to profit,' is not altogether the most agreeable partner in a dispute, whether as opponent or respondent. I confess, however, that the authority of a surgeon, and one who was reputed a good one, may seem a weighty one to my prejudice: but still I must plead my experience, which was greater than his greatest by 7000 drops a day; and, though it was not possible to suppose a medical man unacquainted with characteristic symptoms of vinous intoxication, it yet struck me that he might proceed on a logical error of using the word intoxication with too great latitude, and extending it generically to all modes of nervous excitement, instead of restricting it as the expression for a specific sort of excitement, connected with certain diagnostics. Some people have maintained, in my hearing, that they had been drunk upon green tea: and a medical student in London, for whose knowledge in his profession I have reason to feel great respect, assured me, the other day, that a patient, in recovering from an illness, had got drunk on a beef-steak.

Having dwelt so much on this first and leading error, in respect to opium, I shall notice very briefly a second and a third; which are, that the elevation of spirits produced by opium is necessarily followed by a proportionate depression, and that the natural and even immediate consequence of opium is torpor and stagnation, animal and mental. The first of these errors I shall content myself with simply denying; assuring my reader, that for ten years, during which I took opium at intervals, the day succeeding to that on which I allowed myself this luxury was always a day of unusually good spirits.

With respect to the torpor supposed to follow, or rather (if we were to credit the numerous pictures of Turkish opium-eaters) to accompany the practice of opium-eating, I deny that also. Certainly, opium is classed under the head of narcotics; and some such effect it may produce in the end: but the primary effects of opium are always, and in the highest degree, to excite and stimulate the system: this first stage of its action always lasted with me, during my noviciate, for upwards of eight hours; so that it must be the fault of the opium-eater himself if he does not so time his exhibition of the dose (to speak medically) as that the whole weight of its narcotic influence may descend upon his sleep. Turkish opium-eaters, it seems, are absurd enough to sit, like so many equestrian statues, on logs of wood as stupid as themselves. But that the reader may judge of the degree in which opium is likely to stupify the faculties of an Englishman, I shall (by way of treating the question illustratively, rather than argumentatively) describe the way in which I myself often passed an opium evening in London, during the period between 1804 and 1812. It will be seen, that at least opium did not move me to seek solitude, and much less to seek inactivity, or the torpid state of self-involution ascribed to the Turks. I give this account at the risk of being pronounced a crazy enthusiast or visionary: but I regard *that* little: I must desire my reader to bear in mind, that I was a hard student, and at severe studies for all the rest of my time: and certainly I had a right occasionally to relaxations as well as other people: these, however, I allowed myself but seldom.

The late Duke of ——[62] used to say, 'Next Friday, by the blessing of Heaven, I purpose to be drunk': and in like manner I used to fix beforehand how often, within a given time, and when, I would commit a debauch of opium. This was seldom more than once in three weeks : for at that time I could not have ventured to call every day (as I did afterwards) for *"a glass of laudanum nègus, warm, and without sugar."* No : as I have said, I seldom drank laudanum, at that time, more than once in three weeks : this was usually on a Tuesday or a Saturday night; my reason for which was this. In those days Grassini[63] sang at the Opera : and her voice was delightful to me beyond all that I had ever heard. I know not what may be the state of the Opera-house now, having never been within its walls for seven or eight years, but at that time it was by much the most pleasant place of public resort in London for passing an evening. Five shillings admitted one to the gallery, which was subject to far less annoyance than the pit of the theatres : the orchestra was distinguished by its sweet and melodious grandeur from all English orchestras, the composition of which, I confess, is not acceptable to my ear, from the pre-dominance of the clangorous instruments, and the absolute tyranny of the violin. [XX] The choruses were divine to hear : and when Grassini appeared in some interlude, as she often did, and poured forth her passionate soul as Andromache, at the tomb of Hector, &c. I question whether any Turk, of all that ever entered the paradise of opium-eaters, can have had half the pleasure I had. But, indeed, I honour the Barbarians too much by supposing them capable of any pleasures approaching to the intellectual ones of an Englishman. For music is an intellectual or a sensual pleasure, according to the temperament of him who hears it. And, by the by, with the exception of the fine extrava-ganza on that subject in Twelfth Night,[64] I do not recollect more than one thing said adequately on the subject of music in all literature : it is a passage in the *Religio Medici*\*[65] of Sir T. Brown; and, though chiefly remarkable for its sublimity, has also a philo-sophic value, inasmuch as it points to the true theory of musical effects. The mistake of most people is to suppose that it is by the

---

\*I have not the book at this moment to consult : but I think the passage begins – 'And even that [vulgar and] tavern music, which makes one man merry, another mad, strikes in me a deep fit of devotion,' &c.

ear, they communicate with music, and, therefore, that they are purely passive to its effects. But this is not so : it is by the reaction of the mind upon the notices of the ear, (the *matter* coming by the senses, the *form* from the mind) that the pleasure is constructed : and therefore it is that people of equally good ear differ so much in this point from one another. Now opium, by greatly increasing the activity of the mind generally, increases, of necessity, that particular mode of its activity by which we are able to construct out of the raw material of organic sound an elaborate intellectual pleasure. But, says a friend, a succession of musical sounds is to me like a collection of Arabic characters : I can attach no ideas to them ! Ideas ! my good sir? there is no occasion for them : all that class of ideas, which can be available in such a case, has a language of representative feelings. But this is a subject foreign to my present purposes : it is sufficient to say, that a chorus, &c. of elaborate harmony, displayed before me, as in a piece of arras work, the whole of my past life – not as if recalled by an act of memory, but as if present and incarnated in the music : no longer painful to dwell upon : but the detail of its incidents removed, or blended in some hazy abstraction; and its passions exalted, spiritualized, and sublimed. All this was to be had for five shillings. And over and above the music of the stage and the orchestra, I had all around me, in the intervals of the performance, the music of the Italian language talked by Italian women : for the gallery was usually crowded with Italians : and I listened with a pleasure such as that with which Weld[66] the traveller lay and listened, in Canada, to the sweet laughter of Indian women; for the less you understand of a language, the more sensible you are to the melody or harshness of its sounds : for such a purpose, therefore, it was an advantage to me that I was a poor Italian scholar, reading it but little, and not speaking it at all, nor understanding a tenth part of what I heard spoken.

These were my Opera pleasures : but another pleasure I had which, as it could be had only on a Saturday night, occasionally struggled with my love of the Opera; for, at that time, Tuesday and Saturday were the regular Opera nights. On this subject I am afraid I shall be rather obscure, but, I can assure the reader, not at all more so than Marinus in his life of Proclus,[67] or many other biographers and auto-biographers of fair reputation. This pleasure, I have said, was to be had only on a Saturday night. What then was Saturday night to me more than any other night? I had no labours that I rested from; no wages to receive: what needed I to care for Saturday night, more than as it was a summons to hear Grassini? True, most logical reader: what you say is unanswerable. And yet so it was and is, that, whereas different men throw their feelings into different channels, and most are apt to show their interest in the concerns of the poor, chiefly by sympathy, expressed in some shape or other, with their distresses and sorrows, I, at that time, was disposed to express my interest by sympathising with their pleasures. The pains of poverty I had lately seen too much of; more than I wished to remember: but the pleasures of the poor, their consolations of spirit, and their reposes from bodily toil, can never become oppressive to contemplate. Now Saturday night is the season for the chief, regular, and periodic return of rest to the poor: in this point the most hostile sects unite, and acknowledge a common link of brotherhood: almost all Christendom rests from its labours. It is a rest introductory to another rest: and divided by a whole day and two nights from the renewal of toil. On this account I feel always, on a Saturday night, as though I also were released from some yoke of labour, had some wages to receive, and some luxury of repose to enjoy. For the sake, therefore, of witnessing, upon as large a scale as possible, a spectacle with which my sympathy was so entire, I used often, on Saturday nights, after I had taken opium, to wander forth, without much regarding the direction or the distance, to all the markets, and other parts of London, to which the poor resort on a Saturday night, for laying out their wages. Many a family party, consisting of a man, his wife, and sometimes one or two of his children, have I listened to, as they stood consulting on their ways and means or the strength of their exchequer, or the price of household articles. Gradually I became familiar with their wishes, their difficulties, and their opinions. Sometimes there might be heard murmurs of discontent: but far oftener expressions on the countenance, or uttered in words, of patience, hope, and tranquillity. And, taken generally, I must say, that, in this point at least, the poor are far more philosophic than the rich—that they show a more ready and cheerful submission to what they consider as irremediable evils, or irreparable losses. Whenever I saw occasion, or could do it without appearing to be intrusive, I joined their parties; and gave my opinion upon the matter in discussion, which, if not always judicious, was always received indulgently. If wages were a little higher, or expected to be so, or the quartern loaf a little lower, or it was reported that onions and butter were expected to fall, I was glad: yet, if the contrary were true, I drew from opium some means of consoling myself. For opium (like the bee, that extracts its materials indiscriminately from roses and from the soot of chimneys) can overrule all feelings into a compliance with the master key. Some of these rambles led me to great distances: for an opium-eater is too happy to observe the motion of time. And sometimes in my attempts to steer homewards, upon nautical principles, by fixing my eye on the pole-star, and seeking ambitiously for a north-west passage, instead of circumnavigating all the capes and headlands I had doubled in my outward voyage, I came suddenly upon such knotty problems of alleys, such enigmatical entries, and such sphinx's riddles of streets without thoroughfares, as must, I conceive, baffle the audacity of porters, and confound the intellects of hackney-coachmen. I could almost have believed, at times, that I must be the first discoverer of some of these *terræ incognitæ*, and doubted, whether they had yet been laid down in the modern charts of London. For all this, however, I paid a heavy price in distant years, when the human face tyrannized over my dreams, and the perplexities of my steps in London came back and haunted my sleep, with the feeling of perplexities moral or intellectual, that brought confusion to the reason, or anguish and remorse to the conscience.

Thus I have shown that opium does not, of necessity, produce inactivity or torpor; but that, on the contrary, it often led me into markets and theatres. Yet, in candour, I will admit that markets and theatres are not the appropriate haunts of the opium-eater, when in the divinest state incident to his enjoyment. In that state, crowds become an oppression to him; music even, too sensual and gross. He naturally seeks solitude and silence, as indispensable conditions of those trances, or profoundest reveries, which are the crown and consummation of what opium can do for human nature. I, whose disease it was to meditate too much, and to observe too little, and who, upon my first entrance at college, was nearly falling into a deep melancholy, from brooding too much on the sufferings which I had witnessed in London, was sufficiently aware of the tendencies of my own thoughts to do all I could to counteract them. – I was, indeed, like a person who, according to the old legend, had entered the cave of Trophonius;[68] and the remedies I sought were to force myself into society, and to keep my understanding in continual activity upon matters of science. But for these remedies, I should certainly have become hypochondriacally melancholy. In after years, however, when my cheerfulness was more fully re-established, I yielded to my natural inclination for a solitary life. And, at that time, I often fell into these reveries upon taking opium; and more than once it has happened to me, on a summer night, when I have been at an open window, in a room from which I could overlook the sea at a mile below me, and could command a view of the great town of L—,[69] at about the same distance, that I have sat, from sun-set to sun-rise, motionless, and without wishing to move.

I shall be charged with mysticism, Behmenism, quietism,[70] &c. but *that* shall not alarm me. Sir H. Vane,[71] the younger, was one of our wisest men; and let my readers see if he, in his philosophical works, be half as unmystical as I am. – I say, then, that it has often struck me that the scene itself was somewhat typical of what took place in such a reverie. The town of L— represented the earth, with its sorrows and its graves left behind, yet not out of sight, nor wholly forgotten. The ocean, in everlasting but gentle agitation, and brooded over by a dove-like calm, might not unfitly typify the mind and the mood which then swayed it. For it seemed to me as if then first I stood at a distance, and aloof from the uproar of life; as if the tumult, the fever, and the strife, were suspended; a respite granted from the secret burthens of the heart; a sabbath of repose; a resting from human labours. Here were the hopes which blossom in the paths of life, reconciled with the peace which is in the grave; motions of the intellect as unwearied as the heavens, yet for all anxieties a halcyon calm : a tranquillity that seemed no product of inertia, but as if resulting from mighty and equal antagonisms; infinite activities, infinite repose.

Oh! just, subtle, and mighty opium![72] that to the hearts of poor and rich alike, for the wounds that will never heal, and for "the pangs that tempt the spirit to rebel," bringest an assuaging balm; eloquent opium! that with thy potent rhetoric stealest away the purposes of wrath; and to the guilty man, for one night givest back the hopes of his youth, and hands washed pure from blood; and to the proud man, a brief oblivion for

Wrongs unredress'd, and insults unavenged;

that summonest to the chancery of dreams, for the triumphs of suffering innocence, false witnesses; and confoundest perjury; and dost reverse the sentences of unrighteous judges: – thou buildest upon the bosom of darkness, out of the fantastic imagery of the brain, cities and temples, beyond the art of Phidias and Praxiteles – beyond the splendour of Babylon and Hekatómpy-los:[73] and 'from the anarchy of dreaming sleep,' callest into sunny light the faces of long buried beauties, and the blessed household countenances, cleansed from the 'dishonours of the grave.' Thou only givest these gifts to man; and thou hast the keys of Paradise, oh, just, subtle, and mighty opium!

# Introduction to the Pains of Opium

COURTEOUS, and, I hope, indulgent reader (for all *my* readers must be indulgent ones, or else, I fear, I shall shock them too much to count on their courtesy), having accompanied me thus far, now let me request you to move onwards, for about eight years: that is to say, from 1804 (when I have said that my acquaintance with opium first began) to 1812. The years of academic life are now over and gone – almost forgotten; – the student's cap no longer presses my temples: if my cap exists at all, it presses those of some youthful scholar, I trust, as happy as myself, and as passionate a lover of knowledge. My gown is, by this time, I dare to say, in the same condition with many thousands of excellent books in the Bodleian, viz. diligently perused by certain studious moths and worms: or departed, however (which is all that I know of its fate), to that great reservoir of *somewhere*, to which all the tea-cups, tea-caddies, tea-pots, tea-kettles, &c. have departed (not to speak of still frailer vessels, such as glasses, decanters, bed-makers, &c.) which occasional resemblances in the present generation of tea-cups, &c. remind me of having once possessed, but of whose departure and final fate I, in common with most gownsmen of either university, could give, I suspect, but an obscure and conjectural history. The persecution of the chapel-bell, sounding its unwelcome summons to six o'clock matins, interrupts my slumbers no longer: the porter who rang it, upon whose beautiful nose (bronze, inlaid with copper) I wrote, in retaliation, so many Greek epigrams, whilst I was dressing, is dead, and has ceased to disturb any body: and I, and many others, who suffered much from his tintinnabulous propensities, have now agreed to overlook his errors, and have forgiven him. Even with the bell I am now in charity: it rings, I suppose, as formerly, thrice a-day: and cruelly annoys, I doubt not, many worthy gentlemen, and disturbs their peace of mind: but as to me, in this year 1812, I regard its treacherous voice no longer (treacherous, I call it, for, by some refinement of malice, it spoke in as sweet and silvery tones as if it had been inviting one to a party): its tones have no longer, indeed, power to reach me, let the wind sit as favourable as the malice of the bell itself could wish : for I am 250 miles away from it, and buried in the depth of mountains. And what am I doing amongst the mountains? Taking opium. Yes, but what else? Why, reader, in 1812, the year we are now arrived at, as well as for some years previous, I have been chiefly studying German metaphysics, in the writings of Kant, Fichte, Schelling, &c.[74] And how, and in what manner, do I live? in short, what class or description of men do I belong to? I am at this period, viz. in 1812, living in a cottage; and with a single female servant ('honi soit qui mal y pense'),[75] who, amongst my neighbours, passes by the name of my 'housekeeper.' And, as a scholar and a man of learned education, and in that sense a gentleman, I may presume to class myself as an unworthy member of that indefinite body called *gentlemen*. Partly on the ground I have assigned, perhaps; partly because, from my having no visible calling or business, it is rightly judged that I must be living on my private fortune; I am so classed by my neighbours : and, by the courtesy of modern England, I am usually addressed on letters, &c. *esquire*, though having, I fear, in the rigorous construction of heralds, but slender pretensions to that distinguished honour : yes, in popular estimation, I am X. Y. Z.,[76] esquire, but not Justice of the Peace, nor Custos Rotulorum.[77] Am I married? Not yet. And I still take opium? On Saturday nights. And, perhaps, have taken it unblushingly ever since 'the rainy Sunday,' 'and the stately Pantheon,' and 'the beatific druggist' of 1804? – Even so. And how do I find my health after all this opium-eating? in short, how do I do? Why, pretty well, I thank you, reader : in the phrase of ladies in the straw,[78] 'as well as can be expected.' In fact, if I dared to say the real and simple truth, though, to satisfy the theories of medical men, I *ought* to be ill, I never was better in my life than in the spring of 1812; and I hope sincerely, that the quantity of claret, port, or 'particular Madeira,' which, in all probability, you, good reader, have taken, and design to take for every term of eight years, during your natural life, may as little disorder your health as mine was disordered by the opium I had taken for the eight years, between 1804 and 1812. Hence you may see again the danger of taking any medical advice from *Anastasius*;[79] in divinity, for aught I know, or law, he may be a safe counsellor; but not in medicine. No: it is far better to consult Dr Buchan;[80] as I did: for I never forgot that worthy man's excellent suggestion: and I was 'particularly careful not to take above five-and-twenty ounces of laudanum.' To this moderation and temperate use of the article, I may ascribe it, I suppose, that as yet, at least, (*i.e.* in 1812,) I am ignorant and unsuspicious of the avenging terrors which opium has in store for those who abuse its lenity. At the same time, it must not be forgotten, that hitherto I have been only a diletante eater of opium: eight years' practice even, with the single precaution of allowing sufficient intervals between every indulgence, has not been sufficient to make opium necessary to me as an article of daily diet. But now comes a different era. Move on, if you please, reader, to 1813. In the summer of the year we have just quitted, I had suffered much in bodily health from distress of mind connected with a very melancholy event.[81] This event, being no ways related to the subject now before me, further than through the bodily illness which it produced, I need not more particularly notice. Whether this illness of 1812 had any share in that of 1813, I know not: but so it was, that in the latter year I was attacked by a most appalling irritation of the stomach, in all respects the same as that which had caused me so much suffering in youth, and accompanied by a revival of all the old dreams. This is the point of my narrative on which, as respects my own self-justification, the whole of what follows may be said to hinge. And here I find myself in a perplexing dilemma: – Either, on the one hand, I must exhaust the reader's patience, by such a detail of my malady, and of my struggles with it, as might suffice to establish the fact of my inability to wrestle any longer with irritation and constant suffering: or, on the other hand, by passing lightly over this critical part of my story, I must forego the benefit of a stronger impression left on the mind of the reader, and must lay myself open to the misconstruction of having slipped by the easy and gradual steps of self-indulging persons, from the first to the final stage of opium-eating (a misconstruction to which there will be a lurking predisposition in most readers, from my previous acknowledgments). This is the dilemma: the first horn of which would be sufficient to toss and gore any column of patient readers, though drawn up sixteen deep and constantly relieved by fresh men : consequently *that* is not to be thought of. It remains then, that I *postulate* so much as is necessary for my purpose. And let me take as full credit for what I postulate as if I had demonstrated it, good reader, at the expense of your patience and my own. Be not so ungenerous as to let me suffer in your good opinion through my own forbearance and regard for your comfort. No : believe all that I ask of you, viz. that I could resist no longer; believe it liberally and as an act of grace : or else in mere prudence : for, if not, then in the next edition of my Opium Confessions revised and enlarged, I will make you believe and tremble : and *à force d'ennuyer*, by mere dint of pandiculation[82] I will terrify all readers of mine from ever again questioning any postulate that I shall think fit to make.

This then, let me repeat, I postulate – that, at the time I began to take opium daily, I could not have done otherwise. Whether indeed, afterwards I might not have succeeded in breaking off the habit, even when it seemed to me that all efforts would be unavailing, and whether many of the innumerable efforts which I *did* make might not have been carried much further, and my gradual re-conquests of ground lost might not have been followed up much more energetically – these are questions which I must decline. Perhaps I might make out a case of palliation; but, shall I speak ingenuously? I confess it, as a besetting infirmity of mine, that I am too much of an Eudæmonist :[83] I hanker too much after a state of happiness, both for myself and others : I cannot face misery, whether my own or not, with an eye of sufficient firmness : and am little capable of encountering present pain for the sake of any reversionary benefit. On some other matters, I can agree with the gentlemen in the cotton-trade* at Manchester in affecting the Stoic[84] philosophy : but not in this. Here I take

---

* A handsome news-room, of which I was very politely made free in passing through Manchester by several gentlemen of that place, is called, I think, *The Porch:* whence I, who am a stranger in Manchester, inferred that the subscribers meant to profess themselves followers of Zeno. But I have been since assured that this is a mistake.

the liberty of an Eclectic[85] philosopher, and I look out for some courteous and considerate sect that will condescend more to the infirm condition of an opium-eater; that are 'sweet men,' as Chaucer says, 'to give absolution,' and will show some conscience in the penances they inflict, and the efforts of abstinence they exact, from poor sinners like myself. An inhuman moralist I can no more endure in my nervous state than opium that has not been boiled. At any rate, he, who summons me to send out a large freight of self-denial and mortification upon any cruising voyage of moral improvement, must make it clear to my understanding that the concern is a hopeful one. At my time of life (six and thirty years of age) it cannot be supposed that I have much energy to spare : in fact, I find it all little enough for the intellectual labours I have on my hands : and, therefore, let no man expect to frighten me by a few hard words into embarking any part of it upon desperate adventures of morality.

Whether desperate or not, however, the issue of the struggle in 1813 was what I have mentioned; and from this date, the reader is to consider me as a regular and confirmed opium-eater, of whom to ask whether on any particular day he had or had not taken opium, would be to ask whether his lungs had performed respiration, or the heart fulfilled its functions. – You understand now, reader, what I am : and you are by this time aware, that no old gentleman, 'with a snow-white beard,' will have any chance of persuading me to surrender 'the little golden receptacle of the pernicious drug.' No : I give notice to all, whether moralists or surgeons, that, whatever be their pretensions and skill in their respective lines of practice, they must not hope for any countenance from me, if they think to begin by any savage proposition for a Lent or Ramadan[86] of abstinence from opium. This then being all fully understood between us, we shall in future sail before the wind. Now then, reader, from 1813, where all this time we have been sitting down and loitering – rise up, if you please, and walk forward about three years more. Now draw up the curtain, and you shall see me in a new character.

If any man, poor or rich, were to say that he would tell us what had been the happiest day in his life, and the why, and the wherefore, I suppose that we should all cry out – Hear him ! Hear him !

– As to the happiest *day*, that must be very difficult for any wise man to name: because any event, that could occupy so distinguished a place in a man's retrospect of his life, or be entitled to have shed a special felicity on any one day, ought to be of such an enduring character, as that (accidents apart) it should have continued to shed the same felicity, or one not distinguishably less, on many years together. To the happiest *lustrum*, however, or even to the happiest *year*, it may be allowed to any man to point without discountenance from wisdom. This year, in my case, reader, was the one which we have now reached; though it stood, I confess, as a parenthesis between years of a gloomier character. It was a year of brilliant water (to speak after the manner of jewellers), set as it were, and insulated, in the gloom and cloudy melancholy of opium. Strange as it may sound, I had a little before this time descended suddenly, and without any considerable effort, from 320 grains of opium (*i.e.* eight* thousand drops of laudanum) per day, to forty grains, or one eighth part. Instantaneously, and as if by magic, the cloud of profoundest melancholy which rested upon my brain, like some black vapours that I have seen roll away from the summits of mountains, drew off in one day ($\nu\nu\chi\theta\eta\mu\varepsilon\varrho o\nu$);[87] passed off with its murky banners as simultaneously as a ship that has been stranded, and is floated off by a spring tide –

That moveth altogether, if it move at all.

Now, then, I was again happy: I now took only 1000 drops of laudanum per day: and what was that? A latter spring had come to close up the season of youth: my brain performed its functions as healthily as ever before: I read Kant again; and again I understood him, or fancied that I did. Again my feelings of

---

* I here reckon twenty-five drops of laudanum as equivalent to one grain of opium, which, I believe, is the common estimate. However, as both may be considered variable quantities (the crude opium varying much in strength, and the tincture still more), I suppose that no infinitesimal accuracy can be had in such a calculation. Tea-spoons vary as much in size as opium in strength. Small ones hold about 100 drops: so that 8,000 drops are about eighty times a tea-spoonful. The reader sees how much I kept within Dr Buchan's indulgent allowance.

pleasure expanded themselves to all around me : and if any man from Oxford or Cambridge, or from neither, had been announced to me in my unpretending cottage, I should have welcomed him with as sumptuous a reception as so poor a man could offer. Whatever else was wanting to a wise man's happiness, – of laudanum I would have given him as much as he wished, and in a golden cup. And, by the way, now that I speak of giving laudanum away, I remember, about this time, a little incident, which I mention, because, trifling as it was, the reader will soon meet it again in my dreams, which it influenced more fearfully than could be imagined. One day a Malay knocked at my door. What business a Malay could have to transact amongst English mountains, I cannot conjecture : but possibly he was on his road to a sea-port about forty miles distant.

The servant[88] who opened the door to him was a young girl born and bred amongst the mountains, who had never seen an Asiatic dress of any sort : his turban, therefore, confounded her not a little : and, as it turned out, that his attainments in English were exactly of the same extent as hers in the Malay, there seemed to be an impassable gulf fixed between all communication of ideas, if either party had happened to possess any. In this dilemma, the girl, recollecting the reputed learning of her master (and, doubtless, giving me credit for a knowledge of all the languages of the earth, besides, perhaps, a few of the lunar ones), came and gave me to understand that there was a sort of demon below, whom she clearly imagined that my art could exorcise from the house. I did not immediately go down : but, when I did, the group which presented itself, arranged as it was by accident, though not very elaborate, took hold of my fancy and my eye in a way that none of the statuesque attitudes exhibited in the ballets at the Opera House, though so ostentatiously complex, had ever done. In a cottage kitchen, but panelled on the wall with dark wood that from age and rubbing resembled oak, and looking more like a rustic hall of entrance than a kitchen, stood the Malay – his turban and loose trowsers of dingy white relieved upon the dark panelling : he had placed himself nearer to the girl than she seemed to relish; though her native spirit of mountain intrepidity contended with the feeling of simple awe which her countenance expressed as she gazed upon the tiger-cat before her. And a more striking picture there could not be imagined, than the beautiful English face of the girl, and its exquisite fairness, together with her erect and independent attitude, contrasted with the sallow and bilious skin of the Malay, enamelled or veneered with mahogany, by marine air, his small, fierce, restless eyes, thin lips, slavish gestures and adorations. Half-hidden by the ferocious looking Malay, was a little child from a neighbouring cottage who had crept in after him, and was now in the act of reverting its head, and gazing upwards at the turban and the fiery eyes beneath it, whilst with one hand he caught at the dress of the young woman for protection. My knowledge of the Oriental tongues is not remarkably extensive, being indeed confined to two words – the Arabic word for barley, and the Turkish for opium (madjoon), which I have learnt from Anastasius. And, as I had neither a Malay dictionary, nor even Adelung's *Mithridates*,[89] which might have helped me to a few words, I addressed him in some lines from the Iliad; considering that, of such languages as I possessed, Greek, in point of longitude came geographically nearest to an Oriental one. He worshipped me in a most devout manner, and replied in what I suppose was Malay. In this way I saved my reputation with my neighbours : for the Malay had no means of betraying the secret. He lay down upon the floor for about an hour, and then pursued his journey. On his departure, I presented him with a piece of opium. To him, as an Orientalist, I concluded that opium must be familiar : and the expression of his face convinced me that it was. Nevertheless, I was struck with some little consternation when I saw him suddenly raise his hand to his mouth, and (in the school-boy phrase) bolt the whole, divided into three pieces, at one mouthful. The quantity was enough to kill three dragoons and their horses : and I felt some alarm for the poor creature : but what could be done? I had given him the opium in compassion for his solitary life, on recollecting that if he had travelled on foot from London, it must be nearly three weeks since he could have exchanged a thought with any human being. I could not think of violating the laws of hospitality, by having him seized and drenched with an emetic, and thus frightening him into a notion that we were going to sacrifice him to some

English idol. No: there was clearly no help for it: – he took his leave: and for some days I felt anxious: but as I never heard of any Malay being found dead, I became convinced that he was used* to opium: and that I must have done him the service I designed, by giving him one night of respite from the pains of wandering.

This incident I have digressed to mention, because this Malay (partly from the picturesque exhibition he assisted to frame, partly from the anxiety I connected with his image for some days) fastened afterwards upon my dreams, and brought other Malays with him worse than himself, that ran 'a-muck'* at me, and led me into a world of troubles. – But to quit this episode, and to return to my intercalary year[90] of happiness. I have said already, that on a subject so important to us all as happiness, we should listen with pleasure to any man's experience or experiments, even though he were but a plough-boy, who cannot be supposed to have ploughed very deep into such intractable soil as that of human pains and pleasures, or to have conducted his researches upon any very enlightened principles. But I, who have taken happiness, both in a solid and a liquid shape, both boiled and unboiled, both East India and Turkey – who have conducted my experiments upon this interesting subject with a sort of galvanic battery – and have, for the general benefit of the world, inoculated

---

*This, however, is not a necessary conclusion: the varieties of effect produced by opium on different constitutions are infinite. A London magistrate (Harriott's *Struggles through Life*, vol. iii. p. 391, third edition), has recorded that, on the first occasion of his trying laudanum for the gout, he took *forty* drops, the next night *sixty*, and on the fifth night *eighty*, without any effect whatever: and this at an advanced age. I have an anecdote from a country surgeon, however, which sinks Mr Harriott's case into a trifle; and in my projected medical treatise on opium, which I will publish provided the College of Surgeons will pay me for enlightening their benighted understandings upon this subject, I will relate it: but it is far too good a story to be published gratis.

*See the common accounts in any Eastern traveller or voyager of the frantic excesses committed by Malays who have taken opium, or are reduced to desperation by ill luck at gambling.

myself, as it were, with the poison of 8000 drops of laudanum per day (just, for the same reason, as a French surgeon inoculated himself lately with cancer – an English one, twenty years ago, with plague – and a third, I know not of what nation, with hydrophobia[91]), – I (it will be admitted) must surely know what happiness is, if any body does. And, therefore, I will here lay down an analysis of happiness; and as the most interesting mode of communicating it, I will give it, not didactically, but wrapt up and involved in a picture of one evening, as I spent every evening during the intercalary year when laudanum, though taken daily, was to me no more than the elixir of pleasure. This done, I shall quit the subject of happiness altogether, and pass to a very different one – the *pains of opium*.

Let there be a cottage,[92] standing in a valley, [XXI] 18 miles from any town – no spacious valley, but about two miles long, by three-quarters of a mile in average width; the benefit of which provision is, that all the families resident within its circuit will compose, as it were, one larger household personally familiar to your eye, and more or less interesting to your affections. Let the mountains be real mountains, between 3 and 4000 feet high; and the cottage, a real cottage; not (as a witty author has it) 'a cottage with a double coach-house:' let it be, in fact (for I must abide by the actual scene), a white cottage, embowered with flowering shrubs, so chosen as to unfold a succession of flowers upon the walls, and clustering round the windows through all the months of spring, summer, and autumn – beginning, in fact, with May roses, and ending with jasmine. Let it, however, *not* be spring, nor summer, nor autumn – but winter, in his sternest shape. This is a most important point in the science of happiness. And I am surprised to see people overlook it, and think it matter of congratulation that winter is going; or, if coming, is not likely to be a severe one. On the contrary, I put up a petition annually, for as much snow, hail, frost, or storm, of one kind or other, as the skies can possibly afford us. Surely every body is aware of the divine pleasures which attend a winter fire-side : candles at four o'clock, warm hearth-rugs, tea, a fair tea-maker, shutters closed, curtains flowing in ample draperies on the floor, whilst the wind and rain are raging audibly without,

And at the doors and windows seem to call,
As heav'n and earth they would together mell;
Yet the least entrance find they none at all;
Whence sweeter grows our rest secure in massy hall.
*Castle of Indolence*

All these are items in the description of a winter evening, which must surely be familiar to everybody born in a high latitude. And it is evident, that most of these delicacies, like ice-cream, require a very low temperature of the atmosphere to produce them: they are fruits which cannot be ripened without weather stormy or inclement, in some way or other. I am not *'particular,'* as people say, whether it be snow, or black frost, or wind so strong, that (as Mr ——[93] says) 'you may lean your back against it like a post.' I can put up even with rain, provided it rains cats and dogs: but something of the sort I must have: and, if I have it not, I think myself in a manner ill-used: for why am I called on to pay so heavily for winter, in coals, and candles, and various privations that will occur even to gentlemen, if I am not to have the article good of its kind? No: a Canadian winter for my money: or a Russian one, where every man is but a co-proprietor with the north wind in the fee-simple[94] of his own ears. Indeed, so great an epicure am I in this matter, that I cannot relish a winter night fully if it be much past St Thomas's day,[95] and have degenerated into disgusting tendencies to vernal appearances: no: it must be divided by a thick wall of dark nights from all return of light and sunshine. – From the latter weeks of October to Christmas-eve, therefore, is the period during which happiness is in season, which, in my judgment, enters the room with the tea-tray: for tea, though ridiculed by those who are naturally of coarse nerves, or are become so from wine-drinking, and are not susceptible of influence from so refined a stimulant, will always be the favourite beverage of the intellectual: and, for my part, I would have joined Dr Johnson in a *bellum internecinum* against Jonas Hanway,[96] or any other impious person who should presume to disparage it. – But here, to save myself the trouble of too much verbal description, I will introduce a painter; and give him directions for the rest of the picture. Painters do not like white cottages, unless a good deal weather-stained: but as the reader now understands that it is a winter night, his services will not be required, except for the inside of the house.

Paint me, then, a room seventeen feet by twelve, and not more than seven and a half feet high. This, reader, is somewhat ambitiously styled, in my family, the drawing-room: but, being contrived 'a double debt to pay,' it is also, and more justly, termed the library; for it happens that books are the only article of property in which I am richer than my neighbours. Of these, I have about five thousand, collected gradually since my eighteenth year. Therefore, painter, put as many as you can into this room. Make it populous with books: and, furthermore, paint me a good fire; and furniture, plain and modest, befitting the unpretending cottage of a scholar. And, near the fire, paint me a tea-table; and (as it is clear that no creature can come to see one such a stormy night,) place only two cups and saucers on the tea-tray: and, if you know how to paint such a thing symbolically, or otherwise, paint me an eternal teapot—eternal *à parte ante*, and *à parte post*; for I usually drink tea from eight o'clock at night to four o'clock in the morning. And, as it is very unpleasant to make tea, or to pour it out for oneself, paint me a lovely young woman, sitting at the table. Paint her arms like Aurora's, and her smiles like Hebe's: – But no, dear M., not even in jest let me insinuate that thy power to illuminate my cottage rests upon a tenure so perishable as mere personal beauty; or that the witchcraft of angelic smiles lies within the empire of any earthly pencil. Pass, then, my good painter, to something more within its power: and the next article brought forward should naturally be myself – a picture of the Opium-eater, with his 'little golden receptacle of the pernicious drug,' lying beside him on the table. As to the opium, I have no objection to see a picture of *that*, though I would rather see the original: you may paint it, if you choose; but I apprize you, that no 'little' receptacle would, even in 1816, answer *my* purpose, who was at a distance from the 'stately Pantheon,' and all druggists (mortal or otherwise). No: you may as well paint the real receptacle, which was not of gold, but of glass, and as much like a wine-decanter as possible. Into this you may put a quart of ruby-coloured laudanum: that, and a book of German metaphysics placed by its side, will sufficiently attest my being in the neighbourhood; but, as to myself, – there I demur. I admit that, naturally, I ought to occupy the foreground of the picture; that being the hero of the piece, or (if you choose) the criminal at the bar, my body should be had into court. This seems reasonable : but why should I confess, on this point, to a painter? or why confess at all? If the public (into whose private ear I am confidentially whispering my confessions, and not into any painter's) should chance to have framed some agreeable picture for itself of the Opium-eater's exterior, – should have ascribed to him, romantically, an elegant person, or a handsome face, why should I barbarously tear from it so pleasing a delusion – pleasing both to the public and to me? No : paint me, if at all, according to your own fancy : and, as a painter's fancy should teem with beautiful creations, I cannot fail, in that way, to be a gainer. And now, reader, we have run through all the ten categories of my condition, as it stood about 1816–17 : up to the middle of which latter year I judge myself to have been a happy man : and the elements of that happiness I have endeavoured to place before you, in the above sketch of the interior of a scholar's library, in a cottage among the mountains, on a stormy winter evening.

But now farewell – a long farewell to happiness – winter or summer ! farewell to smiles and laughter ! farewell to peace of mind ! farewell to hope and to tranquil dreams, and to the blessed consolations of sleep ! for more than three years and a half I am summoned away from these : I am now arrived at an Iliad of woes : for I have now to record

### THE PAINS OF OPIUM

– as when some great painter dips
His pencil in the gloom of earthquake and eclipse.
*Shelley's* REVOLT OF ISLAM

Reader, who have thus far accompanied me, I must request your attention to a brief explanatory note on three points : [XXII]

1. For several reasons, I have not been able to compose the notes for this part of my narrative into any regular and connected shape. I give the notes disjointed as I find them, or have now

drawn them up from memory. Some of them point to their own date; some I have dated; and some are undated. Whenever it could answer my purpose to transplant them from the natural or chronological order, I have not scrupled to do so. Sometimes I speak in the present, sometimes in the past tense. Few of the notes, perhaps, were written exactly at the period of time to which they relate; but this can little affect their accuracy; as the impressions were such that they can never fade from my mind. Much has been omitted. I could not, without effort, constrain myself to the task of either recalling, or constructing into a regular narrative, the whole burthen of horrors which lies upon my brain. This feeling partly I plead in excuse, and partly that I am now in London, and am a helpless sort of person, who cannot even arrange his own papers without assistance; and I am separated from the hands[97] which are wont to perform for me the offices of an amanuensis.

2. You will think, perhaps, that I am too confidential and com-municative of my own private history. It may be so. But my way of writing is rather to think aloud, and follow my own humours, than much to consider who is listening to me; and, if I stop to consider what is proper to be said to this or that person, I shall soon come to doubt whether any part at all is proper. The fact is, I place myself at a distance of fifteen or twenty years ahead of this time, and suppose myself writing to those who will be interested about me hereafter; and wishing to have some record of a time, the entire history of which no one can know but myself, I do it as fully as I am able with the efforts I am now capable of making, because I know not whether I can ever find time to do it again.

3. It will occur to you often to ask, why did I not release myself from the horrors of opium, by leaving it off, or diminishing it? To this I must answer briefly: it might be supposed that I yielded to the fascinations of opium too easily; it cannot be supposed that any man can be charmed by its terrors. The reader may be sure, therefore, that I made attempts innumerable to reduce the quantity. I add, that those who witnessed the agonies of those attempts, and not myself, were the first to beg me to desist. But could not I have reduced it a drop a day, or by adding water, have bisected or trisected a drop? A thousand drops bisected would

thus have taken nearly six years to reduce; and that way would certainly not have answered. But this is a common mistake of those who know nothing of opium experimentally; I appeal to those who do, whether it is not always found that down to a certain point it can be reduced with ease and even pleasure, but that, after that point, further reduction causes intense suffering. Yes, say many thoughtless persons, who know not what they are talking of, you will suffer a little low spirits and dejection for a few days. I answer, no; there is nothing like low spirits; on the contrary, the mere animal spirits are uncommonly raised: the pulse is improved: the health is better. It is not there that the suffering lies. It has no resemblance to the sufferings caused by renouncing wine. It is a state of unutterable irritation of stomach (which surely is not much like dejection), accompanied by intense perspirations, and feelings such as I shall not attempt to describe without more space at my command.

I shall now enter 'in *medias res*,' and shall anticipate, from a time when my opium pains might be said to be at their *acmè*, an account of their palsying effects on the intellectual faculties.

*

My studies have now been long interrupted.[98] I cannot read to myself with any pleasure, hardly with a moment's endurance. Yet I read aloud sometimes for the pleasure of others; because, reading is an accomplishment of mine; and, in the slang use of the word *accomplishment* as a superficial and ornamental attainment, almost the only one I possess: and formerly, if I had any vanity at all connected with any endowment or attainment of mine, it was with this; for I had observed that no accomplishment was so rare. Players are the worst readers of all: —— reads vilely: and Mrs ——,[99] who is so celebrated, can read nothing well but dramatic compositions: Milton she cannot read sufferably. People in general either read poetry without any passion at all, or else overstep the modesty of nature, and read not like scholars. Of late, if I have felt moved by any thing in books, it has been by the grand lamentations of Samson Agonistes, or the great harmonies of the Satanic speeches in *Paradise Regained*, when read aloud by myself. A young lady sometimes comes and drinks tea with us: at her request and M.'s I now and then read W—'s[100] poems to them. (W., by the by, is the only poet I ever met who could read his own verses: often indeed he reads admirably.)

For nearly two years I believe that I read no book but one: and I owe it to the author, in discharge of a great debt of gratitude, to mention what that was. The sublimer and more passionate poets I still read, as I have said, by snatches, and occasionally. But my proper vocation, as I well knew, was the exercise of the analytic understanding. Now, for the most part, analytic studies are continuous, and not to be pursued by fits and starts, or fragmentary efforts. Mathematics, for instance, intellectual philosophy, &c. were all become insupportable to me; I shrunk from them with a sense of powerless and infantine feebleness that gave me an anguish the greater from remembering the time when I grappled with them to my own hourly delight; and for this further reason, because I had devoted the labour of my whole life, and had dedicated my intellect, blossoms and fruits, to the slow and elaborate toil of constructing one single work, to which I had presumed to give the title of an unfinished work of Spinoza's; viz. *De Emendatione Humani Intellectus.*[101] This was now lying locked up, as by frost, like any Spanish bridge or aqueduct, begun upon too great a scale for the resources of the architect; and, instead of surviving me as a monument of wishes at least, and aspirations, and a life of labour dedicated to the exaltation of human nature in that way in which God had best fitted me to promote so great an object, it was likely to stand a memorial to my children of hopes defeated, or baffled efforts, of materials uselessly accumulated, of foundations laid that were never to support a superstructure, – of the grief and the ruin of the architect. In this state of imbelicity, I had, for amusement, turned my attention to political economy; my understanding, which formerly had been as active and restless as a hyena, could not, I suppose (so long as I lived at all) sink into utter lethargy; and political economy offers this advantage to a person in my state, that though it is eminently an organic science (no part, that is to say, but what acts on the whole, as the whole again reacts on each part), yet the several parts may be detached and contemplated singly. Great as was the prostration of my powers at this time, yet I could not forget my knowledge; and my understanding had been for too many years intimate with severe thinkers, with logic, and the great masters of knowledge, not to be aware of the utter feebleness of the main herd of modern economists. I had been led in 1811 to look into loads of books and pamphlets on many branches of economy; and, at my desire, M. sometimes read to me chapters from more recent works, or parts of parliamentary debates. I saw that these were generally the very dregs and rinsings of the human intellect; and that any man of sound head, and practised in wielding logic with a scholastic adroitness, might take up the whole academy of modern economists, and throttle them between heaven and earth with his finger and thumb, or bray their fungus heads to powder with a lady's fan. At length, in 1819, a friend in Edinburgh sent me down Mr Ricardo's book:[102] and recurring to my own prophetic anticipation of the advent of some legislator for this science, I said, before I had finished the first chapter, 'Thou art the man!' Wonder and curiosity were emotions that had long been dead in me. Yet I wondered once more: I wondered at myself that I could once again be stimulated to the effort of reading: and much more I wondered at the book. Had this profound work been really written in England during the nineteenth century? Was it possible? I supposed thinking* had been extinct in England. Could it be that an Englishman, and he not in academic bowers, but oppressed by mercantile and senatorial cares, had accomplished what all the universities of Europe, and a century of thought, had failed even to advance by one hair's breadth? All other writers had been crushed and overlaid by the enormous weight of facts and documents; Mr Ricardo had deduced, *à priori*, from the understanding itself, laws which first gave a ray of light into the unwieldy chaos of materials, and

---

*The reader must remember what I here mean by *thinking*: because, else this would be a very presumptuous expression. England, of late, has been rich to excess in fine thinkers, in the departments of creative and combining thought: but there is a sad dearth of masculine thinkers in any analytic path. A Scotchman of eminent name has lately told us, that he is obliged to quit even mathematics, for want of encouragement.

had constructed what had been but a collection of tentative discussions into a science of regular proportions, now first standing on an eternal basis.

Thus did one single work of a profound understanding avail to give me a pleasure and an activity which I had not known for years: – it roused me even to write, or, at least, to dictate, what M. wrote for me. It seemed to me, that some important truths had escaped even 'the inevitable eye' of Mr Ricardo: and, as these were, for the most part, of such a nature that I could express or illustrate them more briefly and elegantly by algebraic symbols than in the usual clumsy and loitering diction of economists, the whole would not have filled a pocket-book; and being so brief, with M. for my amanuensis, even at this time, incapable as I was of all general exertion, I drew up my *Prolegomena to all future Systems of Political Economy*.[103] I hope it will not be found redolent of opium; though, indeed, to most people, the subject itself is a sufficient opiate.

This exertion, however, was but a temporary flash; as the sequel showed – for I designed to publish my work: arrangements were made at a provincial press, about eighteen miles distant, for printing it. An additional compositor was retained, for some days, on this account. The work was even twice advertised: and I was, in a manner, pledged to the fulfilment of my intention. But I had a preface to write; and a dedication, which I wished to make a splendid one, to Mr Ricardo. I found myself quite unable to accomplish all this. The arrangements were countermanded: the compositor dismissed: and my 'Prolegomena' rested peacefully by the side of its elder and more dignified brother.

I have thus described and illustrated my intellectual torpor, in terms that apply, more or less, to every part of the four years during which I was under the Circean spells of opium. But for misery and suffering, I might, indeed, be said to have existed in a dormant state. I seldom could prevail on myself to write a letter; an answer of a few words, to any that I received, was the utmost that I could accomplish; and often *that* not until the letter had lain weeks, or even months, on my writing table. Without the aid of M. all records of bills paid, or *to be* paid, must have perished:

and my whole domestic economy, whatever became of Political Economy, must have gone into irretrievable confusion. – I shall not afterwards allude to this part of the case: it is one, however, which the opium-eater will find, in the end, as oppressive and tormenting as any other, from the sense of incapacity and feebleness from the direct embarrassments incident to the neglect or procrastination of each day's appropriate duties, and from the remorse which must often exasperate the stings of these evils to a reflective and conscientious mind. The opium-eater loses none of his moral sensibilities, or aspirations: he wishes and longs, as earnestly as ever, to realize what he believes possible, and feels to be exacted by duty; but his intellectual apprehension of what is possible infinitely outruns his power, not of execution only, but even of power to attempt. He lies under the weight of incubus and night-mare: he lies in sight of all that he would fain perform, just as a man forcibly confined to his bed by the mortal languor of a relaxing disease, who is compelled to witness injury or outrage offered to some object of his tenderest love: – he curses the spells which chain him down from motion: – he would lay down his life if he might but get up and walk; but he is powerless as an infant, and cannot even attempt to rise.

I now pass to what is the main subject of these latter confessions, to the history and journal of what took place in my dreams; for these were the immediate and proximate cause of my acutest suffering.

The first notice I had of any important change going on in this part of my physical economy, was from the re-awakening of a state of eye[104] generally incident to childhood, or exalted states of irritability. I know not whether my reader is aware that many children, perhaps most, have a power of painting, as it were, upon the darkness, all sorts of phantoms: in some, that power is simply a mechanic affection of the eye; others have a voluntary, or a semi-voluntary power to dismiss or to summon them; or, as a child once said to me when I questioned him on this matter, 'I can tell them to go, and they go; but sometimes they come, when I don't tell them to come.' Whereupon I told him that he had almost as unlimited a command over apparitions, as a Roman centurion over his soldiers. – In the middle of 1817, I think it was, that this faculty became positively distressing to me: at night, when I lay awake in bed, vast processions passed along in mournful pomp; friezes of never-ending stories, that to my feelings were as sad and solemn as if they were stories drawn from times before Œdipus or Priam – before Tyre – before Memphis. And, at the same time, a corresponding change took place in my dreams; a theatre seemed suddenly opened and lighted up within my brain, which presented nightly spectacles of more than earthly splendour. And the four following facts may be mentioned, as noticeable at this time:

1. That, as the creative state of the eye increased, a sympathy seemed to arise between the waking and the dreaming states of the brain in one point – that whatsoever I happened to call up and to trace by a voluntary act upon the darkness was very apt to transfer itself to my dreams; so that I feared to exercise this faculty; for, as Midas turned all things to gold, that yet baffled his hopes and defrauded his human desires, so whatsoever things capable of being visually represented I did but think of in the darkness, immediately shaped themselves into phantoms of the eye; and, by a process apparently no less inevitable, when thus once traced in faint and visionary colours, like writings in sympathetic ink, they were drawn out by the fierce chemistry of my dreams, into insufferable splendour that fretted my heart.

2. For this, and all other changes in my dreams, were accompanied by deep-seated anxiety and gloomy melancholy, such as are wholly incommunicable by words. I seemed every night to descend, not metaphorically, but literally to descend, into chasms and sunless abysses, depths below depths, from which it seemed hopeless that I could ever reascend. Nor did I, by waking, feel that I *had* reascended. This I do not dwell upon; because the state of gloom which attended these gorgeous spectacles, amounting at least to utter darkness, as of some suicidal despondency, cannot be approached by words.

3. The sense of space, and in the end, the sense of time, were both powerfully affected. Buildings, landscapes, &c. were exhibited in proportions so vast as the bodily eye is not fitted to receive. Space swelled, and was amplified to an extent of unutterable infinity. This, however, did not disturb me so much as the vast

expansion of time; I sometimes seemed to have lived for 70 or 100 years in one night; nay, sometimes had feelings representative of a millennium passed in that time, or, however, of a duration far beyond the limits of any human experience.

4. The minutest incidents of childhood, or forgotten scenes of later years, were often revived: I could not be said to recollect them; for if I had been told of them when waking, I should not have been able to acknowledge them as parts of my past experience. But placed as they were before me, in dreams like intuitions, and clothed in all their evanescent circumstances and accompanying feelings, I *recognized* them instantaneously. I was once told by a near relative of mine, that having in her childhood fallen into a river, and being on the very verge of death but for the critical assistance which reached her, she saw in a moment her whole life, in its minutest incidents, arrayed before her simultaneously as in a mirror; and she had a faculty developed as suddenly for comprehending the whole and every part. [XXIII] This, from some opium experiences of mine, I can believe; I have, indeed, seen the same thing asserted twice in modern books, and accompanied by a remark which I am convinced is true; viz. that the dread book of account, which the Scriptures speak of, is, in fact, the mind itself of each individual. Of this, at least, I feel assured, that there is no such thing as *forgetting* possible to the mind; a thousand accidents may, and will interpose a veil between our present consciousness and the secret inscriptions on the mind; accidents of the same sort will also rend away this veil; but alike, whether veiled or unveiled, the inscription remains for ever; just as the stars seem to withdraw before the common light of day, whereas, in fact, we all know that it is the light which is drawn over them as a veil – and that they are waiting to be revealed, when the obscuring daylight shall have withdrawn.

Having noticed these four facts as memorably distinguishing my dreams from those of health, I shall now cite a case illustrative of the first fact; and shall then cite any others that I remember, either in their chronological order, or any other that may give them more effect as pictures to the reader.

I had been in youth, and even since, for occasional amusement, a great reader of Livy, whom, I confess, that I prefer, both for style and matter, to any other of the Roman historians; and I had often felt as most solemn and appalling sounds, and most emphatically representative of the majesty of the Roman people, the two words so often occurring in Livy – *Consul Romanus;* especially when the consul is introduced in his military character. I mean to say, that the words king – sultan, regent, &c. or any other titles of those who embody in their own persons the collective majesty of a great people, had less power over my reverential feelings. I had also, though no great reader of history, made myself minutely and critically familiar with one period of English history, viz. the period of the Parliamentary War, having been attracted by the moral grandeur of some who figured in that day, and by the many interesting memoirs which survived those unquiet times. Both these parts of my lighter reading, having furnished me often with matter of reflection, now furnished me with matter for my dreams. Often I used to see, after painting upon the blank darkness a sort of rehearsal whilst waking, a crowd of ladies, and perhaps a festival, and dances. And I heard it said, or I said to myself, 'These are English ladies from the unhappy times of Charles I. These are the wives and the daughters of those who met in peace, and sat at the same tables, and were allied by marriage or by blood; and yet, after a certain day in August 1642, never smiled upon each other again, nor met but in the field of battle; and at Marston Moor, at Newbury, or at Naseby, cut asunder all ties of love by the cruel sabre, and washed away in blood the memory of ancient friendship.' – The ladies danced, and looked as lovely as the court of George IV. Yet I knew, even in my dream, that they had been in the grave for nearly two centuries. – This pageant would suddenly dissolve: and, at a clapping of hands, would be heard the heart-quaking sound of *Consul Romanus:* and immediately came 'sweeping by,' in gorgeous paludaments, Paulus or Marius, girt round by a company of centurions, with the crimson tunic hoisted on a spear, and followed by the *alalagmos*[105] of the Roman legions.

Many years ago, when I was looking over Piranesi's[106] *Antiquities of Rome*, Mr Coleridge, who was standing by, described to me a set of plates by that artist, called his *Dreams*, and which record the scenery of his own visions during the delirium of a fever. Some of them (I describe only from memory of Mr Coleridge's account) represented vast Gothic halls : on the floor of which stood all sorts of engines and machinery, wheels, cables, pulleys, levers, catapults, &c. &c. expressive of enormous power put forth and resistance overcome. Creeping along the sides of the walls, you perceived a staircase; and upon it, groping his way upwards, was Piranesi himself : follow the stairs a little further, and you perceive it come to a sudden abrupt termination, without any balustrade, and allowing no step onwards to him who had reached the extremity, except into the depths below. Whatever is to become of poor Piranesi, you suppose, at least, that his labours must in some way terminate here. But raise your eyes, and behold a second flight of stairs still higher : on which again Piranesi is perceived, by this time standing on the very brink of the abyss. Again elevate your eye, and a still more aerial flight of stairs is beheld : and again is poor Piranesi busy on his aspiring labours : and so on, until the unfinished stairs and Piranesi both are lost in the upper gloom of the hall. – With the same power of endless growth and self-reproduction did my architecture proceed in dreams. In the early stage of my malady, the splendours of my dreams were indeed chiefly architectural : and I beheld such pomp of cities and palaces as was never yet beheld by the waking eye, unless in the clouds. From a great modern poet[107] [XXIV] I cite part of a passage which describes, as an appearance actually beheld in the clouds, what in many of its circumstances I saw frequently in sleep :

> The appearance, instantaneously disclosed,
> Was of a mighty city – boldly say
> A wilderness of building, sinking far
> And self-withdrawn into a wondrous depth,
> Far sinking into splendour – without end !
> Fabric it seem'd of diamond, and of gold,
> With alabaster domes, and silver spires,
> And blazing terrace upon terrace, high
> Uplifted; here, serene pavilions bright
> In avenues disposed; there towers begirt
> With battlements that on their restless fronts
> Bore stars – illumination of all gems !

By earthly nature had the effect been wrought
Upon the dark materials of the storm
Now pacified: on them, and on the coves,
And mountain-steeps and summits, whereunto
The vapours had receded, – taking there
Their station under a cerulean sky, &c. &c.

The sublime circumstance – 'battlements that on their *restless* fronts bore stars,' – might have been copied from my architectural dreams, for it often occurred. – We hear it reported of Dryden, and of Fuseli[108] in modern times, that they thought proper to eat raw meat for the sake of obtaining splendid dreams: how much better for such a purpose to have eaten opium, which yet I do not remember that any poet is recorded to have done, except the dramatist Shadwell:[109] and in ancient days, Homer is, I think, rightly reputed to have known the virtues of opium.

To my architecture succeeded dreams of lakes – and silvery expanses of water: – these haunted me so much, that I feared (though possibly it will appear ludicrous to a medical man) that some dropsical state or tendency of the brain might thus be making itself (to use a metaphysical word) *objective;* and the sentient organ *project* itself as its own object. – For two months I suffered greatly in my head – a part of my bodily structure which had hitherto been so clear from all touch or taint of weakness (physically, I mean) that I used to say of it, as the last Lord Orford[110] said of his stomach, that it seemed likely to survive the rest of my person. – Till now I had never felt a headache even, or any the slightest pain, except rheumatic pains caused by my own folly. However, I got over this attack, though it must have been verging on something very dangerous.

The waters now changed their character, – from translucent lakes, shining like mirrors, they now became seas and oceans. And now came a tremendous change, which, unfolding itself slowly like a scroll, through many months, promised an abiding torment; and, in fact, it never left me until the winding up of my case. Hitherto the human face had mixed often in my dreams, but not despotically, nor with any special power of tormenting. But now that which I have called the tyranny of the human face began to unfold itself. Perhaps some part of my London life might be answerable for this.[111] Be that as it may, now it was that upon the rocking waters of the ocean the human face began to appear: the sea appeared paved with innumerable faces, upturned to the heavens: faces, imploring, wrathful, despairing, surged upwards by thousands, by myriads, by generations, by centuries: – my agitation was infinite, – my mind tossed – and surged with the ocean.

*

*May 1818.*

The Malay has been a fearful enemy for months. I have been every night, through his means, transported into Asiatic scenes. I know not whether others share in my feelings on this point; but I have often thought that if I were compelled to forego England, and to live in China, and among Chinese manners and modes of life and scenery, I should go mad. The causes of my horror lie deep; and some of them must be common to others. Southern Asia, in general, is the seat of awful images and associations. As the cradle of the human race, it would alone have a dim and reverential feeling connected with it. But there are other reasons. No man can pretend that the wild, barbarous, and capricious superstitions of Africa, or of savage tribes elsewhere, affect him in the way that he is affected by the ancient, monumental, cruel, and elaborate religions of Indostan, &c. The mere antiquity of Asiatic things, of their institutions, histories, modes of faith, &c. is so impressive, that to me the vast age of the race and name overpowers the sense of youth in the individual. A young Chinese seems to me an antediluvian man renewed. Even Englishmen, though not bred in any knowledge of such institutions, cannot but shudder at the mystic sublimity of *castes* that have flowed apart, and refused to mix, through such immemorial tracts of time; nor can any man fail to be awed by the names of the Ganges, or the Euphrates. It contributes much to these feelings, that Southern Asia is, and has been for thousands of years, the part of the earth most swarming with human life; the great *officina gentium*.[112] Man is a weed in those regions. The vast empires also, into which the enormous population of Asia has always been cast, give a further sublimity to the feelings associated with all Oriental names or images. In China, over and above what it has in common with the rest of Southern Asia, I am terrified by the modes of life, by the manners, and the barrier of utter abhorrence, and want of sympathy, placed between us by feelings deeper than I can analyze. I could sooner live with lunatics, or brute animals. All this, and much more than I can say, or have time to say, the reader must enter into before he can comprehend the unimaginable horror which these dreams of Oriental imagery, and mythological tortures, impressed upon me. Under the connecting feeling of tropical heat and vertical sun-lights, I brought together all creatures, birds, beasts, reptiles, all trees and plants, usages and appearances, that are found in all tropical regions, and assembled them together in China or Indostan. From kindred feelings, I soon brought Egypt and all her gods under the same law. I was stared at, hooted at, grinned at, chattered at, by monkeys, by paroquets, by cockatoos. I ran into pagodas: and was fixed, for centuries, at the summit, or in secret rooms; I was the idol; I was the priest; I was worshipped; I was sacrificed. I fled from the wrath of Brama through all the forests of Asia: Vishnu hated me: Seeva laid wait for me. I came suddenly upon Isis and Osiris: I had done a deed, they said, which the ibis and the crocodile trembled at. I was buried, for a thousand years, in stone coffins, with mummies and sphinxes, in narrow chambers at the heart of eternal pyramids. I was kissed, with cancerous kisses, by crocodiles; and laid, confounded with all unutterable slimy things, amongst reeds and Nilotic mud.

I thus give the reader some slight abstraction of my Oriental dreams, which always filled me with such amazement at the monstrous scenery, that horror seemed absorbed, for a while, in sheer astonishment. Sooner or later, came a reflux of feeling that swallowed up the astonishment, and left me, not so much in terror, as in hatred and abomination of what I saw. Over every form, and threat, and punishment, and dim sightless incarceration, brooded a sense of eternity and infinity that drove me into an oppression as of madness. Into these dreams only, it was, with one or two slight exceptions, that any circumstances of physical horror entered. All before had been moral and spiritual terrors.

But here the main agents were ugly birds, or snakes, or crocodiles; especially the last. The cursed crocodile became to me the object of more horror than almost all the rest. I was compelled to live with him; and (as was always the case almost in my dreams) for centuries. I escaped sometimes, and found myself in Chinese houses, with cane tables, &c. All the feet of the tables, sofas, &c. soon became instinct with life : the abominable head of the crocodile, and his leering eyes, looked out at me, multiplied into a thousand repetitions : and I stood loathing and fascinated. And so often did this hideous reptile haunt my dreams, that many times the very same dream was broken up in the very same way : I heard gentle voices speaking to me (I hear every thing when I am sleeping); and instantly I awoke : it was broad noon; and my children were standing, hand in hand, at my bed-side; come to show me their coloured shoes, or new frocks, or to let me see them dressed for going out. I protest that so awful was the transition from the damned crocodile, and the other unutterable monsters and abortions of my dreams, to the sight of innocent *human* natures and of infancy, that, in the mighty and sudden revulsion of mind, I wept, and could not forbear it, as I kissed their faces.

*June 1819.*

I have occasion to remark, at various periods of my life, that the deaths of those whom we love, and indeed the contemplation of death generally, is (*cæteris paribus*)[113] more affecting in summer than in any other season of the year. And the reasons are these three, I think : first, that the visible heavens in summer appear far higher, more distant, and (if such a solecism may be excused) more infinite; the clouds, by which chiefly the eye expounds the distance of the blue pavilion stretched over our heads, are in summer more voluminous, massed, and accumulated in far grander and more towering piles : secondly, the light and the appearances of the declining and the setting sun are much more fitted to be types and characters of the Infinite; and, thirdly, (which is the main reason) the exuberant and riotous prodigality of life naturally forces the mind more powerfully upon the antagonist thought of death, and the wintry sterility of the grave.

For it may be observed, generally, that wherever two thoughts stand related to each other by a law of antagonism, and exist, as it were, by mutual repulsion, they are apt to suggest each other. On these accounts it is that I find it impossible to banish the thought of death when I am walking alone in the endless days of summer; and any particular death, if not more affecting, at least haunts my mind more obstinately and besiegingly in that season. Perhaps this cause, and a slight incident which I omit, might have been the immediate occasions of the following dream; to which, however, a predisposition must always have existed in my mind; but having been once roused, it never left me, and split into a thousand fantastic varieties, which often suddenly re-united, and composed again the original dream.

I thought that it was a Sunday morning in May, that it was Easter Sunday, and as yet very early in the morning. I was standing, as it seemed to me, at the door of my own cottage. Right before me lay the very scene which could really be commanded from that situation, but exalted, as was usual, and solemnized by the power of dreams. There were the same mountains, and the same lovely valley at their feet; but the mountains were raised to more than Alpine height, and there was interspace far larger between them of meadows and forest lawns; the hedges were rich with white roses; and no living creature was to be seen, excepting that in the green churchyard there were cattle tranquilly reposing upon the verdant graves, and particularly round about the grave of a child [114] whom I had tenderly loved, just as I had really beheld them, a little before sun-rise in the same summer, when that child died. I gazed upon the well-known scene, and I said aloud (as I thought) to myself, 'It yet wants much of sun-rise; and it is Easter Sunday; and that is the day on which they celebrate the first-fruits of resurrection. I will walk abroad; old griefs shall be forgotten today; for the air is cool and still, and the hills are high, and stretch away to heaven; and the forest-glades are as quiet as the churchyard; and, with the dew, I can wash the fever from my forehead, and then I shall be unhappy no longer.' And I turned, as if to open my garden gate; and immediately I saw upon the left a scene far different; but which yet the power of dreams had reconciled into harmony with the other. The scene was an Oriental one; and there also it was Easter Sunday, and very early in the morning. And at a vast distance were visible, as a stain upon the horizon, the domes and cupolas of a great city – an image or faint abstraction, caught perhaps in childhood from some picture of Jerusalem. And not a bow-shot from me, upon a stone, and shaded by Judean palms, there sat a woman; and I looked; and it was – Ann! She fixed her eyes upon me earnestly; and I said to her at length: 'So then I have found you at last.' I waited: but she answered me not a word. Her face was the same as when I saw it last, and yet again how different! Seventeen years ago, when the lamp-light fell upon her face, as for the last time I kissed her lips (lips, Ann, that to me were not polluted), her eyes were streaming with tears: the tears were now wiped away; she seemed more beautiful than she was at that time, but in all other points the same, and not older. Her looks were tranquil, but with unusual solemnity of expression; and I now gazed upon her with some awe, but suddenly her countenance grew dim, and, turning to the mountains I perceived vapours rolling between us; in a moment all had vanished; thick darkness came on; and, in the twinkling of an eye, I was far away from mountains, and by lamp-light in Oxford-street, walking again with Ann – just as we walked seventeen years before, when we were both children.

As a final specimen, I cite one of a different character, from 1820.

The dream commenced with a music which now I often heard in dreams – a music of preparation and of awakening suspense; a music like the opening of the Coronation Anthem,[115] and which, like *that*, gave the feeling of a vast march – of infinite calvalcades filing off – and the tread of innumerable armies. The morning was come of a mighty day – a day of crisis and of final hope for human nature, then suffering some mysterious eclipse, and labouring in some dread extremity. Somewhere, I knew not where – somehow, I knew not how – by some beings, I knew not whom – a battle, a strife, an agony, was conducting, – was evolving like a great drama, or piece of music; with which my sympathy was the more insupportable from my confusion as to its place, its cause, its nature, and its possible issue. I, as is usual in dreams (where, of necessity, we make ourselves central to every movement), had the power, and yet had not the power, to decide it. I had the power, if I could raise myself, to will it; and yet again had not the power, for the weight of twenty Atlantics was upon me, or the oppression of inexpiable guilt. 'Deeper than ever plummet sounded,' I lay inactive. Then, like a chorus, the passion deepened. Some greater interest was at stake; some mightier cause than ever yet the sword had pleaded, or trumpet had proclaimed. Then came sudden alarms; hurryings to and fro: trepidations of innumerable fugitives, I knew not whether from the good cause or the bad: darkness and lights: tempest and human faces: and at last, with the sense that all was lost, female forms, and the features that were worth all the world to me, and but a moment allowed, – and clasped hands, and heart-breaking partings, and then – everlasting farewells! and with a sigh, such as the caves of hell sighed when the incestuous mother[116] uttered the abhorred name of death, the sound was reverberated – everlasting farewells! and again, and yet again reverberated – everlasting farewells!

And I awoke in struggles, and cried aloud – 'I will sleep no more!' [XXV]

But I am now called upon to wind up a narrative which has already extended to an unreasonable length. Within more spacious limits, the materials which I have used might have been better unfolded; and much which I have not used might have been added with effect. Perhaps, however, enough has been given. It now remains that I should say something of the way in which this conflict of horrors was finally brought to its crisis. The reader is already aware (from a passage near the beginning of the introduction to the first part) that the opium-eater has, in some way or other, 'unwound, almost to its final links, the accursed chain which bound him.' By what means? To have narrated this, according to the original intention, would have far exceeded the space which can now be allowed. It is fortunate, as such a cogent reason exists for abridging it, that I should, on a maturer view of the case, have been exceedingly unwilling to injure, by any such unaffecting details, the impression of the history itself, as an appeal to the prudence and the conscience of the yet unconfirmed opium-eater – or even (though a very inferior consideration) to injure its effect as a composition. The interest of the judicious reader will not attach itself chiefly to the subject of the fascinating spells, but to the fascinating power. Not the opium-eater, but the opium, is the true hero of the tale; and the legitimate centre on which the interest revolves. The object was to display the marvellous agency of opium, whether for pleasure or for pain: if that is done, the action of the piece has closed.

However, as some people, in spite of all laws to the contrary, will persist in asking what became of the opium-eater, and in what state he now is, I answer for him thus: The reader is aware that opium had long ceased to found its empire on spells of pleasure; it was solely by the tortures connected with the attempt to abjure it, that it kept its hold. Yet, as other tortures, no less it may be thought, attended the non-abjuration of such a tyrant, a choice only of evils was left: and *that* might as well have been adopted, which, however terrific in itself, held out a prospect of final restoration to happiness. This appears true; but good logic gave the author no strength to act upon it. However, a crisis arrived for the author's life, and a crisis for other objects still dearer to him – and which will always be far dearer to him than his life, even now that it is again a happy one – I saw that I must die if I continued the opium: I determined, therefore, if that should be required, to die in throwing it off. How much I was at that time taking I cannot say; for the opium which I used had been purchased for me by a friend who afterwards refused to let me pay him; so that I could not ascertain even what quantity I had used within the year. I apprehend, however, that I took it very irregularly: and that I varied from about fifty or sixty grains, to 150 a-day. My first task was to reduce it to forty, to thirty, and, as fast as I could, to twelve grains.

I triumphed: but think not, reader, that therefore my sufferings were ended; nor think of me as of one sitting in a *dejected* state. Think of me as of one, even when four months had passed, still agitated, writhing, throbbing, palpitating, shattered; and much, perhaps, in the situation of him who has been racked, as I collect the torments of that state from the affecting account of them left by the most innocent sufferer* (of the times of James I). Meantime, I derived no benefit from any medicine, except one prescribed to me by an Edinburgh surgeon of great eminence, viz. ammoniated tincture of Valerian. Medical account, therefore, of my emancipation I have not much to give: and even that little, as managed by a man so ignorant of medicine as myself, would probably tend only to mislead. At all events, it would be misplaced in this situation. The moral of the narrative is addressed to the opium-eater; and therefore, of necessity, limited in its application. If he is taught to fear and tremble, enough has been effected. But he may say, that the issue of my case is at least a proof that opium, after a seventeen years' use, and an eight years' abuse of its powers, may still be renounced: and that *he* may chance to bring to the task greater energy than I did, or that with a stronger constitution than mine he may obtain the same results with less. This may be true: I would not presume to measure the efforts of other men by my own: I heartily wish him more energy: I wish him the same success. Nevertheless, I had motives external to myself which he may unfortunately want: and these supplied me with conscientious supports which mere personal interests might fail to supply to a mind debilitated by opium.

Jeremy Taylor[117] conjectures that it may be as painful to be born as to die: I think it probable: and, during the whole period of diminishing the opium, I had the torments of a man passing out of one mode of existence into another. The issue was not death, but a sort of physical regeneration: and I may add, that ever since, at intervals, I have had a restoration of more than youthful spirits, though under the pressure of difficulties, which, in a less happy state of mind, I should have called misfortunes.

One memorial of my former condition still remains: my dreams are not yet perfectly calm: the dread swell and agitation of the storm have not wholly subsided: the legions that encamped

---

*William Lithgow: his book (*Travels*, &c.) is ill and pedantically written: but the account of his own sufferings on the rack at Malaga is overpoweringly affecting.

in them are drawing off, but not all departed: my sleep is still tumultuous, and, like the gates of Paradise to our first parents when looking back from afar, it is still (in the tremendous line of Milton) –

With dreadful faces throng'd and fiery arms.

# APPENDIX

## *De Quincey's Second Thoughts About the* Confessions

### A. NOTES, LETTERS AND ARTICLES COMMENTING ON THE 'CONFESSIONS', 1821–55

[*When the second part of the* Confessions *was published in the London Magazine of October 1821, De Quincey attached to it a 'Notice to the Reader' explaining that the different periods at which the sections of the* Confessions *had been written had caused some confusion in its dates.*]

The incidents recorded in the Preliminary Confessions, lie within a period of which the earlier extreme is now rather more, and the latter extreme less, than nineteen years ago: consequently, in a popular way of computing dates, many of the incidents might be indifferently referred to a distance of eighteen or nineteen years; and, as the notes and memoranda for this narrative were drawn up originally about last Christmas, it seemed most natural in all cases to prefer the former date. In the hurry of composing the narrative, though some months had then elapsed, this date was every where retained: and, in many cases, perhaps, it leads to no error, or to none of importance. But in one instance, viz. where the author speaks of his own birth-day, this adoption of one uniform date has led to a positive inaccuracy of an entire year: for, during the very time of composition, the *nineteenth* year from the earlier term of the whole period revolved to its close. It is, therefore, judged proper to mention, that the period of that narrative lies between the early part of July, 1802, and the beginning or middle of March, 1803.

*London Magazine*, vol. iv, no. xxii, October 1821

[*After the appearance of the second part of the* Confessions *in*

C.E.O.–6                    117

*October 1821, many reviews of the work appeared in newspapers and magazines. De Quincey commented on some of these, gave a further explanation of his motives in writing the Confessions, and promised to produce a Third Part of them, in a letter from 'X.Y.Z.' dated 27 November 1821 published in the December 1821 London Magazine.*]

... I have seen in the Sheffield Iris[118] a notice of my two papers entitled *Confessions of an English Opium Eater*. Notice of any sort from Mr Montgomery[119] could not have failed to gratify me, by proving that I had so far succeeded in my efforts as to catch the attention of a distinguished man of genius: a notice so emphatic as this, and introduced by an exordium of so much beauty as that contained in the two first paragraphs on the faculty of dreaming, I am bound in gratitude to acknowledge as a more flattering expression and memorial of success than any which I had allowed myself to anticipate.

I am not sorry that a passage in Mr Montgomery's comments enables me to take notice of a doubt which had reached me before: the passage I mean is this: in the fourth page of the Iris, amongst the remarks with which Mr Montgomery has introduced the extracts, which he has done me the honour to make, it is said – 'whether this character' (the character in which the Opium-eater speaks) 'be real or imaginary, we know not.' The same doubt was reported to me as having been made in another quarter; but, in that instance, as clothed in such discourteous expressions, that I do not think it would have been right for me, or that on a principle of just self-respect, I could have brought myself to answer it at all; which I say in no anger, and I hope with no other pride than that which may reasonably influence any man in refusing an answer to all direct impeachments of his veracity. From Mr Montgomery, however, this scruple on the question of authenticity comes in the shape which might have been anticipated from his own courteous and honourable nature, and implies no more than a suggestion (in one view perhaps complimentary to myself) that the whole might be professedly and intentionally a fictitious case as respected the incidents – and chosen as a more impressive form for communicating some moral or medical admonitions to the unconfirmed Opium-eater. Thus shaped – I cannot have any right to quarrel with this scruple. But on many accounts I should be sorry that such a view were taken of the narrative by those who may have happened to read it. And therefore, I assure Mr Montgomery, in this public way, that the entire Confessions were designed to convey a narrative of my own experience as an Opium-eater, drawn up with entire simplicity and fidelity to the facts; from which they can in no respect have deviated, except by such trifling inaccuracies of date, etc. as the memoranda I have with me in London would not, in all cases, enable me to reduce to certainty. Over and above the want of these memoranda, I laboured sometimes (as I will acknowledge) under another, and a graver embarrassment: To tell nothing *but* the truth – must, in all cases, be an unconditional moral law: to tell the *whole* truth is not equally so: in the earlier narrative I acknowledge that I could not always do this: regards of delicacy towards some who are yet living, and of just tenderness to the memory of others who are dead, obliged me, at various points of my narrative, to suppress what would have added interest to the story, and sometimes, perhaps, have left impressions on the reader favourable to other purposes of an auto-biographer. In cases which touch too closely on their own rights and interests, all men should hesitate to trust their own judgment: thus far I imposed a restraint upon myself, as all just and conscientious men would do: in everything else I spoke fearlessly, and as if writing private memoirs for my own dearest friends. Events, indeed, in my life, connected with so many remembrances of grief, and sometimes of self-reproach, had become too sacred from habitual contemplation to be altered or distorted for the unworthy purposes of scenical effect and display, without violating those feelings of self-respect which all men should cherish, and giving a lasting wound to my conscience.

Having replied to the question involved in the passage quoted from the Iris, I ought to notice an objection, conveyed to me through many channels, and in too friendly terms to have been overlooked if I had thought it unfounded: whereas, I believe it is a very just one: – it is this: that I have so managed the second narrative, as to leave an overbalance on the side of the *pleasures* of opium; and that the very horrors themselves, described as connected with the use of opium, do not pass the limits of pleasure. I know not how to excuse myself on this head, unless by alleging (what is obvious enough) that to describe any pains, of any class, and that at perfect leisure for choosing and rejecting thoughts and expressions, is a most difficult task: in my case I scarcely know whether it is competent to me to allege further, that I was limited, both as to space and time, so long as it appears on the face of my paper, that I did not turn all that I had of either to the best account. It is known to you, however, that I wrote in extreme haste, and under very depressing circumstances in other respects. – On the whole, perhaps, the best way of meeting this objection will be to send you a Third Part of my Confessions:* drawn up with such assistance from fuller memoranda, and the recollections of my only companion during those years,[120] as I shall be able to command on my return to the north: I hope that I shall be able to return thither in the course of next week: and, therefore, by the end of January, or thereabouts, I shall have found leisure from my other employments, to finish it to my own satisfaction. I do not venture to hope, that it will realise the whole of what is felt to be wanting: but it is fit that I should make the effort, if it were only to meet the expressions of interest in my previous papers, which have reached me from all quarters, or to mark my sense of the personal kindness which, in many cases, must have dictated the terms in which that interest was conveyed.

This, I think, is what I had to say. Some things, which I might have been disposed to add, would not be fitting in a public letter. Let me say, however, generally, that these two papers of mine, short and inconsiderable as they are, have, in one way, produced a disproportionate result though but of a personal nature, by leading to many kind acts, and generous services, and expressions of regard, in many shapes, from men of talent in London. ...

*London Magazine*, vol. iv, no. xxiv, December 1821

---

*In the Third Part I will fill up an omission noticed by the *Medical Intelligencer*[121] (No. 24) viz. – The omission to record the particular effects of the Opium between 1804–12 ...

[*The December 1821 London Magazine also contained an editorial announcement that the Third Part of the Confessions would be published in the magazine during 1822. But De Quincey never succeeded in writing this Third Part. When the Confessions first appeared in book form in 1822, he added an Appendix, dated 30 September 1822, apologizing for his failure to produce the promised Third Part, and giving detailed advice, based on his own experience, on how to reduce opium dosage, and an account of the withdrawal symptoms that accompany the process. This Appendix was reprinted in the December 1822 number of the London Magazine, with an introductory note by the Editors apologizing to their readers who had been eagerly awaiting the promised sequel to the extraordinary narrative which had aroused such interest.*]

The proprietors of this little work having determined on reprinting it, some explanation seems called for, to account for the non-appearance of a Third Part promised in the London Magazine of December last; and the more so, because the proprietors, under whose guarantee that promise was issued, might otherwise be implicated in the blame – little or much – attached to its non-fulfilment. This blame, in mere justice, the author takes wholly upon himself. ... For any purpose of self-excuse, it might be sufficient to say that intolerable bodily suffering had totally disabled him for almost any exertion of mind, more especially for such as demand and presuppose a pleasurable and genial state of feeling: but, as a case that may by possibility contribute a trifle to the medical history of Opium in a further stage of its action than can often have been brought under the notice of professional men, he has judged that it might be acceptable to some readers to have it described more at length ...

Those who have read the Confessions will have closed them with the impression that I had wholly renounced the use of Opium. This impression I meant to convey: and that for two reasons: first, because the very act of deliberately recording such a state of suffering necessarily presumes in the recorder a power of surveying his own case as a cool spectator, and a degree of spirits for adequately describing it, which it would be inconsistent to suppose in any person speaking from the station of an actual sufferer: secondly, because I, who had descended from so large a quantity as 8000 drops to so small a one (comparatively speaking) as a quantity ranging between 300 and 160 drops, might well suppose that the victory was in effect achieved. In suffering my readers therefore to think of me as a reformed opium-eater, I left no impression but what I shared myself; and, as may be seen, even this impression was left to be collected from the general tone of the conclusion, and not from any specific words – which are in no instance at variance with the literal truth. In no long time after that paper was written, I became sensible that the effort which remained would cost me far more energy than I had anticipated: and the necessity for making it was more apparent every month. ... Opium therefore I resolved wholly to abjure, as soon as I should find myself at liberty to bend my undivided attention and energy to this purpose. It was not however until the 24th of June last that any tolerable concurrence of facilities for such an attempt arrived. On that day I began my experiment, having previously settled in my own mind that I would not flinch, but would 'stand up to the scratch' – under any possible 'punishment'. I must premise that about 170 or 180 drops had been my ordinary allowance for many months: occasionally I had run up as high as 500; and once nearly to 700: in repeated preludes to my final experiment I had also gone as low as 100 drops; but had found it impossible to stand it beyond the 4th day – which, by the way, I have always found more difficult to get over than any of the preceding 3. I went off under easy sail – 130 drops a day for 3 days: on the 4th I plunged at once to 80: the misery which I now suffered 'took the conceit' out of me at once: and for about a month I continued off and on about this mark: then I sunk to 60: and the next day to – none at all. This was the first day for nearly ten years that I had existed without opium. I persevered in my abstinence for 90 hours; i.e. upwards of half a week. Then I took – ask me not how much: say, ye severest, what would ye have done? then I abstained again: then took about 25 drops: then abstained: and so on.

Meantime the symptoms which attended my case for the first six weeks of the experiment were these: – enormous irritability and excitement of the whole system: the stomach in particular restored to a full feeling of vitality and sensibility; but often in great pain: unceasing restlessness night and day: sleep – I scarcely knew what it was: 3 hours out of the 24 was the utmost I had, and that so agitated and shallow that I heard every sound that was near me: lower jaw constantly swelling: mouth ulcerated: and many other distressing symptoms that would be tedious to repeat; amongst which however I must mention one, because it had never failed to accompany any attempt to renounce opium – viz. violent sternutation.[122] This now became exceedingly troublesome: sometimes lasting for 2 hours at once, and recurring at least twice or three times a day.... In an unfinished fragment of a letter begun about this time ... I find these words: '... I protest to you that I have a greater influx of thoughts in one hour at present than in a whole year under the reign of opium. It seems as though all the thoughts which had been frozen up for a decad of years by opium, had now according to the old fable been thawed at once – such a multitude stream in on me from all quarters. Yet such is my impatience and hideous irritability – that, for one which I detain and write down, 50 escape me: in spite of my weariness from suffering and want of sleep, I cannot stand still or sit for two minutes together.' ...

From this account, rambling as it may be, it is evident that thus much of benefit may arise to the persons most interested in such a history of opium – viz. to opium-eaters in general – that it establishes, for their consolation and encouragement, the fact that opium may be renounced; and without greater sufferings than an ordinary resolution may support; and by a pretty rapid course of descent.

Appendix to *Confessions of an English Opium Eater*, 1822

[*Sixteen years later, in a reminiscent article about Charles Lamb, De Quincey recalled his sufferings from opium at the time when he wrote the* Confessions *and, generalizing from his and Coleridge's experiences, gave some of his most important conclusions as to the effect of opium addiction on a writer's powers.*]

I was ill at that time, and for years after – ill from the effects of opium upon the liver; and one primary indication of any illness felt in that organ is peculiar depression of spirits. Hence arose a singular effect of reciprocal action, in maintaining a state of dejection. From the original physical depression caused by the derangement of the liver arose a sympathetic derangement of the mind, disposing me to believe that I never *could* extricate myself; and from this belief arose, by reaction, a thousand-fold increase of the physical depression. I began to view my unhappy London life – a life of literary toils, odious to my heart – as a permanent state of exile from my Westmoreland home. My three eldest children, at that time in the most interesting stages of childhood and infancy, were in Westmoreland; and so powerful was my feeling (derived merely from a deranged liver) of some long, never-ending separation from my family, that at length, in pure weakness of mind, I was obliged to relinquish my daily walks in Hyde Park and Kensington Gardens, from the misery of seeing children in multitudes, that too forcibly recalled my own. The picture of Fox-ghyll,[123] my Westmoreland abode, and the solitary fells about it, upon which those were roaming whom I could not see, was for ever before my eyes. . . .

In any state of health, I do not write with rapidity. Under the influence of opium, however, when it reaches its maximum in diseasing the liver and deranging the digestive functions, all exertion whatever is revolting in excess; intellectual exertion, above all, is connected habitually, when performed under opium influence, with a sense of disgust the most profound for the subject (no matter what) which detains the thoughts; all that morning freshness of animal spirits which, under ordinary circumstances, consumes, as it were, and swallows up the interval between one's self and one's distant object (consumes, that is, in the same sense as Virgil describes a high-blooded horse, on the fret for starting, as traversing the ground with his eye, and devouring the distance in fancy before it is approached): all that dewy freshness is exhaled and burnt off by the parching effects of opium on the animal economy. You feel like one of Swift's *Strulbrugs*,[124] prematurely exhausted of life; and molehills are inevitably exaggerated by the feelings into mountains. Not that it was molehills exactly that I had then to surmount – they were moderate hills; but that made it all the worse in the result, since my judgment could not altogether refuse to go along with my feelings. I was, besides, and had been for some time, engaged in the task of unthreading the labyrinth by which I had reached, unawares, my present state of slavery to opium. I was descending the mighty ladder, stretching to the clouds as it seemed, by which I had imperceptibly attained my giddy altitude – that point from which it had seemed equally impossible to go forward or backward. To wean myself from opium I had resolved inexorably; and finally I accomplished my vow. But the transition state was the worst of all to support. All the pains of martyrdom were there: all the ravages in the economy of the great central organ, the stomach, which had been wrought by opium; the sickening disgust which attended each separate respiration; and the rooted depravation of the appetite and the digestion – all these must be weathered for months upon months, and without the stimulus (however false and treacherous) which, for some part of each day, the old doses of laudanum would have supplied. . . . If twenty-five to fifty drops were withdrawn on each day (that is, from one to two grains of opium), inevitably within three, four, or five days, the deduction began to tell grievously; and the effect was to restore the craving for opium more keenly than ever. There was the collision from both evils – that from the laudanum, and that from the want of laudanum. The last was a state of distress perpetually increasing; the other was one which did not sensibly diminish – no, not for a long period of months. Irregular motions, impressed by a potent agent upon the blood or other processes of life, are slow to subside; they maintain themselves long after the exciting cause has been partially or even wholly withdrawn; and, in my case, they did not perfectly subside into the motion of tranquil health for several years. . . .

Over and above the principal operation of my suffering state, as felt in the enormous difficulty with which it loaded every act of exertion, there was another secondary effect which always followed as a reaction from the first. And that this was no accident or peculiarity attached to my individual temperament, I may presume from the circumstance that Mr Coleridge experienced the very same sensations, in the same situation, throughout his literary life, and has often noticed it to me with surprise and vexation. The sensation was that of powerful disgust with any subject upon which he had occupied his thoughts, or had exerted his powers of composition for any length of time, and an equal disgust with the result of his exertions – powerful abhorrence I may call it, absolute loathing, of all that he had produced. ... Reverting to my own case, which was pretty nearly the same as his, there was, however, this difference – that, at times, when I had slept at more regular hours for several nights consecutively, and had armed myself by a sudden increase of the opium for a few days running, I recovered, at times, a remarkable glow of jovial spirits. In some such artificial respites it was from my usual state of distress, and purchased at a heavy price of subsequent suffering, that I wrote the greater part of the Opium Confessions in the autumn of 1821. The introductory part (i.e. the narrative part) written for the double purpose of creating an interest in what followed, and of making it intelligible, since, without this narration, the dreams (which were the real object of the whole work) would have had no meaning, but would have been mere incoherencies – this narrative part was written with singular rapidity. The rest might be said to have occupied an unusual length of time; since, though the mere penmanship might have been performed within moderate limits (and in fact under some pressure from the printer), the dreams had been composed slowly, and by separate efforts of thought, at wide intervals of time, according to the accidental prevalence, at any particular time, of the separate elements of such dream in my own real dream-experience. These circumstances I mention to account for my having written anything in a happy or genial state of mind, when I was in a general state so opposite, by my own description, to anything like enjoyment. That description, as a *general* one, states most truly the unhappy condition, and the somewhat extra-ordinary condition of feeling, to which opium had brought me. I, like Mr Coleridge, could not endure what I had written for some time after I had written it. I also shrank from treating any subject which I had much considered; but more, I believe, as recoiling from the intricacy and the elaborateness which had been made known to me in the course of considering it, and on account of the difficulty or the toilsomeness which might be fairly presumed from the mere fact that I *had* long considered it, or could have found it necessary to do so, than from any blind, mechanical feeling inevitably associated (as in Coleridge it was) with a second survey of the same subject.

One other effect there was from the opium, and I believe it had some place in Coleridge's list of morbid affections caused by opium, and of disturbances extended even to the intellect – which was, that the judgment was for a time grievously impaired, sometimes even totally abolished, as applied to anything which I had recently written. Fresh from the labour of composition, I believe, indeed, that almost every man, unless he has had a very long and close experience in the practice of writing, finds himself a little dazzled and bewildered in computing the effect, as it will appear to neutral eyes, of what he has produced. This result from the hurry and effort of composition doubtless we all experience, or at some time *have* experienced. But the incapacitation which I speak of here, as due to opium, is of another kind and another degree. It is mere childish helplessness, or senile paralysis, of the judgment, which distresses the man in attempting to grasp the upshot and the total effect (the *tout ensemble*) of what he has himself so recently produced. There is the same imbecility in attempting to hold things steadily together, and to bring them under a comprehensive or unifying act of the judging faculty, as there is in the efforts of a drunken man to follow a chain of reasoning. Opium is said to have some specific effect of debilitation upon the memory;* that is, not merely the general one which might be supposed to accompany its morbid effects upon the bodily system, but some other, more direct, subtle, and exclusive; and this, of whatever nature, may possibly extend to the faculty of judging.

*Recollections of Charles Lamb, Collected Writings of Thomas de Quincey*, ed. David Masson, 1890, vol. iii, pp. 71–7

---

*The *technical memory*, or that which depends upon purely arbitrary links of connexion, and therefore more upon a *nisus* or separate activity of the mind – that memory, for instance, which recalls names – is undoubtedly affected, and most powerfully, by opium. On the other hand, the *logical* memory, or that which recalls facts that are connected by fixed relations, and where, A being given, B must go before or after – historical memory, for instance – is not much, if at all, affected by opium.

[*In the late 1830s, letters and reminiscences of Coleridge were published in which De Quincey was blamed for having persisted in opium-eating for the sake of the pleasurable sensations which it gave him. This provoked De Quincey into writing an article,* Coleridge and Opium-Eating, *published in 1845, to claim that there was no difference between his case and Coleridge's, and to make some further deductions as to how opium addiction affected writers.*]

... it will not follow, because, with a relation to happiness and tranquillity, a man may have found opium his curse, that therefore, as a creature of energies and great purposes, he must have been the wreck which he [Coleridge] seems to suppose. Opium gives and takes away. It defeats the *steady* habit of exertion; but it creates spasms of irregular exertion. It ruins the natural power of life; but it develops preternatural paroxysms of intermitting power. ... Whenever Coleridge (being highly charged, or saturated, with opium) had written with distempered vigour upon any question, there occurred soon after a recoil of intense disgust, not from his own paper only, but even from the entire subject. All opium-eaters are tainted with the infirmity of leaving works unfinished, and suffering reactions of disgust. ... Coleridge raises ... a distinction, perfectly perplexing to us, between himself and the author of the *Opium Confessions*, upon the question why they severally began the practice of opium-eating. In himself, it seems, this motive was to relieve pain, whereas the confessor was surreptitiously seeking for pleasure. Ay, indeed! where did he learn *that*? We have no copy of the *Confessions* here; so we cannot quote chapter and verse; but we distinctly remember that toothache is recorded in that book as the particular occasion which first introduced the author to the knowledge of opium. Whether afterwards, having been thus initiated by the demon of pain, the opium-confessor did not apply powers thus discovered to purposes of mere pleasure, is a question for himself; and the same question applies with the same cogency to Coleridge. Coleridge began in rheumatic pains. What then? This is no proof that he did not end in voluptuousness. For our part, we are slow to believe that ever any man did or could learn the somewhat awful truth, that in a certain ruby-coloured elixir there lurked a divine power to chase away the genius of pain, or secondly, of *ennui* (which it is, far more than pain, that saddens our human life), without sometimes, and to some extent, abusing this power. To taste but once from the tree of knowledge is fatal to the subsequent power of abstinence. True it is that generations have used laudanum as an anodyne (for instance, hospital patients) who have not afterwards courted its powers as a voluptuous stimulant; but that, be sure, has arisen from no abstinence in *them*. There are, in fact, two classes of temperaments as to this terrific drug – those which are, and those which are not, preconformed to its power; those which genially expand to its temptations, and those which frostily exclude them. Not in the energies of the will, but in the qualities of the nervous organisation, lies the dread arbitration of – Fall or stand: doomed thou art to yield, or strengthened constitutionally to resist. Most of those who have but a low sense of the spells lying couchant in opium have practically none at all; for the initial fascination is for *them* effectually defeated by the sickness which nature has associated with the first stages of opium-eating. But to that other class whose nervous sensibilities vibrate to their profoundest depths under the first touch of the angelic poison, even as a lover's ear thrills on hearing unexpectedly the voice of her whom he loves, opium is the Amreeta[125] cup of beatitude. You know the *Paradise Lost*: and you remember from the eleventh book, in its earlier part, that laudanum must already have existed in Eden – nay, that it was used medicinally by an archangel: for, after Michael had 'purged with euphrasy and rue' the eyes of Adam, lest he should be unequal to the mere *sight* of the great visions about to unfold their draperies before him, next he fortifies his fleshly spirits against the *affliction* of these visions, of which visions the first was death. And how?

'He from the well of life three drops instilled.'

What was their operation?

> 'So deep the power of these ingredients pierced,
> *Even to the inmost seat of mental sight,*
> That Adam, now enforced to close his eyes,
> Sank down, and all his spirits became entranced
> But him the gentle angel by the hand
> Soon raised. . . .'

129

The second of these lines it is which betrays the presence of laudanum. It is in the faculty of mental vision, it is in the increased power of dealing with the shadowy and the dark, that the characteristic virtue of opium lies. Now, in the original higher sensibility is found some palliation for the *practice* of opium-eating; in the greater temptation lies a greater excuse. And in this faculty of self-revelation is found some palliation for *reporting* the case to the world; which palliation both Coleridge and his biographer have overlooked.

*Coleridge and Opium Eating*, a review of James Gillman's *Life of Samuel Taylor Coleridge* in *Blackwood's Magazine*, January 1845, reprinted in *Collected Writings of Thomas de Quincey*, ed. David Masson, 1890, vol. v, pp. 179–211

[*In the same year, De Quincey defended himself against the charge that by the fascination of the* Confessions *he had tempted others to become opium eaters.*]

Whatever were the impelling principles to the publication of the opium "Confessions", whether motive that was distinctly contemplated or impulse that was obscurely felt, there will remain a perfectly separate question as to the practical result. For a conscientious man will grieve over those consequences from his acts which he never could have designed, and will charge upon himself those seductions which he had not even suspected.

Here, then, opens an admirable occasion for the extent of my power by laying bare the world of mischief which I have caused; and, secondly, the fairest excuse possible for resuming my enchanter's wand in order that I may exorcise the evil spirits which I have evoked. Listening to others, as Coleridge for instance, I ought first to be horror-struck at the havoc which my revelations have produced; and next, under the coercion of conscience, I ought to find the necessity for redressing this havoc by revelations still more appalling. There in 1822 is your bane; here in 1845 is your antidote. Oh, stratagems of vanity! but I reject both. I have neither done the evil in past times with which I am charged, nor am I at present seeking to repair it. The first is not a fact; the second is not a possibility.... It is past all denying that in 1822 very many people ... did procure copies, and cause copies to be multiplied, of the opium "Confessions". But I have yet to learn that any one of these people was inoculated by me, or could have been, with a first love for a drug so notorious as opium. Teach opium-eating! Did I teach wine-drinking? Did I reveal the mystery of sleeping? Did I inaugurate the infirmity of laughter?

Yet still I may have sharpened the attention, or I may have pointed a deeper interest, to this perilous medicine. But these cases are accidents perhaps in a world where comparatively so few can be left to their own free choice in matters of daily habit – are such slight undulations upon the face of society as we see arising on the sea from the passing of a steamboat; they subside almost immediately into the mighty levels around them. In any ten cases of this nature, five will probably cure themselves by original defect of natural preconformity to the drug – four by coercion of circumstances barring all means of procuring opium. The opium-eater goes to sea, to jail, to the hulks,[126] to a hospital, or he is ordered off on a march; and in any of these cases the chain is broken violently. But then for the one case remaining? As to *that*, there is reason to think, from the vast diffusion of opium in all its forms, that any individual temptation must have been the *causa occasionalis* only, and not the *causa sine qua non* of such a habit.[127] A man has read a description of the powers lodged in opium; or, which is still more striking, he has found these powers heraldically emblazoned in some magnificent dream due to that agency. This by accident has been his own introduction to opium-eating. But if he never *had* seen the gorgeous description or the gorgeous dream, he would (fifty to one) have tried opium on the recommendation of a friend for toothache, which is as general as the air, or for ear-ache, or (as Coleridge) for rheumatism; and thus, without either description or dream, he would have learned the powers of opium on the surer basis of his own absolute experience.

Consequently, I deny the opening to any large range of mischief; and not believing in any mischief caused by my "Confessions", equally I deny the opening to any compensating power of detaining men from opium. My faith is, that no man is likely to adopt opium or lay it aside in consequence of anything he may read in a book. A book may suggest it; but, in default of the book, every day's intercourse with men, and every day's experience of pain, would have made the same suggestion.

*Thomas de Quincey: His Life and Writings* by H. A. Page (A. H. Japp), 1877, vol. ii, pp. 271–3.

[*The subject was much in his mind at that time, since he was working on* Suspiria de Profundis, *the never-finished sequel to the* Confessions, *in which he planned to develop to the full the study of the dreaming faculty which he had begun in the earlier work. The first part of* Suspiria de Profundis, *published in Blackwood's in March 1845, began with an Introductory Notice which put into perspective – and slightly distorted – his motives in writing the* Confessions.]

The object of that work was to reveal something of the grandeur which belongs *potentially* to human dreams. Whatever may be the number of those in whom this faculty of dreaming splendidly can be supposed to lurk, there are not perhaps very many in whom it is developed. He whose talk is of oxen, will probably dream of oxen; and the condition of human life, which yokes so vast a majority to a daily experience incompatible with much elevation of thought, oftentimes neutralises the tone of grandeur in the reproductive faculty of dreaming, even for those whose minds are populous with solemn imagery. Habitually to dream magnificently, a man must have a constitutional determination to reverie. This in the first place, and even this, where it exists strongly, is too much liable to disturbance from the gathering agitation of our present English life. . . .

Among the powers in man which suffer by this too intense life of the *social* instincts, none suffers more than the power of dreaming. Let no man think this a trifle. The machinery for dreaming planted in the human brain was not planted for nothing. That faculty, in alliance with the mystery of darkness, is the one great tube through which man communicates with the shadowy. And the dreaming organ, in connection with the heart, the eye and the ear, compose the magnificent apparatus which forces the infinite into the chambers of a human brain, and throws dark reflections from eternities below all life upon the mirrors of that mysterious *camera obscura*[128] – the human mind.

But if this faculty suffers from the decay of solitude, which is becoming a visionary idea in England, on the other hand it is certain that some merely physical agencies can and do assist the faculty of dreaming almost preternaturally. Amongst these is intense exercise; to some extent at least, and for some persons; but beyond all others is opium, which indeed seems to possess a *specific* power in that direction; not merely for exalting the colours of dream-scenery, but for deepening its shadows; and, above all, for strengthening the sense of its fearful *realities*.

The *Opium Confessions* were written with some slight secondary purpose of exposing this specific power of opium upon the faculty of dreaming, but much more with the purpose of displaying the faculty itself: and the outline of the work travelled in this course. Supposing a reader acquainted with the true object of the *Confessions* as here stated, namely, the revelation of dreaming, to have put this question:

'But how came you to dream more splendidly than others?'

The answer would have been –

'Because (*praemissis praemittendis*)[129] I took excessive quantities of opium.'

Secondly, suppose him to say, 'But how came you to take opium in this excess?'

The answer to *that* would be, 'Because some early events in my life had left a weakness in one organ which required (or seemed to require) that stimulant.'

Then, because the opium dreams could not always have been understood without a knowledge of these events, it became necessary to relate them. Now, these two questions and answers exhibit the *law* of the work; that is, the principle which determined its form, but precisely in the inverse or regressive order. The work itself opened with the narration of my early adventures. These, in the natural order of succession, led to the opium as a resource for healing their consequences; and the opium as naturally led to the dreams. But in the synthetic order of presenting the facts, what stood last in the succession of developments stood first in the order of my purposes.

Introductory Notice to *Suspiria de Profundis*, *Blackwood's Magazine*, March 1845

[*In 1853 a collected edition of De Quincey's works began to appear in Edinburgh under the title* Selections Grave and Gay. *Any selection, grave or gay, of De Quincey's works obviously had eventually to include the* Confessions of an English Opium Eater, *and in 1855, for the fifth volume of the selections, De Quincey addressed himself to the task of revising the* Confessions. *Old and tired as he then was, he found it a crushing task, and when he had finished it, he was doubtful whether after all it really was an improvement, as he confided to his daughter Emily in a letter of 30 September 1855.*]

Volume V is on the point of closing, viz., "The Confessions". It is almost rewritten; and there cannot be much doubt that here and there it is enlivened, and so far improved. To justify the enormous labour it has cost me, most certainly it *ought* to be improved. And yet, reviewing the volume as a *whole,* now that I can look back from nearly the end to the beginning, greatly I doubt whether many readers will not prefer it in its original fragmentary state to its present full-blown development. ... I should, however, be misleading you if any impression were left upon your mind that I had eked out the volume by any wire-drawing process: on the contrary, nothing has been added which did not originally belong to my outline of the work, having been left out chiefly through hurry at the period of first, i.e., original, publication in the autumn of 1821. ... As a book of *amusement* it is undoubtedly improved; what I doubt is, whether also as a book to *impress.* ... Here again, as in thousands of similar cases, is a conflict – is a call for a choice – between an almost *extempore* effort, having the faults, the carelessness, possibly the graces, of a fugitive inspiration – this on the one side, and on the other a studied and mature presentation of the same thoughts, facts, and feelings, but without the same benefit from extemporaneous excitement.

*Thomas de Quincey: His Life and Writings by* H. A. Page (A. H. Japp), 1877, vol. ii, pp. 109–11

## Appendix B

### B. SELECTED PASSAGES FROM THE 1856 REVISION

[*The following passage was added at the end of the original Preface, into which De Quincey also inserted the names of famous contemporary opium eaters left blank in the original version, and notes on their personalities (see Note 4).*]

[1] At this point I shall say no more than that opium, as the one sole *catholic* anodyne which hitherto has been revealed to man; secondly, as the one sole anodyne which in a vast majority of cases is *irresistible*; thirdly, as by many degrees the most potent of all known counter-agents to nervous irritation, and to the formidable curse of *tædium vitæ*;[130] fourthly, as by possibility, under an argument undeniably plausible, alleged by myself, the sole known agent – not for curing *when* formed, but for intercepting whilst likely to be formed – the great English scourge of pulmonary consumption; – I say that opium, as wearing these, or *any* of these, four beneficent characteristics – I say that any agent whatever making good such pretensions, no matter what its name, is entitled haughtily to refuse the ordinary classification and treatment which opium receives in books. I say that opium, or any agent of equal power, is entitled to assume that it was revealed to man for some higher object than that it should furnish a target for moral denunciations, ignorant where they are not hypocritical, childish where not dishonest; that it should be set up as a theatrical scarecrow for superstitious terrors, of which the *result* is oftentimes to defraud human suffering of its readiest alleviation, and of which the *purpose* is, 'Ut pueris placeant et declamatio fiant.'*

In one sense, and remotely, all medicines and modes of medical treatment offer themselves as anodynes – that is, so far as they promise ultimately to relieve the suffering connected with physical maladies or infirmities. But we do not, in the special and

---

*That they may win the applause of schoolboys, and furnish matter for a prize essay.

135

ordinary sense, designate as 'anodynes' those remedies which obtain the relief from pain only as a secondary and distant effect following out from the *cure* of the ailment; but those only we call anodynes which obtain this relief and pursue it as the *primary* and *immediate* object. If, by giving tonics to a child suffering periodic pains in the stomach, we were ultimately to banish those pains, this would not warrant us in calling such tonics by the name of anodynes; for the neutralisation of the pains would be a circuitous process of nature, and might probably require weeks for its evolution. But a true anodyne (as, for instance, half-a-dozen drops of laudanum, or a dessert-spoonful of some warm carminative mixed with brandy) will often banish the misery suffered by a child in five or six minutes. Amongst the most potent of anodynes, we may rank hemlock, henbane, chloroform, and opium. But unquestionably the three first have a most narrow field of action, by comparison with opium. This, beyond all other agents made known to man, is the mightiest for its command, and for the extent of its command, over pain; and so much mightier than any other, that I should think, in a Pagan land, supposing it to have been adequately made known* through experimental acquaintance with its revolutionary magic, opium would have had altars and priests consecrated to its benign and tutelary powers. But this is not my own object in the present little work. Very many people have thoroughly misconstrued this object; and therefore I beg to say here, in closing my Original

---

*'Adequately made known': – Precisely this, however, was impossible. No feature of ancient Pagan life has more entirely escaped notice than the extreme rarity, costliness, and circuitous accessibility of the more powerful drugs, especially of mineral drugs; and of drugs requiring elaborate preparation, or requiring much manufacturing skill. When the process of obtaining any manufactured drug was slow and intricate it could most rarely be called for. And rarely called for, why should it be produced? By looking into the history and times of Herod the Great, as reported by Josephus, the reader will gain some notion of the mystery and the suspicion surrounding all attempts at importing such drugs as could be applied to murderous purposes, consequently of the delay, the difficulty, and the peril in forming any familiar acquaintance with opium.

Preface, a little remodelled, that what I contemplated in these Confessions was to emblazon the power of opium – not over bodily disease and pain, but over the grander and more shadowy world of dreams.

(*He also added a 'Prefatory Notice to the New Edition.'*)

[11] When it had been settled that, in the general series of these republications, the *Confessions of an English Opium-Eater* should occupy the Fifth Volume, I resolved to avail myself most carefully of the opening thus made for a revision of the entire work. By accident, a considerable part of the Confessions (all, in short, except the Dreams) had originally been written hastily; and, from various causes, had never received any strict revision, or, *virtually*, so much as an ordinary verbal correction. But a great deal more was wanted than this. The main narrative should naturally have moved through a succession of secondary incidents; and with leisure for recalling these, it might have been greatly inspirited. Wanting all opportunity for such advantages, this narrative had been needlessly impoverished. And thus it had happened, that not so properly correction and retrenchment were called for, as integration of what had been left imperfect, or amplification of what, from the first, had been insufficiently expanded.

With these views, it would not have been difficult (though toilsome) to re-cast the little work in a better mould; and the result might, in all reason, count upon the approbation at least of its own former readers. Compared with its own former self, the book must certainly tend, by its very principle of change, whatever should be the *execution* of that change, to become better: and in my own opinion, after all drawbacks and allowances for the faulty exemplification of a good principle, it is better. This should be a matter of mere logical or inferential necessity; since, in pure addition to everything previously approved, there would now be a clear surplus of extra matter – all that might be good in the old work, and a great deal beside that was new. Meantime this improvement has been won at a price of labour and suffering that, if they could be truly stated, would seem incredible. A nervous malady, of very peculiar character, which has attacked me intermittingly for the last eleven years, came on in May last, almost concurrently with the commencement of this revision; and so obstinately has this malady pursued its noiseless, and what I may call subterraneous siege, since none of the symptoms are externally manifested, that, although pretty nearly dedicating myself to this one solitary labour, and not intermitting or relaxing it for a single day, I have yet spent, within a very few days, six calendar months upon the re-cast of this one small volume.

The consequences have been distressing to all concerned. The press has groaned under the chronic visitation; the compositors shudder at the sight of my handwriting, though not objectionable on the score of legibility; and I have much reason to fear that, on days when the pressure of my complaint has been heaviest, I may have so far given way to it, as to have suffered greatly in clearness of critical vision. Sometimes I may have overlooked blunders, mis-statements, or repetitions, implicit or even express. But more often I may have failed to appreciate the true effects from faulty management of style and its colourings. Sometimes, for instance, a heavy or too intricate arrangement of sentences may have defeated the tendency of what, under its natural presentation, would have been affecting; or it is possible enough that, by unseasonable levity at other times, I may have repelled the sympathy of my readers – all or some. Endless are the openings for such kinds of mistake – that is, of mistakes not fully seen *as* such. But even in a case of unequivocal mistake, seen and acknowledged, yet when it is open to remedy only through a sudden and energetic act, then or never, the press being for twenty minutes, suppose, free to receive an alteration, but beyond that time closed and sealed inexorably: such being supposed the circumstances, the humane reader will allow for the infirmity which even wilfully and consciously surrenders itself to the error, acquiescing in it deliberately, rather than face the cruel exertion of correcting it most elaborately at a moment of sickening misery, and with the prevision that the main correction must draw after it half-a-dozen others for the sake of decent consistency. I am not speaking under any present consciousness of such a case existing against myself: I believe there is none such. But I choose to suppose an extreme case of even conscious error, in order that venial cases of oversight may, under shelter of such an *outside* license, find toleration from a liberal critic. To fight up against the wearying siege of an abiding sickness, imposes a fiery combat. I attempt no description of this combat, knowing the unintelligibility and the repulsiveness of all attempts to communicate the Incommunicable. But the generous reader will not, for that forbearance on my part, the less readily show his indulgence, if a case should (unexpectedly to myself) arise for claiming it. ... The case of poor Ann the Outcast formed not only the most memorable and the most suggestively pathetic incident, but also *that* which, more than any other, coloured – or (more truly I should say) shaped, moulded and remoulded, composed and decomposed – the great body of opium dreams. The search after the lost features of Ann, which I spoke of as pursued in the crowds of London, was in a more proper sense pursued through many a year in dreams. The general idea of a search and a chase reproduced itself in many shapes. The person, the rank, the age, the scenical position, all varied themselves for ever; but the same leading traits more or less faintly remained of a lost Pariah woman, and of some shadowy malice which withdrew her, or attempted to withdraw her, from restoration and from hope. ...

[In his revision De Quincey cut out the opening paragraphs of the original 'Preliminary Confessions' except for the phrase 'I have often been asked how I first came to be a regular opium-eater', but then inserted a long passage about his and Coleridge's motives and case-histories as opium addicts.]

[III] I have often been asked – how it was, and through what series of steps, that I became an opium-eater. Was it gradually, tentatively, mistrustingly, as one goes down a shelving beach into a deepening sea, and with a knowledge from the first of the dangers lying on that path; half-courting those dangers, in fact, whilst seeming to defy them? Or was it, secondly, in pure ignorance of such dangers, under the misleadings of mercenary fraud? Since oftentimes lozenges, for the relief of pulmonary affections, found their efficacy upon the opium which they contain, upon this, and this only, though clamorously disavowing so suspicious an alliance: and under such treacherous disguises multitudes are seduced into a dependency which they had not foreseen upon a drug which they had not known; not known even by name or by sight: and thus the case is not rare – that the chain of abject slavery is first detected when it has inextricably wound itself about the constitutional system. Thirdly, and lastly, was it (*Yes*, by passionate anticipation, I answer, before the question is finished) – was it on a sudden overmastering impulse derived from bodily anguish? Loudly I repeat, *Yes*; loudly and indignantly – as in answer to a wilful calumny. Simply as an anodyne it was, under the mere coercion of pain the severest, that I first resorted to opium; and precisely that same torment it is, or some variety of that torment, which drives most people to make acquaintance with that same insidious remedy. Such was the fact; such by accident. Meantime, without blame it might have been otherwise. If in early days I had fully understood the subtle powers lodged in this mighty drug (when judiciously regulated), (1) to tranquillise all irritations of the nervous system; (2) to stimulate the capacities of enjoyment; and (3) under any call for extraordinary exertion (such as all men meet at times), to sustain through twenty-four consecutive hours the else drooping animal energies – most certainly, knowing or suspecting all this, I should have inaugurated my opium career in the character of one seeking *extra* power and enjoyment, rather than of one shrinking from *extra* torment. And why not? If *that* argued any fault, is it not a fault that most of us commit every day with regard to alcohol? Are we entitled to use *that* only as a medicine? Is wine unlawful, except as an anodyne? I hope not: else I shall be obliged to counterfeit and to plead some anomalous *tic* in my little finger; and thus gradually, as in any Ovidian metamorphosis, I, that am at present a truth-loving man, shall change by daily inches into a dissembler. No: the whole race of man proclaim it lawful to drink wine without pleading a medical certificate as a qualification. That same license extends itself therefore to the use of opium; what a man may lawfully seek in wine surely he may lawfully find in opium; and much more so in those many cases (of which mine happens to be one) where opium deranges the animal economy less by a great deal than an equivalent quantity of alcohol. Coleridge, therefore, was doubly in error when he allowed himself to aim most unfriendly blows at my supposed voluptuousness in the use of opium; in error as to a principle, and in error as to a fact. A letter of his,[131] which I will hope that he did not design to have published, but which, however, *has* been published, points the attention of his correspondent to a broad distinction separating my case as an opium-eater from his own: he, it seems, had fallen excusably (because unavoidably) into this habit of eating opium – as the one sole therapeutic resource available against his particular malady; but I, wretch that I am, being so notoriously charmed by fairies against pain, must have resorted to opium in the abominable character of an adventurous voluptuary, angling in all streams for variety of pleasures. Coleridge is wrong to the whole extent of what was possible; wrong in his fact, wrong in his doctrine; in his little fact, and his big doctrine. I did not do the thing which he charges upon me; and if I *had* done it, this would not convict me as a citizen of Sybaris or Daphne.[132] There never was a distinction more groundless and visionary than that which it has pleased him to draw between my motives and his own; nor could Coleridge have possibly owed this mis-statement to any false information; since no man surely, on a question of my own private experience, could have pretended to be better informed than myself. Or, if there really is such a person, perhaps he will not think it too much trouble to re-write these Confessions from first to last, correcting their innumerable faults; and, as it happens that some parts of the unpublished sections for the present are missing, would he kindly restore them – brightening the colours that may have faded, rekindling the inspiration that may have drooped; filling up all those chasms which else are likely to remain as permanent disfigurations of my little work? Meantime the reader, who takes any interest in such a question, will find that I myself (upon such a theme not simply the best, but surely the sole authority) have, without a shadow of variation, always given a different account of the matter. Most truly I have told the reader, that not any search after pleasure, but mere extremity of pain from rheumatic toothache – this and nothing else it was that first drove me into the use of opium. Coleridge's bodily affliction was simple rheumatism. Mine, which intermittingly raged for ten years, was rheumatism in the face combined with toothache. ... I was thrown passively upon chance advice, and therefore, by a natural consequence, upon opium – that being the one sole anodyne that is almost notoriously such, and which in that great function is universally appreciated.

Coleridge, therefore, and myself, as regards our baptismal initiation into the use of that mighty drug, occupy the very same position. We are embarked in the self-same boat; nor is it within the compass even of angelic hair-splitting, to show that the dark shadow thrown by our several trespasses in this field, mine and his, had by so much as a pin's point any assignable difference. Trespass against trespass (if any trespass there were) – shadow against shadow (if any shadow were really thrown by this trespass over the snowy disk of pure ascetic morality), in any case, that act in either of us would read into the same meaning, would count up as a debt into the same value, would measure as a delinquency into the same burden of responsibility. And vainly, indeed, does Coleridge attempt to differentiate two cases which ran into absolute identity, differing only as rheumatism differs from toothache. Amongst the admirers of Coleridge, I at all times stood in the foremost rank; and the more was my astonishment at being summoned so often to witness his carelessness in the management of controversial questions, and his demoniac inaccuracy in the statement of facts. The more also was my sense of Coleridge's wanton injustice in relation to myself individually. Coleridge's gross mis-statement of facts, in regard to our several opium experiences, had its origin, sometimes in flighty reading, sometimes in partial and incoherent reading, sometimes in subsequent forgetfulness; and any one of these lax habits (it will occur to the reader) is a venial infirmity. Certainly it is; but surely *not* venial, when it is allowed to operate disadvantageously upon the character for self-control of a brother, who had never spoken of *him* but in the spirit of enthusiastic admiration; of that admiration which his exquisite works so amply challenge. Imagine the case that I really *had* done something wrong, still it would have been ungenerous – me it would have saddened, I confess, to see Coleridge rushing forward with a public denunciation of my fault: – 'Know all men by these presents, that I, S. T. C., a *noticeable man with large grey eyes,* am a licensed opium-eater, whereas this other man is a buccaneer, a pirate, a flibustier,† and can have none but a forged licence in his disreputable pocket. In the name of Virtue, arrest him!' But the truth is, that inaccuracy as to facts and citations from books was in Coleridge a mere necessity of nature. . . .

This case, therefore, might now be counted on as disposed of; and what sport it could yield might reasonably be thought exhausted. Meantime, on consideration, another and much deeper oversight of Coleridge's becomes apparent; and as this connects itself with an aspect of the case that furnishes the foundation to the whole of these ensuing Confessions, it cannot altogether be neglected. Any attentive reader, after a few moments' reflection, will perceive that, whatever may have been the casual *occasion* of mine or Coleridge's opium-eating, this could not have been the permanent *ground* of opium-eating; because neither rheumatism nor toothache is any *abiding* affection of the system. Both are intermitting maladies, and not at all capable of accounting for a *permanent* habit of opium-eating. Some months are requisite to found *that.* Making allowance for constitutional differences, I should say that *in less than 120 days* no habit of opium-eating could be formed strong enough to call for any extraordinary self-conquest in renouncing it, and even suddenly renouncing it. On Saturday you are an opium-eater, on Sunday no longer such. What then was it, after all, that made Coleridge a slave to opium, and a slave that could not break his chain? He fancies, in his headlong carelessness, that he has accounted for this habit and this slavery; and in the meantime he has accounted for nothing

---

*See Wordsworth's exquisite picture of S. T. C. and himself as occasional denizens in the *Castle of Indolence.*

†This word – in common use, and so spelled as I spell it, amongst the grand old French and English buccaneers contemporary with our own admirable Dampier, at the close of the seventeenth century – has recently been revived in the journals of the United States, with a view to the special case of Cuba, but (for what reason I know not) is now written always as *fillibusters.* Meantime, written in whatsoever way, it is understood to be a Franco-Spanish corruption of the English word *freebooter.*

at all about which any question has arisen. Rheumatism, he says, drove him to opium. Very well; but with proper medical treatment the rheumatism would soon have ceased; or even, without medical treatment, under the ordinary oscillations of natural causes. And when the pain ceased, then the opium should have ceased. Why did it not? Because Coleridge had come to taste the genial pleasure of opium; and thus the very impeachment, which he fancied himself in some mysterious way to have evaded, recoils upon him in undiminished force. The rheumatic attack would have retired before the habit could have had time to form itself. Or suppose that I underrate the strength of the possible habit – this tells equally in *my* favour; and Coleridge was not entitled to forget in *my* case a plea remembered in his own. It is really memorable in the annals of human self-deceptions, that Coleridge could have held such language in the face of such facts. I, boasting not at all of my self-conquests, and owning no moral argument against the free use of opium, nevertheless on mere *prudential* motives break through the vassalage more than once,[133] and by efforts which I have recorded as modes of transcendent suffering. Coleridge, professing to believe (without reason assigned) that opium-eating is criminal, and in some mysterious sense more criminal than wine-drinking or porter-drinking, having, therefore, the strongest *moral* motive for abstaining from it, yet suffers himself to fall into a captivity to this same wicked opium, deadlier than was ever heard of, and under no coercion whatever that he has anywhere explained to us. A slave he was to this potent drug not less abject than Caliban to Prospero – his detested and yet despotic master. Like Caliban, he frets his very heart-strings against the rivets of his chain. Still, at intervals through the gloomy vigils of his prison, you hear muttered growls of impotent mutineering swelling upon the breeze:

'Irasque leonum
Vincla recusantum' –[134]

*recusantum*, it is true, still refusing yet still accepting, protesting for ever against the fierce, overmastering curb-chain, yet for ever submitting to receive it into the mouth. It is notorious that in Bristol (to *that* I can speak myself, but probably in many other places) he went so far as to hire men – porters, hackney-coachmen, and others – to oppose by force his entrance into any druggist's shop. But, as the authority for stopping him was derived simply from himself, naturally these poor men found themselves in a metaphysical fix, not provided for even by Thomas Aquinas or by the prince of Jesuitical casuists. And in this excruciating dilemma would occur such scenes as the following : –

'Oh, sir,' would plead the suppliant porter – suppliant, yet semi-imperative (for equally if he *did*, and if he did *not*, show fight, the poor man's daily 5s. seemed endangered) – 'really you must not; consider, sir, your wife and – '

*Transcendental Philosopher.* – 'Wife ! what wife? I have no wife.'*

*Porter.* – 'But, really now, you must not, sir. Didn't you say no longer ago than yesterday – '

*Transcend. Philos.* – 'Pooh, pooh ! yesterday is a long time ago. Are you aware, my man, that people are known to have dropped down dead for timely want of opium?'

*Porter.* – 'Ay, but you tell't me not to hearken – '

*Transcend. Philos.* – 'Oh, nonsense. An emergency, a shocking emergency, has arisen – quite unlooked for. No matter what I told you in times long past. That which I *now* tell you, is – that, if you don't remove that arm of yours from the doorway of this most respectable druggist, I shall have a good ground of action against you for assault and battery.'

Am I the man to reproach Coleridge with this vassalage to opium? Heaven forbid ! Having groaned myself under that yoke, I pity, and blame him not. But undeniably, such a vassalage must have been created wilfully and consciously by his own craving after genial stimulation; a thing which I do not blame, but Coleridge *did*. For my own part, duly as the torment relaxed in relief of which I had resorted to opium, I laid aside the opium, not under any meritorious effort of self-conquest; nothing of that sort do I pretend to; but simply on a prudential instinct warning me not to trifle with an engine so awful of consolation and support, nor to waste upon a momentary uneasiness what might

---

*Vide Othello.*

eventually prove, in the midst of all-shattering hurricanes, the great elixir of resurrection. What was it that did in reality make me an opium-eater? That affection which finally drove me into the *habitual* use of opium, what was it? Pain was it? No, but misery. Casual overcasting of sunshine was it? No, but blank desolation. Gloom was it that might have departed? No, but settled and abiding darkness.

'Total eclipse,
Without all hope of day!'*

Yet whence derived? Caused by what? Caused, as I might truly plead, by youthful distresses in London; were it not that these distresses were due, in their ultimate origin, to my own unpardonable folly; and to that folly I trace many ruins. Oh, spirit of merciful interpretation, angel of forgiveness to youth and its aberrations, that hearkenest for ever as if to some sweet choir of far-off female intercessions! will ye, choir that intercede – wilt thou, angel that forgivest – join together and charm away that mighty phantom, born amidst the gathering mists of remorse, which strides after me in pursuit from forgotten days – towering for ever into proportions more and more colossal, overhanging and overshadowing my head as if close behind, yet dating its nativity from hours that are fled by more than half-a-century? Oh heavens! that it should be possible for a child not seventeen years old, by a momentary blindness, by listening to a false, false whisper from his own bewildered heart, by one erring step, by a motion this way or that, to change the currents of his destiny, to poison the fountains of his peace, and in the twinkling of an eye to lay the foundations of a life-long repentance! Yet, alas! I must abide by the realities of the case. And one thing is clear, that amidst such bitter self-reproaches as are now extorted from me by the anguish of my recollections, it cannot be with any purpose of weaving plausible excuses, or of evading blame, that I trace the origin of my confirmed opium-eating to a necessity growing out of my early sufferings in the streets of London. Because, though true it is that the re-agency of these London sufferings did

------

*\* Samson Agonistes.*

in after years *enforce* the use of opium, equally it is true that the sufferings themselves grew out of my own folly. What really calls for excuse, is not the recourse to opium, when opium had become the one sole remedy available for the malady, but those follies which had themselves produced that malady.

I, for my part, after I had become a regular opium-eater, and from mismanagement had fallen into miserable excesses in the use of opium, did nevertheless, four several times, contend successfully against the dominion of this drug; did four several years renounce it; renounced it for long intervals; and finally resumed it upon the warrant of my enlightened and deliberate judgment, as being of two evils by very much the least. In this I acknowledge nothing that calls for excuse. I repeat again and again, that not the application of opium, with its deep tranquillising powers to the mitigation of evils, bequeathed by my London hardships, is what reasonably calls for sorrow, but that extravagance of childish folly which precipitated me into scenes naturally producing such hardships.

These scenes I am now called upon to retrace. Possibly they are sufficiently interesting to merit, even on their own account, some short record; but at present, and at this point, they have become indispensable as a key to the proper understanding of all which follows. For in these incidents of my early life is found the entire substratum, together with the secret and underlying motive of those pompous dreams and dream-sceneries which were in reality the true objects – first and last – contemplated in these Confessions.

[After a long digression on the history and dangers of guardianship, and descriptions of three of his guardians after his father's death, De Quincey gave a fuller account of the fourth, the Reverend Samuel Hall, a Manchester clergyman and a friend of De Quincey's father, who was also De Quincey's tutor for some years. He also describes a sojourn in the house of John Kelsall, formerly a clerk in De Quincey's father's business, and afterwards business agent to the De Quincey family. Of Samuel Hall he writes:]

[IV] This gentleman represented a class – large enough at all times by necessity of human nature, but in those days far larger than at present – that class, I mean, who sympathise with no spiritual sense or spiritual capacities in man; who understand by religion simply a respectable code of ethics – leaning for support upon some great mysteries dimly traced in the background, and commemorated in certain great church festivals by the *elder* churches of Christendom; as, *e.g.*, by the English, which does not stand as to age on the Reformation epoch, by the Romish and by the Greek. He had composed a body of about 330 sermons, which thus, at the rate of two every Sunday, revolved through a cycle of three years; that period being modestly assumed as sufficient for insuring to their eloquence total oblivion. Possibly to a cynic, some shorter cycle might have seemed equal to that effect, since their topics rose but rarely above the level of prudential ethics; and the style, though scholarly, was not impressive. As a preacher, Mr H. was sincere, but not earnest. He was a good and conscientious man; and he made a high valuation of the pulpit as an organ of civilisation for co-operating with books; but it was impossible for any man, starting from the low ground of themes so unimpassioned and so desultory as the benefits of industry, the danger from bad companions, the importance of setting a good example, or the value of perseverance – to pump up any persistent stream of earnestness either in himself or in his auditors. These auditors, again, were not of a class to desire much earnestness. There were no naughty people among them: most of them were rich, and came to church in carriages: and, as a natural result of their esteem for my reverend guardian, a number of them combined to build a church for him – viz., St Peter's, at the point of confluence between Moseley Street and the newly projected Oxford Street – then existing only as a sketch in the portfolio of a surveyor. But what connected myself individually with Mr H. was, that two or three years previously I, together with one of my brothers (five years my senior), had been placed under his care for classical instruction. This was done, I believe, in obedience to a dying injunction of my father, who had a just esteem for Mr S. H. as an upright man, but apparently too exalted an opinion of his scholarship: for he was but an indifferent Grecian. In whatever way the appointment arose, so it was that this gentleman, previously *tutor* in the Roman sense to all of us, now became to my brother and myself tutor also in the common English sense. From the age of eight, up to eleven and a-half, the character and intellectual attainments of Mr H. were therefore influentially important to myself in the development of my powers, such as they were. Even his 330 sermons, which rolled overhead with such slender effect upon his general congregation, to me became a real instrument of improvement. One-half of these, indeed, were all that I heard; for, as my father's house (Greenhay) stood at this time in the country, Manchester not having yet overtaken it, the distance obliged us to go in a carriage, and only to the morning service; but every sermon in this morning course was propounded to me as a textual basis upon which I was to raise a mimic duplicate – sometimes a pure miniature abstract – sometimes a rhetorical expansion – but preserving as much as possible of the original language, and also (which puzzled me painfully) preserving the exact succession of the thoughts; which might be easy where they stood in some dependency upon each other, as, for instance, in the development of an argument, but in arbitrary or chance arrangements was often as trying to my powers as any feat of rope-dancing. I, therefore, amongst that whole congregation,* was the one sole care-

---

*'That whole congregation': – Originally at churches which I do not remember, where, however, in consideration of my tender age, the demands levied upon my memory were much lighter. Two or three years later, when I must have been nearing my tenth year, and when St Peter's had been finished, occurred the opening, and consequently (as an indispensable pre-condition) the consecration of that edifice by the bishop of the diocese (viz., Chester). I, as a ward of the incumbent, was naturally amongst those specially invited to the festival; and I remember a little incident which exposed broadly the conflict of feelings inherited by the Church of England from the Puritans of the seventeenth century. The architecture of the church was Grecian; and certainly the enrichments, inside or outside, were few enough, neither florid nor obtrusive. But in the centre of the ceiling, for the sake of breaking the monotony of so large a blank white surface, there was moulded, in plaster-of-Paris, a large tablet or shield, charged with a cornucopia of fruits and flowers. And yet, when we were all assembled in the vestry waiting – rector, churchwardens, architect, and trains of dependants – there arose a deep buzz of anxiety, which soon ripened into an articulate expression of fear, that the bishop

worn auditor – agitated about that which, over all other heads, flowed away like water over marble slabs – viz., the somewhat torpid sermon of my somewhat torpid guardian. But this annoyance was not wholly lost: and those same $\frac{330}{2}$ sermons, which (lasting only through sixteen minutes each) were approved and forgotten by everybody else, for me became a perfect palæstra[136] of intellectual gymnastics far better suited to my childish weakness than could have been the sermons of Isaac Barrow or Jeremy Taylor.[137] In these last, the gorgeous imagery would have dazzled my feeble vision, and in both the gigantic thinking would have crushed my efforts at apprehension. I drew, in fact, the deepest benefits from this weekly exercise. Perhaps, also, in the end it ripened into a great advantage for me, though long and bitterly I complained of it, that I was not allowed to use a pencil in taking notes: all was to be charged upon the memory. But it is notorious that the memory strengthens as you lay burdens upon it, and becomes trustworthy as you trust it. So that, in my third year of practice, I found my abstracting and condensing powers sensibly enlarged. My guardian was gradually better satisfied; for unfortunately (and in the beginning it *was* unfortunate) always one witness could be summoned against me upon any impeachment of my fidelity – viz., the sermon itself; since, though lurking amongst the 330, the wretch was easily forked out. But these appeals grew fewer; and my guardian, as I have said, was continually better satisfied. Meantime, might not I be continually less satisfied with *him* and his 330 sermons? Not at all: loving and trusting, without doubt or reserve, and with the deepest principles of veneration rooted in my nature, I never, upon meeting something more impressive than the average complexion of my guardian's discourses, for one moment thought of him as worse or feebler than others, but simply as different; and no more

---

would think himself bound, like the horrid eikonoclasts of 1645, to issue his decree of utter *averruncation*[135] to the simple decoration overhead. Fearfully did we all tread the little aisles in the procession of the prelate. Earnestly my lord looked upwards; but finally – were it courtesy, or doubtfulness as to his ground, or approbation – he passed on.

quarrelled with him for his characteristic languor, than with a green riband for not being blue. By mere accident, I one day heard quoted a couplet which seemed to me sublime. It described a preacher such as sometimes arises in difficult times, or in fermenting times, a son of thunder, that looks all enemies in the face, and volunteers a defiance even when it would have been easy to evade it. The lines were written by Richard Baxter[138] – who battled often with self-created storms from the first dawn of the Parliamentary War in 1642, through the period of Cromwell (to whom he was personally odious), and, finally, through the trying reigns of the second Charles and of the second James. As a pulpit orator, he was perhaps the Whitfield of the seventeenth century – the *Leuconomos* of Cowper.[139] And thus it is that he describes the impassioned character of his own preaching –

'I preach'd, as never sure to preach again;

[Even *that* was telling; but then followed this thunder-*peal*]

And as a dying man to dying men.'

This couplet, which seemed to me equally for weight and for splendour like molten gold, laid bare another aspect of the Catholic church; revealed it as a Church militant and crusading.

Not even thus, however, did I descry any positive imperfection in my guardian. He and Baxter had fallen upon different generations. Baxter's century, from first to last, was revolutionary. Along the entire course of that seventeenth century, the great principles of representative government and the rights of conscience* were passing through the anguish of conflict and fiery trial. Now again

---

*'*The rights of conscience*': – With which it is painful to know that Baxter did not sympathise. Religious toleration he called 'Soulmurder'. And, if you reminded him that the want of this toleration had been his own capital grievance, he replied, 'Ah, but the cases were very different: I was in the right; whereas the vast majority of those who will benefit by this newfangled toleration are shockingly in the wrong.'

in my own day, at the close of the eighteenth century, it is true that all the elements of social life were thrown into the crucible – but on behalf of our neighbours, no longer of ourselves. No longer, therefore, was invoked the heroic pleader, ready for martyrdom, preaching, therefore, 'as never sure to preach again'; and I no more made it a defect in my guardian that he wanted energies for combating evils now forgotten, than that he had not in patriotic fervour leaped into a gulf, like the fabulous Roman martyr Curtius,[140] or in zeal for liberty had not mounted a scaffold, like the real English martyr Algernon Sidney.[141] Every Sunday, duly as it revolved, brought with it this cruel anxiety. On Saturday night under sad anticipation, on Sunday night under sadder experimental knowledge, of my trying task, I slept ill : my pillow was stuffed with thorns; and until Monday morning's inspection and *armilustrium*[142] had dismissed me from parade to 'stand at ease,' verily I felt like a false steward summoned to some killing audit. Then suppose Monday to be invaded by some horrible intruder, visitor perhaps from a band of my guardian's poor relations, that in some undiscovered nook of Lancashire seemed in fancy to blacken all the fields, and suddenly at a single note of *'caw, caw,'* rose in one vast cloud like crows, and settled down for weeks at the table of my guardian and his wife, whose noble hospitality would never allow the humblest among them to be saddened by a faint welcome. In such cases, very possibly the whole week did not see the end of my troubles.

On these terms, for upwards of three-and-a-half years – that is, from my eighth to beyond my eleventh birth-day – my guardian and I went on cordially : he never once angry, as indeed he never had any reason for anger; I never once treating my task either as odious (which in the most abominable excess it was), or, on the other hand, as costing but a trivial effort, which practice might have taught me to hurry through with contemptuous ease. To the very last I found no ease at all in this weekly task, which never ceased to be 'a thorn in the flesh' : and I believe that my guardian, like many of the grim Pagan divinities, inhaled a flavour of fragrant incense, from the fretting and stinging of anxiety which, as it were some holy vestal fire, he kept alive by this periodic exaction. It gave him pleasure that he could reach me in the very recesses of my dreams, where even a Pariah might look for rest; so that the Sunday, which to man, and even to the brutes within his gates, offered an interval of rest, for me was signalized as a day of martyrdom. Yet in this, after all, it is possible that he did me a service: for my constitutional infirmity of mind ran but too determinately towards the sleep of endless reveries, and of dreamy abstraction from life and its realities.

Whether serviceable or not, however, the connexion between my guardian and myself was now drawing to its close. Some months after my eleventh birth-day, Greenhay* was sold, and my mother's establishment – both children and servants – was translated to Bath: only that for a few months I and one brother were still left under the care of Mr Samuel H.; so far, that is, as regarded our education. Else, as regarded the luxurious comforts of a thoroughly English home, we became the guests, by special invitation, of a young married couple in Manchester – viz., Mr and Mrs K—l. This incident, though otherwise without results, I look back upon with feelings inexpressibly profound, as a jewelly parenthesis of pathetic happiness – such as emerges but once in any man's life. Mr K. was a young and rising American merchant; by which I mean, that he was an Englishman who exported to the United States. He had married about three years previously a pretty and amiable young woman – well educated, and endowed with singular compass of intellect. But the distinguishing feature in this household was the spirit of love which, under the benign superintendence of the mistress, diffused itself through all its members. ...

She had won the gratitude of her servants from the first, by making the amplest provision for their comfort; their confidence, by listening with patience, and counselling with prudence; and their respect, by refusing to intermeddle with gossiping person-

---

* 'Greenhay': – A country-house built by my father; and at the time of its foundation (say in 1791 or 1792) separated from the last outskirts of Manchester by an entire mile; but now, and for many a year, overtaken by the hasty strides of this great city, and long since (I presume) absorbed into its mighty uproar.

alities always tending to slander. To this extent, perhaps, most mistresses might follow her example. But the happiness which reigned in Mrs K—'s house at this time depended very much upon special causes. All the eight persons had the advantage of youth; and the three young female servants were under the spell of fascination, such as could rarely be counted on, from a spectacle held up hourly before their eyes, that spectacle which of all others is the most touching to womanly sensibilities, and which any one of these servants might hope, without presumption, to realise for herself – the spectacle, I mean, of a happy marriage union between two persons, who lived in harmony so absolute with each other, as to be independent of the world outside. How tender and self-sufficing such an opinion might be, they saw with their own eyes. The season was then midwinter, which of itself draws closer all household ties. Their own labours, as generally in respectable English services, were finished for the most part by two o'clock; and as the hours of evening drew nearer, when the master's return might be looked for without fail, beautiful was the smile of anticipation upon the gentle features of the mistress: even more beautiful the reflex of that smile, half-unconscious, and half-repressed, upon the features of the sympathising hand-maidens. One child, a little girl of two years old, had then crowned the happiness of the K—s. She naturally lent her person at all times, and apparently in all places at once, to the improvement of the family groups. My brother and myself, who had been trained from infancy to the courteous treatment of servants, filled up a vacancy in the graduated scale of ascending ages, and felt in varying degrees the depths of a peace which we could not adequately understand or appreciate. Bad tempers there were none amongst us; nor any opening for personal jealousies; nor, through the privilege of our common youth, either angry recollections breathing from the past, or fretting anxieties gathering from the future. The spirit of hope and the spirit of peace (so it seemed to me, when looking back upon this profound calm) had, for their own enjoyment, united in a sisterly league to blow a solitary bubble of visionary happiness – and to sequester from the unresting hurricanes of life one solitary household of eight persons within a four months' lull, as if within some Arabian tent on some untrodden wilderness, withdrawn from human intrusion, or even from knowledge, by worlds of mist and vapour.

How deep was that lull! and yet, as in a human atmosphere, how frail! Did the visionary bubble burst at once? Not so: but silently and by measured steps, like a dissolving palace of snow, it collapsed. In the superb expression of Shakspere, minted by himself, and drawn from his own aerial fancy, like a cloud it '*dislimned*'; lost its lineaments by stealthy steps. Already the word '*parting*' (for myself and my brother were under summons for Bath) hoisted the first signal for breaking up. Next, and not very long afterwards, came a mixed signal: alternate words of joy and grief – marriage and death severed the sisterly union amongst the young female servants. Then, thirdly, but many years later, vanished from earth, and from peace the deepest that can support itself on earth, summoned to a far deeper peace, the mistress of the household herself, together with her first-born child. Some years later, perhaps twenty from this time, as I stood sheltering myself from rain in a shop within the most public street of Manchester, the master of the establishment drew my attention to a gentleman on the opposite side of the street – roaming along in a reckless style of movement, and apparently insensible to the notice which he attracted. 'That,' said the master of the shop, 'was once a leading merchant in our town; but he met with great commercial embarrassments. There was no impeachment of his integrity, or (as I believe) of his discretion. But what with these commercial calamities, and deaths in his family, he lost all hope; and you see what sort of consolation it is that he seeks' – meaning to say that his style of walking argued intoxication. I did not think so. There was a settled misery in his eye, but complicated with *that* an expression of nervous distraction, that, if it should increase, would make life an intolerable burden. I never saw him again, and thought with horror of his being called in old age to face the fierce tragedies of life. For many reasons, I recoiled from forcing myself upon his notice: but I had ascertained, some time previously to this casual rencontre, that he and myself were, at that date, all that remained of the once joyous household. At present, and for many a year, I am myself the sole relic from that household sanctuary – sweet, solemn, profound – that concealed, as in some ark floating on solitary seas, eight persons, since called away, all except myself, one after one, to that rest which only could be deeper than ours was then.

[*De Quincey enormously expanded the section on his experiences at Manchester Grammar School. His description of the Headmaster, Charles Lawson, showed more sympathetic understanding than the brief dismissal of him in the original* Confessions *as 'coarse, clumsy, and inelegant'.*]

[v] On a day, therefore, it was in the closing autumn (or rather in the opening winter) of 1800 that my first introduction took place to the Manchester Grammar School. The school-room showed already in its ample proportions some hint of its pretensions as an endowed school, or school of that class which I believe peculiar to England. To this limited extent had the architectural sense of power been timidly and parsimoniously invoked. Beyond that, nothing had been attempted; and the dreary expanse of whitewashed walls, that at so small a cost might have been embellished by plaster-of-Paris friezes and large medallions, illustrating to the eye of the youthful student the most memorable glorifications of literature – these were bare as the walls of a poor-house or a lazaretto; buildings whose functions, as thoroughly sad and gloomy, the mind recoils from drawing into relief by sculpture or painting. But this building was dedicated to purposes that were noble. The naked walls clamoured for decoration : and how easily might tablets have been moulded – exhibiting (as a first homage to literature) Athens, with the wisdom of Athens, in the person of Pisistratus, concentrating the general energies upon the revisal and recasting of the *Iliad*. Or (second) the Athenian captives in Sicily, within the fifth century B.C., as winning noble mercy for themselves by some

> 'Repeated air
> Of sad Electra's poet.'

Such, and so sudden, had been the oblivion of earthly passions wrought by the contemporary poet of Athens that in a moment the wrath of Sicily, with all its billows, ran down into a heavenly calm; and he that could plead for his redemption no closer relation to Euripides than the accident of recalling some scatterings from his divine verses, suddenly found his chains dropping to the ground; and himself, that in the morning had risen a despairing slave in a stone-quarry, translated at once as a favoured brother into a palace of Syracuse. Or, again, how easy to represent (third) 'the great Emathian conqueror,' that in the very opening of his career, whilst visiting Thebes with vengeance, nevertheless relented at the thought of literature, and

> 'Bade spare
> The house of Pindarus, when Temple and tower
> Went to the ground.'

Alexander might have been represented amongst the colonnades of some Persian capital – Ecbatana or Babylon, Susa or Persepolis – in the act of receiving from Greece, as a *nuzzur* more awful than anything within the gift of the 'barbaric East,' a jewelled casket containing the *Iliad* and the *Odyssey*; creations that already have lived almost as long as the Pyramids.

Puritanically bald and odious therefore, in my eyes, was the hall up which my guardian and myself paced solemnly – though not Miltonically 'riding up to the Soldan's chair,' yet in fact, within a more limited kingdom, advancing to the chair of a more absolute despot. This potentate was the head-master, or *archididascalus*, of the Manchester Grammar School; and that school was variously distinguished. It was (1) ancient, having in fact been founded by a bishop of Exeter in an early part of the sixteenth century, so as to be now, in 1856, more than 330 years old; (2) it was rich, and was annually growing richer; and (3) it was dignified by a beneficial relation to the magnificent University of Oxford.

The head-master at that time was Mr Charles Lawson. ... Mr Lawson was in some degree interesting by his position and his recluse habits. Life was over with him, for its hopes and for its trials. Or at most one trial yet awaited him, which was – to fight with a painful malady, and fighting to die. He still had his dying to do : he was in arrear as to *that:* else all was finished. It struck me (but, with such limited means for judging, I might easily be wrong) that his understanding was of a narrow order. But that did not disturb the interest which surrounded him now in his old age (probably seventy-five, or more), nor make any drawback from the desire I had to spell backwards and re-compose the text of his life. What had been his fortunes in this world? Had they travelled upwards or downwards? What triumphs had he enjoyed in the sweet and solemn cloisters of Oxford? What mortifications in the harsh world outside? Two only had survived in the malicious traditions of 'his friends.' He was a Jacobite (as were so many amongst my dear Lancastrian compatriots); had drunk the Pretender's health, and drunk it in company with that Dr Byrom[143] who had graced the *symposium* by the famous equivocating *impromptu*\* to the health of that prince. Mr Lawson had therefore been obliged to witness the final prostration of his political party. That was his earliest mortification. His second, about seven years later, was, that he had been jilted; and with circumstances (at least so I heard) of cruel scorn. Was it that *he* had interpreted in a sense too flattering for himself ambiguous expressions of favour in the lady? or that she in cruel caprice had disowned the hopes which she had authorised. However this might be, half-a-century of soothing and reconciling years had cicatrised the wounds of Mr Lawson's heart. The lady of 1752, if living in 1800,

---

\* '*Equivocating impromptu*': – The party had gathered in a tumultuary way; so that some Capulets had mingled with the Montagues, one of whom called upon Dr Byrom to drink *The King, God bless him! and Confusion to the Pretender!* Upon which the doctor sang out –

> 'God bless the king, of church and state defender;
> God bless (no harm in *blessing*) the Pretender !
> But who Pretender is, and who the King –
> God bless us all ! that's quite another thing.'

Dr Byrom was otherwise famous than as a Jacobite – viz., as the author of a very elaborate shorthand, which (according to some who have examined it) rises even to a philosophic dignity. David Hartley in particular said of it that, 'if ever a philosophic language (as projected by Bishop Wilkins, by Leibnitz, etc.) should be brought to bear, in that case Dr Byrom's work would furnish the proper character for its notation.'

must be furiously wrinkled. And a strange metaphysical question arises : Whether, when the object of an impassioned love has herself faded into a shadow, the fiery passion itself can still survive as an abstraction, still mourn over its wrongs, still clamour for redress. I have heard of such cases. In Wordsworth's poem of *Ruth* (which was founded, as I happen to know, upon facts), it is recorded as an affecting incident, that, some months after the first frenzy of her disturbed mind had given way to medical treatment, and had lapsed into a gentler form of lunacy, she was dismissed from confinement; and upon finding herself uncontrolled among the pastoral scenes where she played away her childhood, she gradually fell back to the original habits of her life whilst yet undisturbed by sorrow. Something similar had happened to Mr Lawson; and some time after his first shock, amongst other means for effacing that deep-grooved impression, he had laboured to replace himself, as much as was possible, in the situation of a college student. In this effort he was assisted considerably by the singular arrangement of the house attached to his official station. For an English house it was altogether an oddity, being, in fact, built upon a Roman plan. All the rooms on both storeys had their windows looking down upon a little central court. This court was quadrangular, but so limited in its dimensions, that by a Roman it would have been regarded as the *impluvium*.[144] For Mr Lawson, however, with a little exertion of fancy, it transmuted itself into a college quadrangle. Here, therefore, were held the daily 'callings-over,' at which every student was obliged to answer upon being named. And thus the unhappy man, renewing continually the fancy that he was still standing in an Oxford quadrangle, perhaps cheated himself into the belief that all had been a dream which concerned the caprices of the lady, and the lady herself a phantom. College usages also, which served to strengthen this fanciful *alibi* – such, for instance, as the having two plates arranged before him at dinner (one for the animal, the other for the vegetable, food) – were reproduced in Millgate. One sole luxury also, somewhat costly, which, like most young men of easy income, he had allowed himself at Oxford, was now retained long after it had become practically useless. This was a hunter for himself, and another for his groom, which he continued to keep, in spite of the increasing war-taxes, many a year after he had almost ceased to ride. Once in three or four months he would have the horses saddled and brought out. Then, with considerable effort, he swung himself into the saddle, moved off at a quiet amble, and, in about fifteen or twenty minutes, might be seen returning from an excursion of two miles, under the imagination that he had laid in a stock of exercise sufficient for another period of a hundred days. Meantime Mr Lawson had sought his main consolation in the great classics of elder days. His senior *alumni* were always working their way through some great scenic poet that had shaken the stage of Athens; and more than one of his classes, never-ending, still beginning, were daily solacing him with the gaieties of Horace, in his Epistles or in his Satires. The Horatian jests indeed to *him* never grew old. On coming to the *plagosus Orbilius*,[145] or any other sally of pleasantry, he still threw himself back in his arm-chair, as he *had* done through fifty years, with what seemed heart-shaking bursts of sympathetic merriment. Mr Lawson, indeed, could afford to be sincerely mirthful over the word *plagosus*. There are gloomy tyrants, exulting in the discipline of fear, to whom and to whose pupils this word must call up remembrances too degrading for any but affected mirth. Allusions that are too fearfully personal cease to be subjects of playfulness. Sycophancy only it is that laughs; and the artificial merriment is but the language of shrinking and grovelling deprecation. Different, indeed, was the condition of the Manchester Grammar School. It was honourable both to the masters and the upper boys, through whom only such a result was possible, that in that school, during my knowledge of it (viz., during the closing year of the eighteenth century, and the two opening years of the nineteenth), all punishments, that appealed to the sense of bodily pain, had fallen into disuse; and this at a period long before any public agitation had begun to stir in that direction. How then was discipline maintained? It was maintained through self-discipline of the senior boys, and through the efficacy of their example, combined with their system of rules. Noble are the impulses of opening manhood, where they are not utterly ignoble : at that period, I mean, when the poetic sense begins to blossom, and when boys are first made sensible of the paradise that lurks in female smiles.

Had the school been entirely a day-school, too probable it is that the vulgar brawling tendencies of boys left to themselves would have prevailed. But it happened that the elder section of the school – those on the brink of manhood, and by incalculable degrees the more scholar-like section, all who read, meditated, or began to kindle into the love of literature – were boarders in Mr Lawson's house. The students, therefore, of the house carried an overwhelming influence into the school. They were bound together by links of brotherhood; whereas the day-scholars were disconnected.

[*De Quincey passed his entrance examination to the school with great success and found his fellow pupils congenial from the start. He describes his installation there.*]

[VI] I succeeded, and beyond my expectation. For once – being the first time that he had been known to do such a thing, but also the very last – Mr Lawson did absolutely pay me a compliment. And with another compliment more than verbal he crowned his gracious condescensions – viz., with my provisional instalment in his highest class; not the highest at that moment, since there was one other class above us; but this other was on the wing for Oxford within some few weeks; which change being accomplished, we (viz., I and two others) immediately moved up into the supreme place.

Two or three days after this examination – viz., on the Sunday following – I transferred myself to head-quarters at Mr Lawson's house. About nine o'clock in the evening, I was conducted by a servant up a short flight of stairs, through a series of gloomy and unfurnished little rooms, having small windows but no doors, to the common room (as in Oxford it would technically be called) of the senior boys. Everything had combined to depress me. To leave the society of accomplished women [146] – *that* was already a signal privation. The season besides was rainy, which in itself is a sure source of depression; and the forlorn aspect of the rooms completed my dejection. But the scene changed as the door was thrown open: faces kindling with animation became visible; and from a company of boys, numbering sixteen or eighteen, scattered about the room, two or three, whose age entitled them to the rank of leaders, came forward to receive me with a courtesy which I had not looked for. The grave kindness and the absolute sincerity of their manner impressed me most favourably. I had lived familiarly with boys gathered from all quarters of the island at the Bath Grammar School: and for some time (when visiting Lord Altamont at Eton) with boys of the highest aristocratic pretensions. At Bath and at Eton, though not equally, there prevailed a tone of higher polish; and in the air, speech, deportment of the majority could be traced at once a premature knowledge of the world. They had indeed the advantage over my new friends in graceful self-possession; but, on the other hand, the best of them suffered by comparison with these Manchester boys in the qualities of visible self-restraint and of self-respect. At Eton high rank was distributed pretty liberally; but in the Manchester school the parents of many boys were artisans, or of that rank; some even had sisters that were menial servants; and those who stood higher by pretensions of birth and gentle blood were, at the most, the sons of rural gentry or of clergymen. And I believe that, with the exception of three or four brothers, belonging to a clergyman's family at York, all were, like myself, natives of Lancashire. At that time my experience was too limited to warrant me in expressing any opinion, one way or the other, upon the relative pretensions – moral and intellectual – of the several provinces in our island. But since then I have seen reason to agree with the late Dr Cooke Taylor [147] in awarding the pre-eminence, as regards energy, power to face suffering, and other high qualities, to the natives of Lancashire. Even a century back, they were distinguished for the culture of refined tastes. In musical skill and sensibility, no part of Europe, with the exception of a few places in Germany, could pretend to rival them: and, accordingly, even in Handel's days, but for the chorus-singers from Lancashire, his oratorios must have remained a treasure, if not absolutely sealed, at any rate most imperfectly revealed,

One of the young men, noticing my state of dejection, brought out some brandy – a form of alcohol which I, for my part, tasted now for the first time, having previously taken only wine, and never once in quantities to affect my spirits. So much the greater was my astonishment at the rapid change worked in my state of feeling – a change which at once reinstalled me in my natural advantages for conversation.

[*De Quincey then recounted at great length the learned discussion with his schoolfellows which followed this hospitable reception. But though the intellectual atmosphere of Manchester Grammar School suited him, he was nevertheless wretched there. He expanded his explanation of why he finally ran away by explaining how much his health suffered there, but also admitted that it was a fatal and largely inexplicable decision.*]

[VII] Oh, wherefore, then, was it – through what inexplicable growth of evil in myself or in others – that now in the summer of 1802, when peace was brooding over all the land, peace succeeding to a bloody seven years' war, but peace which already gave signs of breaking into a far bloodier war, some dark sympathising movement within my own heart, as if echoing and repeating in mimicry the political menaces of the earth, swept with storm-clouds across that otherwise serene and radiant dawn which should have heralded my approaching entrance into life? *Inexplicable* I have allowed myself to call this fatal error in my life, because such it *must* appear to others; since, even to myself, so often as I fail to realise the case by reproducing a reflex impression in kind, and in degree, of the suffering before which my better angel gave way – yes, even to myself this collapse of my resisting energies seems inexplicable. Yet again, in simple truth, now that it becomes possible, through changes worked by time, to tell the *whole* truth (and not, as in former editions, only part of it), there really was no absolute mystery at all. But this case, in common with many others, exemplifies to my mind the mere impossibility of making full and frank 'Confessions', whilst many of the persons concerned in the incidents are themselves surviving, or (which is worse still) if themselves dead and buried, are yet vicariously surviving in the persons of near and loving kinsmen. Rather than inflict mortifications upon people so circumstanced, any kind-hearted man will choose to mutilate his narrative; will suppress facts, and will mystify explanations. For instance, at this point in my record, it has become my right, perhaps I might say my duty, to call a particular medical man of the penultimate generation a blockhead; nay, doubtfully, to call him a criminal blockhead. But could I do this without deep compunction, so long as sons and daughters of his were still living, from whom I, when a boy, had received most hospitable attentions? Often, on the very same day which brought home to my suffering convictions the atrocious ignorance of papa, I was benefiting by the courtesies of the daughters, and by the scientific accomplishments of the son. Not the less this man, at that particular moment when a crisis of gloom was gathering over my path, became effectually my evil genius. Not that singly perhaps he could have worked any durable amount of mischief: but he, as a co-operator unconsciously with others, sealed and ratified that sentence of stormy sorrow then hanging over my head. Three separate persons, in fact, made themselves unintentional accomplices in that ruin (a ruin reaching me even at this day by its shadows) which threw me out a homeless vagrant upon the earth before I had accomplished my seventeenth year. Of these three persons, foremost came myself, through my wilful despair and resolute adjuration of all *secondary* hope: since, after all, some mitigation was possible, supposing that perfect relief might *not* be possible. Secondly, came that medical ruffian through whose brutal ignorance it happened that my malady had not been arrested before reaching an advanced stage. Thirdly, came Mr Lawson, through whose growing infirmities it had arisen that this malady ever reached its very earliest stage. Strange it was, but not the less a fact, that Mr Lawson was gradually becoming a curse to all who fell under his influence, through pure zealotry of conscientiousness. Being a worse man, he would have carried far deeper blessings into his circle. If he could have reconciled himself to an imperfect discharge of his duties, he would not have betrayed his insufficiency for those duties. But this he would not hear of. He persisted in travelling over the appointed course to the last inch: and the consequences told most painfully upon the comfort of all around him. By the old traditionary usages of the school, going in at seven A.M., we ought to have been dismissed for breakfast and a full hour's repose at nine. This hour of rest was in strict justice a *debt* to the students – liable to no discount either through the caprice or the tardiness of the supreme master. Yet such were the gradual encroachments

upon this hour that at length the bells of the collegiate church, –
which, by an ancient usage, rang every morning from half-past
nine to ten, and through varying modifications of musical key and
*rhythmus* that marked the advancing stages of the half-hour, –
regularly announced to us, on issuing from the school-room, that
the bread and milk which composed our simple breakfast must be
despatched at a pace fitter for the fowls of the air than students
of Grecian philosophy. But was no compensatory encroachment
for our benefit allowed upon the next hour from ten to eleven?
Not for so much as the fraction of a second. Inexorably as the
bells, by stopping, announced the hour of ten, was Mr Lawson to
be seen ascending the steps of the school; and he that suffered
most by this rigorous exaction of duties could not allege that Mr
Lawson suffered less. If he required others to pay, he also paid up
to the last farthing. The same derangement took place, with the
same refusal to benefit by any indemnification, at what *should*
have been the two-hours' pause for dinner. Only for some mysterious reason, resting possibly upon the family arrangements of the
day-scholars, – which, if once violated, might have provoked a
rebellion of fathers and mothers, – he still adhered faithfully to
five o'clock P.M. as the closing hour of the day's labours.

Here then stood arrayed the whole machinery of mischief in
good working order; and through six months or more, allowing
for one short respite of four weeks,[148] this machinery had been
operating with effect. Mr Lawson, to begin, had (without meaning
it, or so much as perceiving it) barred up all avenues from morning to night through which any bodily exercise could be obtained.
Two or three chance intervals of five minutes each, and even these
not consecutively arranged, composed the whole available fund
of leisure out of which any stroll into the country could have
been attempted. But in a great city like Manchester the very
suburbs had hardly been reached before that little fraction of
time was exhausted. Very soon after Mr Lawson's increasing
infirmities had begun to tell severely in the contraction of our
spare time, the change showed itself powerfully in my drooping
health. Gradually the liver became affected : and connected with
that affection arose, what often accompanies such ailments, profound melancholy. In such circumstances, indeed under any the

slightest disturbance of my health, I had authority from my guardians to call for medical advice : but I was not left to my own discretion in selecting the adviser. This person was not a physician who would of course have expected the ordinary fee of a guinea for every visit; nor a surgeon; but simply an apothecary.[149] In any case of serious illness a physician would have been called in. But a less costly style of advice was reasonably held to be sufficient in any illness which left the patient strength sufficient to walk about. Certainly it ought to have been sufficient here : for no case could possibly be simpler. Three doses of calomel or blue pill,[150] which unhappily I did not then know, would no doubt have re-established me in a week. But far better, as acting always upon me with a magical celerity and a magical certainty, would have been the authoritative prescription (privately notified to Mr Lawson) of seventy miles' walking in each week. Unhappily my professional adviser was a comatose old gentleman, rich beyond all his needs, careless of his own practice, and standing under that painful necessity (according to the custom then regulating medical practice, which prohibited fees to apothecaries) of seeking his remuneration in excessive deluges of medicine. Me, however, out of pure idleness, he forbore to plague with any *variety* of medicines. With sublime simplicity he confined himself to one horrid mixture, that must have suggested itself to him when prescribing for a tiger. In ordinary circumstances, and with plenty of exercise, no creature could be healthier than myself. But my organisation was perilously frail. And to fight simultaneously with such a malady and such a medicine seemed really too much. The proverb tells us that three 'flittings' are as bad as a fire. Very possibly. And I should think that, in the same spirit of reasonable equation, three such tiger-drenches must be equal to one apoplectic fit, or even to the tiger himself. Having taken two of them, which struck me as quite enough for one life, I declined to comply with the injunction of the label pasted upon each several phial – viz., *Repetatur haustus;\** and, instead of doing any such dangerous thing, called upon Mr —— (the apothecary), begging to know if his art had not amongst its reputed infinity of resources any less

---

\* 'Let the draught be repeated.'

166

abominable, and less shattering to a delicate system than this. 'None whatever,' he replied. Exceedingly kind he was; insisted on my drinking tea with his really amiable daughters; but continued at intervals to repeat 'None whatever – none whatever'; then, as if rousing himself to an effort, he sang out loudly 'None whatever,' which in this final utterance he toned down syllabically into 'what*ever – ever – ver – er*.' The whole wit of man, it seems, had exhausted itself upon the preparation of that one infernal mixture.

Now then we three – Mr Lawson, the somnolent apothecary, and myself – had amongst us accomplished a climax of perplexity. Mr Lawson, by mere dint of conscientiousness, had made health for me impossible. The apothecary had subscribed *his* little contribution, by ratifying and trebling the ruinous effects of this sedentariness. And for myself, as last in the series, it now remained to clench the operation by my own little contribution, all that I really had to offer – viz., absolute despair. Those who have ever suffered from a profound derangement of the liver may happen to know that of human despondencies through all their infinite gamut none is more deadly. Hope died within me. I could not look for medical relief, so deep being my own ignorance, so equally deep being that of my official counsellor. I could not expect that Mr Lawson would modify his system – his instincts of duty being so strong, his incapacity to face that duty so steadily increasing. 'It comes then to this,' thought I, 'that in myself only there lurks any arrear of help' : as always for every man the ultimate reliance should be on himself.

[*De Quincey revealed that he had thought of making for Westmorland, to make the acquaintance of Wordsworth, when he decided to run away from Manchester.*]

[VIII] But now, at last, came over me, from the mere excess of bodily suffering and mental disappointments, a frantic and rapturous re-agency. In the United States the case is well known, and many times has been described by travellers, of that furious instinct which, under a secret call for saline variations of diet, drives all the tribes of buffaloes for thousands of miles to the common centre of the 'Salt-licks.' Under such a compulsion does the locust, under such a compulsion does the leeming, traverse its mysterious path. They are deaf to danger, deaf to the cry of battle, deaf to the trumpets of death. Let the sea cross their path, let armies with artillery bar the road, even these terrific powers can arrest only by destroying; and the most frightful abysses, up to the very last menace of engulfment, up to the very instant of absorption, have no power to alter or retard the line of their inexorable advance.

Such an instinct it was, such a rapturous command – even so potent, and alas! even so blind – that, under the whirl of tumultuous indignation and of new-born hope, suddenly transfigured my whole being. In the twinkling of an eye, I came to an adamantine resolution – not as if issuing from any act or any choice of my own, but as if passively received from some dark oracular legislation external to myself. That I would elope from Manchester – this was the resolution. *Abscond* would have been the word, if I had meditated anything criminal. But whence came the indignation, and the hope? The indignation arose naturally against my three tormentors (guardian, Archididascalus, and the professor of tigrology) for those who *do* substantially co-operate to one result, however little designing it, unavoidably the mind unifies as a hostile confederacy. But the hope – how shall I explain *that?* Was it the first-born of the resolution, or was the resolution the first-born of the hope? Indivisibly they went together, like thunder and lightning; or each interchangeably ran before and after the other. Under that transcendent rapture which the prospect of sudden liberation let loose, all that natural anxiety which should otherwise have interlinked itself with my anticipations was actually drowned in the blaze of joy, as the light of the planet Mercury is lost and confounded on sinking too far within the blaze of the solar beams. Practically I felt no care at all stretching beyond two or three weeks. Not being heedless and improvident; my tendencies lay generally in the other direction. No; the cause lurked in what Wordsworth, when describing the festal state of France during the happy morning-tide of her First Revolution (1788–1790), calls *'the senselessness of joy'*: this it was, joy – headlong – frantic – irreflective – and (as Wordsworth truly calls it), for that very reason, *sublime\** – which swallowed up all capacities of rankling care or heart-corroding doubt. I was, I had been long, a captive: I was in a house of bondage: one fulminating word – *Let there be freedom* – spoken from some hidden recess in my own will, had as by an earthquake rent asunder my prison gates. At any minute I could walk out. Already I trod by anticipation the sweet pastoral hills, already I breathed gales from the garden of Paradise; and in that vestibule of an earthly heaven it was no more possible for me to see vividly or in any lingering detail the thorny cares which might hereafter multiply around me than amongst the roses of June, and on the loveliest of June mornings, I could gather depression from the glooms of the last December. . . .

My plan originally had been to travel northwards – viz, to the region of the English Lakes. That little mountainous district, lying stretched like a pavilion between four well-known points – viz., the small towns of Ulverstone and Penrith as its two poles, south and north; between Kendal, again, on the east, and Egremont on the west – measuring on the one diameter about forty miles, and on the other perhaps thirty-five – had for me a secret fascination, subtle, sweet, fantastic, and even from my seventh or eighth year spiritually strong. The southern section of that district, about eighteen or twenty miles long, which bears the name of Furness, figures in the eccentric geography of English law as a section of Lancashire, though separated from that county by the estuary of Morecambe Bay: and therefore, as Lancashire happened to be my own native county, I had from childhood, on the strength of this mere legal fiction cherished as a mystic privilege, slender as a filament of air, some fraction of denizenship in the fairy little domain of the English Lakes. The major part of these lakes lies in Westmoreland and Cumberland: but the sweet reposing little water of Esthwaite, with its few emerald fields, and the grander one of Coniston, with the sublime cluster of mountain groups,

---

\* *'The senselessness of joy was then sublime.'* – Wordsworth at Calais in 1802 (see his sonnets), looking back through thirteen years to the great era of social resurrection, in 1788–89, from a sleep of ten centuries.

and the little network of quiet dells lurking about its head* all the way back to Grasmere, lie in or near the upper chamber of Furness; and all these, together with the ruins of the once glorious abbey, had been brought out not many years before into sunny splendour by the great enchantress of that generation – Anne Radcliffe.[151] But more even than Anne Radcliffe had the landscape painters,[152] so many and so various, contributed to the glorification of the English lake district; drawing out and impressing upon the heart the sanctity of repose in its shy recesses – its alpine grandeurs in such passes as those of Wastdale-head, Langdale-head, Borrowdale, Kirkstone, Hawsdale, etc., together with the monastic peace which seems to brood over its peculiar form of pastoral life, so much nobler (as Wordsworth notices) in its stern simplicity and continual conflict with danger hidden in the vast draperies of mist overshadowing the hills, and amongst the armies of snow and hail arrayed by fierce northern winters, than the effeminate shepherd's life in the classical Arcadia, or in the flowery pastures of Sicily.

---

*'Its head* : – That end of a lake which receives the rivulets and brooks feeding its waters is locally called its *head*; and, in continuation of the same constructive image, the counter terminus, which discharges its surplus water, is called its *foot*. By the way, as a suggestion from this obvious distinction, I may remark that in all cases the very existence of a head and a foot to any sheet of water defeats the malice of Lord Byron's sneer against the lake poets, in calling them by the contemptuous designation of '*pond* poets'; a variation which some part of the public readily caught up as a natural reverberation of that spitefulness, so petty and apparently so groundless, which notoriously Lord Byron cherished against Wordsworth steadily, and more fitfully against Southey. The effect of transforming a living image – an image of restless motion – into an image of foul stagnation was tangibly apprehensible. But what was it that contradistinguished the '*vivi lacus*' of Virgil from rotting ponds mantled with verdant slime? To have, or *not* to have, a head and a foot (*i.e.* a principle of perpetual change) is at the very heart of this distinction; and to substitute for *lake* a term which ignores and negatives the very differential principle that constitutes a lake – viz., its current and its eternal mobility – is to offer an insult in which the insulted party has no interest or concern.

Amongst these attractions that drew me so strongly to the Lakes, there had also by that time arisen in this lovely region the deep deep magnet (as to me *only* in all this world it then was)[153] of William Wordsworth. Inevitably this close connexion of the poetry which most of all had moved me with the particular region and scenery that most of all had fastened upon my affections, and led captive my imagination, was calculated, under ordinary circumstances, to impress upon my fluctuating deliberations a summary and decisive bias. But the very depth of the impressions which had been made upon me, either as regarded the poetry or the scenery, was too solemn and (unaffectedly I may say it) too spiritual, to clothe itself in any hasty or chance movement as at all adequately expressing its strength, or reflecting its hallowed character. If you, reader, were a devout Mahometan, throwing gazes of mystical awe daily towards Mecca, or were a Christian devotee looking with the same rapt adoration to St Peter's at Rome, or to El Kodah, the Holy City of Jerusalem (so called even amongst the Arabs, who hate both Christian and Jew) – how painfully would it jar upon your sensibilities if some friend, sweeping past you upon a high road, with a train (according to the circumstances) of dromedaries or of wheel carriages, should suddenly pull up, and say, 'Come, old fellow, jump up alongside of me; I'm off for the Red Sea, and here's a spare dromedary,' or 'Off for Rome, and here's a well-cushioned barouche.' Seasonable and convenient it might happen that the invitation were; but still it would shock you that a journey which, with or without your consent, could not *but* assume the character eventually of a saintly pilgrimage, should arise and take its initial movement upon a casual summons, or upon a vulgar opening of momentary convenience. In the present case, under no circumstances should I have dreamed of presenting myself to Wordsworth. The principle of 'veneration' (to speak phrenologically) was by many degrees too strong in me for any such overture on my part. Hardly could I have found the courage to meet and to answer such an overture coming from *him*. I could not even tolerate the prospect (as a bare possibility) of Wordsworth's hearing my name first of all associated with some case of pecuniary embarrassment. And, apart from all *that*, it vulgarised the whole 'interest' (no other term can I find to express the case collectively) – the whole 'interest' of poetry and the enchanted land – equally it vulgarised person and thing, the vineyard and the vintage, the gardens and the ladies, of the Hesperides, together with all their golden fruitage, if I should rush upon them in a hurried and thoughtless state of excitement. I remembered the fine caution of this subject involved in a tradition preserved by Pausanias.[154] Those (he tells us) who visited by night the great field of Marathon (where at certain times phantom cavalry careered, flying and pursuing) in a temper of vulgar sight-seeking, and under no higher impulse than the degrading one of curiosity, were met and punished severely in the dark, by the same sort of people, I presume, as those who handled Falstaff so roughly in the venerable shades of Windsor:[155] whilst loyal visitors, who came bringing a true and filial sympathy with the grand deeds of their Athenian ancestors, who came as children of the same hearth, met with the most gracious acceptance, and fulfilled all the purposes of a pilgrimage or sacred mission. Under my present circumstances, I saw that the very motives of love and honour, which would have inclined the scale so powerfully in favour of the northern lakes, were exactly those which drew most heavily in the other direction – the circumstances being what they were as to hurry and perplexity. And just at that moment suddenly unveiled itself another powerful motive against taking the northern direction – viz., consideration for my mother – which made my heart recoil from giving her too great a shock; and in what other way could it be mitigated than by my personal presence in a case of emergency? For such a purpose North Wales would be the best haven to make for, since the road thither from my present home lay through Chester – where at that time my mother had fixed her residence.

[*The description of the last days at Manchester was expanded to include premonitions of 'forms of darkness shrouded within the recesses of blind human hearts'.*]

[IX] The secret sense of a farewell or testamentary act I carried along with me into every word or deed of this memorable day. Agent or patient, singly or one of a crowd, I heard for ever some sullen echo of valediction in every change, casual or periodic, that varied the revolving hours from morning to night. Most of all, I felt this valedictory sound as a pathetic appeal when the closing hour of five P.M. brought with it the solemn evening service of the English Church – read by Mr Lawson; read now, as always, under a reverential stillness of the entire school. Already in itself, without the solemnity of prayers, the decaying light of the dying day suggests a mood of pensive and sympathetic sadness. And, if the changes in the light are less impressively made known so early as five o'clock in the depth of summer-tide, not the less we are sensible of being as near to the hours of repose, and to the secret dangers of the night, as if the season were mid-winter. Even thus far there was something that oftentimes had profoundly impressed me in this evening liturgy, and its special prayer against the perils of darkness. But greatly was that effect deepened by the symbolic treatment which this liturgy gives to this darkness and to these perils. Naturally, when contemplating that treatment, I had been led vividly to feel the memorable *rhab-domancy*[156] or magical power of evocation which Christianity has put forth here and in parallel cases. The ordinary physical rhabdomantist, who undertakes to evoke from the dark chambers of our earth wells of water lying far below its surface, and more rarely to evoke minerals, or hidden deposits of jewels and gold, by some magnetic sympathy between his rod and the occult object of his divination, is able to indicate the spot at which this object can be hopefully sought for. Not otherwise has the marvellous magnetism of Christianity called up from darkness sentiments the most august, previously inconceivable, formless, and without life; for previously there had been no religious philosophy equal to the task of ripening such sentiments; but also, at the same time, by incarnating these sentiments in images of corresponding grandeur, it has so exalted their character as to lodge them eternally in human hearts.

Flowers, for example, that are so pathetic in their beauty, frail as the clouds, and in their colouring as gorgeous as the heavens, had through thousands of years been the heritage of children – honoured as the jewellery of God only by *them* – when suddenly the voice of Christianity, counter-signing the voice of infancy, raised them to a grandeur transcending the Hebrew throne, although founded by God himself, and pronounced Solomon in all his glory not to be arrayed like one of these. Winds again, hurricanes, the eternal breathings, soft or loud, of Æolian power, wherefore had they, raving or sleeping, escaped all moral arrest and detention? Simply because vain it were to offer a nest for the reception of some new moral birth whilst no religion is yet moving amongst men that can furnish such a birth. Vain is the image that should illustrate a heavenly sentiment, if the sentiment is yet unborn. Then, first, when it had become necessary to the purposes of a spiritual religion that the spirit of man, as the fountain of all religion, should in some commensurate reflex image have its grandeur and its mysteriousness emblazoned, suddenly the pomp and mysterious path of winds and tempests, blowing whither they list, and from what fountains no man knows, are cited from darkness and neglect, to give and to receive reciprocally an impassioned glorification, where the lower mystery enshrines and illustrates the higher. Call for the grandest of all earthly spectacles, what is *that?* It is the sun going to his rest. Call for the grandest of all human sentiments, what is *that?* It is that man should forget his anger before he lies down to sleep. And these two grandeurs, the mighty sentiment and the mighty spectacle, are by Christianity married together.

Here again, in his prayer 'Lighten our darkness, we beseech thee, O Lord!' were the darkness and the great shadows of night made symbolically significant: these great powers, Night and Darkness, that belong to aboriginal Chaos, were made representative of the perils that continually menace poor afflicted human nature. With deepest sympathy I accompanied the prayer against the perils of darkness – perils that I seemed to see, in the ambush of midnight solitude, brooding around the beds of sleeping nations; perils from even worse forms of darkness shrouded within the recesses of blind human hearts; perils from temptations weaving unseen snares for our footing; perils from the limitations of our own misleading knowledge.

[*Into the account of his last morning at school, De Quincey introduced the anecdote of his visit as a boy to the Whispering Gallery at*

St Paul's Cathedral, a symbolic experience which had become central in his imagination.]

[x] Happy hours? Yes; and was it certain that ever again I should enjoy hours *as* happy? At this point it is not impossible that, left to my own final impressions, I might have receded from my plan. But it seemed to me, as too often happens in such cases, that no retreat was now open. The confidence which unavoidably I had reposed in a groom of Mr Lawson's made it dangerous. The effect of this distracted view was, not to alter my plan, but to throw despondency for one sad half hour over the whole prospect before me. In that condition, with my eyes open, I dreamed. Suddenly a sort of trance, a frost as of some deathlike revelation, wrapped round me; and I found renewed within me a hateful remembrance derived from a moment that I had long left behind. Two years before, when I wanted about as much of my fifteenth birthday as now of my seventeenth, I happened to be in London for part of a single day, with a friend of my own age.[157] Naturally, amongst some eight or ten great spectacles which challenged our earnest attention, St Paul's Cathedral had been one. This we had visited, and consequently the Whispering Gallery.* More than by all beside I had been impressed by this : and some half-hour later, as we were standing beneath the dome, and I should imagine pretty nearly on the very spot where rather more than five years subsequently Lord Nelson was buried, – a spot from which we saw, pompously floating to and fro in the upper spaces of a great aisle running westwards from ourselves, many flags captured from France, Spain, and Holland, – I, having my previous impressions of awe deepened by these solemn trophies of chance and change amongst mighty nations, had suddenly been surprised by a dream, as profound as at present, in which a thought that often had persecuted me figured triumphantly. This thought turned upon the

---

*To those who have never visited the Whispering Gallery, nor have read any account of it amongst other acoustic phenomena described in scientific treatises, it may be proper to mention, as the distinguishing feature of the case, that a word or a question, uttered at one end of the gallery in the gentlest of whispers, is reverberated at the other end in peals of thunder.

fatality that must often attend an evil choice. As an oracle of fear I remembered that great Roman warning, *Nescit vox missa reverti* (that a word once uttered is irrevocable), a freezing arrest upon the motions of hope too sanguine that haunted me in many shapes. Long before that fifteenth year of mine, I had noticed, as a worm lying at the heart of life and fretting its security, the fact that innumerable acts of choice change countenance and are variously appraised at varying stages of life – shift with the shifting hours. Already, at fifteen, I had become deeply ashamed of judgments which I had once pronounced, of idle hopes that I had once encouraged, false admirations or contempts with which once I had sympathised. And, as to acts which I surveyed with any doubts at all, I never felt sure that after some succession of years I might not feel withering doubts about them, both as to principle and as to inevitable results.

This sentiment of nervous recoil from any word or deed that could not be recalled had been suddenly re-awakened on that London morning by the impressive experience of the Whispering Gallery. At the earlier end of the gallery had stood my friend, breathing in the softest of whispers a solemn but not acceptable truth. At the further end, after running along the walls of the gallery, that solemn truth reached me as a deafening menace in tempestuous uproars. And now in these last lingering moments, when I dreamed ominously with open eyes in my Manchester study, once again that London menace broke angrily upon me as out of a thick cloud with redoubled strength; a voice, too late for warning, seemed audibly to say, 'Once leave this house, and a Rubicon is placed between thee and all possibility of return. Thou wilt not say that what thou doest is altogether approved in thy secret heart. Even now thy conscience speaks against it in sullen whispers; but at the other end of thy long life-gallery that same conscience will speak to thee in volleying thunders.'

A sudden step upon the stairs broke up my dream, and recalled me to myself. Dangerous hours were now drawing near, and I prepared for a hasty farewell.

[*Before starting his walking tour in Wales, De Quincey first went home to his mother's house in Chester, he revealed in the revised*

*Confessions. On the way there he passed through Altrincham; the description of this gay little town which he introduced here is an effective touch of brightness in his shadowy narrative.*]

[XI] On leaving Manchester, by a south-western route, towards Chester and Wales, the first town that I reached (to the best of my remembrance) was Altrincham — colloquially called *Awtrigem*. When a child of three years old, and suffering from the hooping-cough, I had been carried for a change of air to different places on the Lancashire coast; and in order to benefit by as large a compass as possible of varying atmospheres, I and my nurse had been made to rest for the first night of our tour at this cheerful little town of Altrincham. On the next morning, which ushered in a most dazzling day of July, I rose earlier than my nurse fully approved : but in no long time she found it advisable to follow my example; and after putting me through my morning's drill of ablutions and the Lord's prayer, no sooner had she fully arranged my petticoats[158] than she lifted me up in her arms, threw open the window, and let me suddenly look down upon the gayest scene I had ever beheld — viz., the little market-place of Altrincham at eight o'clock in the morning. It happened to be the market-day; and I, who till then had never consciously been in any town whatever, was equally astonished and delighted with the novel gaiety of the scene. Fruits, such as can be had in July, and flowers were scattered about in profusion : even the stalls of the butchers, from their brilliant cleanliness, appeared attractive : and the bonny young women of Altrincham were all tripping about in caps and aprons coquettishly disposed. The general hilarity of the scene at this early hour, with the low murmurings of pleasurable conversation and laughter, that rose up like a fountain to the open window, left so profound an impression upon me that I never lost it. All this occurred, as I have said, about eight o'clock on a superb July morning. Exactly at that time of the morning, on exactly such another heavenly day of July, did I, leaving Manchester at six A.M., naturally enough find myself in the centre of Altrincham market-place. Nothing had altered. There were the very same fruits and flowers; the same bonny young women tripping up and down in the same (no, *not* the same) coquettish bonnets; everything was apparently the same :

perhaps the window of my bedroom was still open, only my nurse and I were not looking out; for alas! on recollection, fourteen years precisely had passed since then. Breakfast-time, however, is always a cheerful stage of the day; if a man can forget his cares at any season, it is then; and after a walk of seven miles it is doubly so. I felt it at the time, and have stopped, therefore, to notice it, as a singular coincidence, that twice, and by the merest accident, I should find myself, precisely as the clocks on a July morning were all striking eight, drawing inspiration of pleasurable feelings from the genial sights and sounds in the little market-place of Altrincham. There I breakfasted; and already by the two hours' exercise I felt myself half restored to health. After an hour's rest, I started again upon my journey: all my gloom and despondency were already retiring to the rear; and, as I left Altrincham, I said to myself, 'All places, it seems, are not Whispering Galleries.'

[*When he reached Chester, De Quincey at first lingered outside the town in the fields by the river Dee, and there, on an artificial mound called the Cop, he suddenly heard a strange 'uproar of tumultuous sounds', the noise of an advancing tidal wave, the Bore, though he could not yet see it.*]

[XII] From this unseen reach it was that the angry clamour, so passionate and so mysterious, arose: and I, for my part, having never heard such a fierce battling outcry, nor even heard of such a cry, either in books or on the stage, in prose or verse, could not so much as whisper a guess to myself upon its probable cause. Only this I felt, that blind, unorganised nature it must be – and nothing in human or in brutal wrath – that could utter itself by such an anarchy of sea-like roars. What was it? Where was it? Whence was it? Earthquake was it? convulsion of the steadfast earth? or was it the breaking loose from ancient chains of some deep morass like that of Solway? More probable it seemed that the ἄνω ποτάμων of Euripides (the flowing backwards of rivers to their fountains) now, at last, after ages of expectation, had been suddenly realised. Not long I needed to speculate; for within half a minute, perhaps, from the first arrest of our attention, the proximate cause of this mystery declared itself to our eyes, although the remote cause (the hidden cause of that visible cause) was still as dark as before. Round that right-angled turn which I have mentioned as wheeling into the next succeeding reach of the river, suddenly as with the trampling of cavalry – but all dressing accurately – and the water at the outer angle sweeping so much faster than that at the inner angle, as to keep the front of advance rigorously in line, violently careered round into our own placid watery vista a huge charging block of waters, filling the whole channel of the river, and coming down upon us at the rate of forty miles an hour. ... In fact, this watery breastwork, a perpendicular wall of water carrying itself as true as if controlled by a mason's plumb-line, rode forward at such a pace, that obviously the fleetest horse or dromedary would have had no chance of escape. Many a decent railway even, among railways since born its rivals, would not have had above the third of a chance. Naturally, I had too short a time for observing much or accurately; and universally I am a poor hand at observing; else I should say, that this riding block of crystal waters did not gallop, but went at a long trot; yes, long trot – that most frightful of paces in a tiger, in a buffalo, or in a rebellion of waters. Even a ghost, I feel convinced, would appal me more if coming up at a long diabolical trot, than at a canter or gallop. ... The preternatural column of waters, running in the very opposite direction to the natural current of the river, came up with us, ran by with the ferocious uproar of a hurricane, sent up the sides of the Cop a salute of waters, as if hypocritically pretending to kiss our feet, but secretly understood by all parties as a vain treachery for pulling us down into the flying deluge; whilst all along both banks the mighty refluent wash was heard as it rode along, leaving memorials, by sight and by sound, of its victorious power.

[*After this De Quincey tried to meet his sister in the garden of his mother's house, the Priory, without attracting the attention of the rest of the family, but his ruse failed.*]

[XIII] Not one minute had I waited, when in glided amongst the ruins – not my fair sister, but my bronzed Bengal uncle![159] A Bengal tiger would not more have startled me. Now, to a dead certainty, I said, here comes a fatal barrier to the prosecution of my scheme. I was mistaken. Between my mother and my uncle there existed the very deepest affection; for they regarded each other as sole reliques of a household once living together in memorable harmony. But in many features of character no human beings could stand off from each other in more lively repulsion. And this was seen on the present occasion. My dear excellent mother, from the eternal quiet of her decorous household, looked upon every violent or irregular movement, and therefore upon mine at present, much as she would have done upon the opening of the seventh seal in the Revelations. But my uncle was thoroughly a man of the world, and what told even more powerfully on my behalf in this instance, he was a man of even morbid activity. It was so exquisitely natural in his eyes that any rational person should prefer moving about amongst the breezy mountains of Wales, to a slavish routine of study amongst books grim with dust and masters too probably still more dusty, that he seemed disposed to regard my conduct as an extraordinary act of virtue. On his advice, it was decided that there could be no hope in any contest with my main wishes, and that I should be left to pursue my original purpose of walking amongst the Welsh mountains; provided I chose to do so upon the slender allowance of a guinea-a-week. My uncle, whose Indian munificence ran riot upon all occasions, would gladly have had a far larger allowance made to me, and would himself have clandestinely given me anything I asked. But I myself, from general ignorance (in which accomplishment I excelled), judged this to be sufficient; and at this point my mother, hitherto passively acquiescent in my uncle's proposals, interfered with a decisive rigour that in my own heart I could not disapprove. Any larger allowance, most reasonably she urged, what was it but to 'make proclamation to my two younger brothers that rebellion bore a premium, and that mutiny was the ready road to ease and comfort'? My conscience smote me at these words: I felt something like an electric shock on this sudden reference, so utterly unexpected, to my brothers; for, to say the truth, I never once admitted them to my thoughts in forecasting the eventual consequences that might possibly unroll themselves from my own headstrong act. Here now, within three days, rang like a solemn knell, reverberating from the sounding-board within my awakened conscience, one of those many self-reproaches so dimly masked, but not circumstantially prefigured, by the secret thought under the dome of St Paul's Cathedral about its dread Whispering Gallery. In this particular instance, I know that the evil consequences from my own example never did take effect. But at the moment of my mother's sorrowful suggestion, the fear that they *might* take effect thrilled me with remorse. My next brother,[160] a boy of generous and heroic temper, was at a school governed by a brutal and savage master. This brother, I well know, had justifying reasons, ten times weightier than any which I could plead, for copying my precedent. Most probable it was that he would do so; but I learned many years subsequently from himself that in fact he did not. The man's diabolical malice at last made further toleration impossible. Without thinking of my example, under very different circumstances my brother won his own emancipation in ways suggested by his own views and limited by his own resources: he got afloat upon the wide, wide world of ocean; ran along a perilous seven-years' career of nautical romance; had his name almost blotted out from all memories in England; became of necessity a pirate amongst pirates; was liable to the death of a pirate wherever taken; then suddenly, on a morning of battle, having effected his escape from the bloody flag, he joined the English storming party at Monte Video, fought under the eye of Sir Home Popham, the commodore, and within twenty-four hours after the victory was rated as a midshipman on board the *Diadem* (a 64-gun ship), which bore Sir Home's flag. All this I have more circumstantially narrated elsewhere. I repeat the sum of it here, as showing that his elopement from a brutal tyrant was not due to any misleading of mine. I happen to know this now – but then I could not know it. And if I had so entirely overlooked one such possible result, full of calamity to my youthful brothers, why might I not have overlooked many hundreds beside, equally probable, – equally full of peril? That consideration saddened me, and deepened more and more the ominous suggestion – the oracle full of woe – that spoke from those Belshazzar thunderings upon the wall of the Whispering Gallery. In fact, every intricate and untried path in life, where it was from the first a matter of arbitrary choice to enter upon it or avoid it, is effectually a path through a vast Hercynian forest,[161] unexplored and unmapped, where each several turn in your advance leaves you open to new anticipations of what is next to be expected, and consequently open to altered valuations of all that has been already traversed. Even the character of your own absolute experience, past and gone, which (if anything in this world) you might surely answer for as sealed and settled for ever – even this you must submit to hold in suspense, as a thing conditional and contingent upon what is yet to come – liable to have its provisional character affirmed or reversed, according to the new combinations into which it may enter with elements only yet perhaps in the earliest stages of development.

Saddened by these reflections, I was still more saddened by the chilling manner of my mother. If I could presume to descry a fault in my mother, it was – that she turned the chilling aspects of her high-toned character too exclusively upon those whom, in any degree, she knew or supposed to be promoters of evil. Sometimes her austerity might seem even unjust. But at present the whole artillery of her displeasure seemed to be unmasked, and *justly* unmasked, against a moral aberration, that offered for itself no excuse that was obvious in one moment, that was legible at one glance, that could utter itself in one word. My mother was predisposed to think ill of all causes that required many words: I, predisposed to subtleties of all sorts and degrees, had naturally become acquainted with cases that could not unrobe their apparellings down to that degree of simplicity. If in this world there is one misery having no relief, it is the pressure on the heart from the *Incommunicable*. And if another Sphinx should arise to propose another enigma to man – saying, What burden is that which only is insupportable by human fortitude? I should answer at once – *It is the burden of the Incommunicable*. At this moment, sitting in the same room of the Priory with my mother, knowing how reasonable she was – how patient of explanations – how candid – how open to pity – not the less I sank away in a hopelessness that was immeasurable from all effort at explanation. She and I were contemplating the very same act; but she from one centre, I from another. Certain I was, that if through one half minute she could realise in one deadly experience the suffering with which I had fought through more than three months, the amount of physical anguish, the desolation of all genial life, she would have uttered a rapturous absolution of that which else must always seem to her a mere explosion of wilful insubordination. 'In this brief experience,' she would exclaim, 'I read the record of your acquittal; in this fiery torment I acknowledge the gladiatorial resistance.' Such in the case supposed would have been her revised verdict. But this case was exquisitely impossible. Nothing which offered itself to my rhetoric gave any but the feeblest and most childish reflection of my past sufferings. Just so helpless did I feel, disarmed into just the same languishing impotence to face (or make an effort at facing) the difficulty before me, as most of us have felt in the dreams of our childhood when lying down without a struggle before some all-conquering lion. I felt that the situation was one without hope; a solitary word, which I attempted to mould upon my lips, died away into a sigh; and passively I acquiesced in the apparent confession spread through all the appearances – that in reality I had no palliation to produce.

One alternative, in the offer made to me, was, that I had permission to stay at the Priory. The Priory, or the mountainous region of Wales, was offered freely to my choice. Either of the two offered an attractive abode. The Priory, it may be fancied, was clogged with the liability to fresh and intermitting reproaches. But this was not so. I knew my mother sufficiently to be assured that, once having expressed her sorrowful condemnation of my act, having made it impossible for me to misunderstand her views, she was ready to extend her wonted hospitality to me, and (as regarded all practical matters) her wonted kindness; but not that sort of kindness which could make me forget that I stood under the deepest shadows of her displeasure, or could leave me for a moment free to converse at my ease upon any and every subject. A man that is talking on simple toleration, and, as it were, under permanent protest, cannot feel himself morally at his ease, unless very obtuse and coarse in his sensibilities.

Mine, under any situation approaching to the present, were so far from being obtuse that they were morbidly and extravagantly acute. I had erred : that I knew, and did not disguise from myself. Indeed, the rapture of anguish with which I had recurred involuntarily to my experience of the Whispering Gallery, and the symbolic meaning which I had given to that experience, manifested indirectly my deep sense of error through the dim misgiving which attended it – that in some mysterious way the sense and the consequences of this error would magnify themselves at every stage of life, in proportion as they were viewed retrospectively from greater and greater distances. I had, besides, through the casual allusion to my brothers, suddenly become painfully aware of another and separate failure in the filial obligations resting on myself. Any mother, who is a widow, has especial claims on the co-operation of her eldest son in all means of giving a beneficial bias to the thoughts and purposes of the younger children : and, if *any* mother, then by a title how special could my own mother invoke such co-operation, who had on *her* part satisfied all the claims made upon her maternal character, by self-sacrifices as varied, as privately I knew them to be exemplary. Whilst yet comparatively young, not more than thirty-six, she had sternly refused all countenance, on at least two separate occasions, to distinguished proposals of marriage, out of pure regard to the memory of my father, and to the interests of his children. Could I fail to read, in such unostentatious exemplifications of maternal goodness, a summons to a corresponding earnestness on my part in lightening, as much as possible, the burden of her responsibilities? Alas ! too certainly, as regarded *that* duty, I felt my own failure: one opportunity had been signally lost, and yet, on the other hand, I also felt that more might be pleaded on my behalf than could by possibility be apparent to a neutral bystander. But this, to be pleaded effectually, needed to be said – not by myself, but by a disinterested advocate: and no such advocate was at hand. In blind distress of mind, conscience-stricken and heart-stricken, I stretched out my arms, seeking for my one sole auxiliary; that was my eldest sister Mary; for my younger sister Jane was a mere infant. Blindly and mechanically, I stretched out my arms as if to arrest her attention; and giving utterance to my labouring thoughts, I was beginning to speak, when all at once I became sensible that Mary was not there. . . .

Had I waited until my sister returned home, which I might have been sure could only have been delayed through the imperfectly concerted system of correspondence, all would have prospered. From her I should have received the cordiality and the genial sympathy which I needed; I could have quietly pursued my studies; and my Oxford matriculation would have followed as a matter of course. But, unhappily, having for so long a time been seriously shaken in health, any interruption of my wild open-air system of life instantly threw me back into nervous derangements. Past all doubt it had now become that the *al fresco* life, to which I had looked with so much hopefulness for a sure and rapid restoration to health, was even more potent than I had supposed it. Literally irresistible it seemed in reorganising the system of my languishing powers. Impatient, therefore, under the absence of my sister, and agitated every hour so long as my home wanted its central charm in some household countenance, some σύντροφον ὄμμα [162] beaming with perfect sympathy, I resolved to avail myself of those wild mountainous and sylvan attractions which at present lay nearest to me.

[*In the revised* Confessions De Quincey *gave a much fuller description of his wanderings in Wales, the friends he made, the beauties of landscape and fresh air that he enjoyed, the hardships that he endured. Wales was then already a place of pilgrimage for tourists, but otherwise rural and unspoilt.*]

[XIV] There were already, even in those days of 1802, numerous inns, erected at reasonable distances from each other, for the accommodation of tourists: and no sort of disgrace attached in Wales, as too generally upon the great roads of England, to the pedestrian style of travelling. Indeed, the majority of those whom I met as fellow-tourists in the quiet little cottage-parlours of the Welsh posting-houses were pedestrian travellers. All the way from Shrewsbury through Llangollen, Llanrwst,* Conway, Bangor, then turning to the left at right angles through Carnarvon, and so on to Dolgelly (the chief town of Merionethshire), Tany-y-Bwlch, Harlech, Barmouth, and through the sweet

---

*'Llanrwst': – This is an alarming word for the eye; one vowel to what the English eye counts as seven consonants: but it is easily pronounced as *Tlanroost*.

solitudes of Cardiganshire, or turning back sharply towards the English border through the gorgeous wood scenery of Montgomeryshire – everywhere at intermitting distances of twelve to sixteen miles, I found the most comfortable inns. One feature indeed of repose in all this chain of solitary resting-houses – viz., the fact that none of them rose above two storeys in height – was due to the modest scale on which the travelling system of the Principality had moulded itself in correspondence to the calls of England, which then (but be it remembered this *then* was in 1802, a year of peace) threw a very small proportion of her vast migratory population annually into this sequestered channel. No huge Babylonian centres of commerce towered into the clouds on these sweet sylvan routes: no hurricanes of haste, or fever-stricken armies of horses and flying chariots, tormented the echoes in these mountain recesses. And it has often struck me that a world-wearied man, who sought for the peace of monasteries separated from their gloomy captivity – peace and silence such as theirs combined with the large liberty of nature – could not do better than revolve amongst these modest inns in the five northern Welsh counties of Denbigh, Montgomery, Carnarvon, Merioneth, and Cardigan. Sleeping, for instance, and breakfasting at Carnarvon; then, by an easy nine-mile walk, going forwards to dinner at Bangor, thence to Aber – nine miles; or to Llanberris; and so on for ever, accomplishing seventy to ninety or one hundred miles in a week. This, upon actual experiment, and for week after week, I found the most delightful of lives. Here was the eternal motion of winds and rivers, or of the Wandering Jew liberated from the persecution which compelled him to move, and turned his breezy freedom into a killing captivity. Happier life I cannot imagine than this vagrancy, if the weather were but tolerable, through endless successions of changing beauty, and towards evening a courteous welcome in a pretty rustic home – that having all the luxuries of a fine hotel (in particular some luxuries* that are almost sacred to Alpine regions), was at the same time liberated from the inevitable

---

*But a luxury of another class, and quite peculiar to Wales, was in those days (I hope in these) the Welsh harp, in attendance at every inn.

accompaniments of such hotels in great cities or at great travelling stations – viz., the tumult and uproar.

Life on this model was but too beautiful; and to myself especially, that am never thoroughly in health unless when having pedestrian exercise to the extent of fifteen miles at the most, and eight to ten miles at the least. Living thus, a man earned his daily enjoyment. But what did it cost? About half a guinea a day: whilst my boyish allowance was not a third of this. The flagrant health, health boiling over in fiery rapture, which ran along, side by side, with exercise on this scale, whilst all the while from morning to night I was inhaling mountain air, soon passed into a hateful scourge. Perquisites to servants and a bed would have absorbed the whole of my weekly guinea. My policy therefore was, if the autumnal air was warm enough, to save this expense of a bed and the chambermaid by sleeping amongst ferns or furze upon a hillside; and perhaps with a cloak of sufficient *weight* as well as compass, or an Arab's burnoose, this would have been no great hardship. But then in the daytime what an oppressive burden to carry! So perhaps it was as well that I had no cloak at all. I did, however, for some weeks try the plan of carrying a canvas tent manufactured by myself, and not larger than an ordinary umbrella: but to pitch this securely I found difficult; and on windy nights it became a troublesome companion. As winter drew near, this bivouacking system became too dangerous to attempt. Still one may bivouack decently, barring rain and wind, up to the end of October. And I counted, on the whole, that in a fortnight I spent nine nights abroad. There are, as perhaps the reader knows by experience, no jaguars in Wales – nor pumas – nor anacondas – nor (generally speaking) any Thugs.[163] What I feared most, but perhaps only through ignorance of zoology, was, lest, whilst my sleeping face was upturned to the stars, some one of the many little Brahminical-looking cows on the Cambrian hills, one or other, might poach her foot into the centre of my face. I do not suppose any fixed hostility of that nature to English faces in Welsh cows: but everywhere I observe in the feminine mind something of beautiful caprice, a floral exuberance of that charming wilfulness which characterises our dear human sisters I fear through all worlds. Against Thugs I had Juvenal's license to be careless in the emptiness of my pockets (*cantabit vacuus\* coram latrone viator*).[164] But I fear that Juvenal's license will not always hold water. There are people bent upon cudgelling one who will persist in excusing one's having nothing but a bad shilling in one's purse, without reading in that Juvenalian *vacuitas* any privilege or license of exemption from the general fate of travellers that intrude upon the solitude of robbers.

Dr Johnson, upon some occasion, which I have forgotten, is represented by his biographers as accounting for an undeserving person's success in these terms : 'Why, I suppose that *his* nonsense suited *their* nonsense.' Can *that* be the humiliating solution of my own colloquial success at this time in Carnarvonshire inns? Do not suggest such a thought, most courteous reader. No matter : won in whatsoever way, success *is* success; and even nonsense, if it is to be victorious nonsense – victorious over the fatal habit of yawning in those who listen, and in some cases over the habit of disputing – must involve a deeper art or more effective secret of power than is easily attained. Nonsense, in fact, is a very difficult thing. Not every seventh son of a seventh son (to use Milton's words) is equal to the task of keeping and maintaining a company of decent men in orthodox nonsense for a matter of two hours. Come from what fountain it may, all talk that succeeds to the extent of raising a wish to meet the talker again, must contain *salt; must* be seasoned with some flavouring element pungent enough to neutralise the natural tendencies of all mixed conversation, not vigilantly tended, to lose itself in insipidities and platitudes. Above all things, I shunned, as I would shun a pestilence, Coleridge's capital error, which through life he practised, of keeping the audience in a state of passiveness. Unjust this was to others, but most of all to himself. This eternal stream of talk which never for one instant intermitted, and allowed no

---

\* '*Vacuus*' : – I am afraid, though many a year has passed since I read Juvenal, that the true classical sense of *vacuus* is, *careless, clear from all burden of anxiety*, so that *vacuitas* will be the *result* of immunity from robbery. But suffer me to understand it in the sense of *free from the burden of property*, in which sense *vacuitas* would be the *cause* of such an immunity.

momentary opportunity of reaction to the persecuted and bated auditor, was absolute ruin to the interests of the talker himself. Always passive – always acted upon, never allowed to react, into what state did the poor afflicted listener – he that played the *rôle* of listener – collapse? He returned home in the exhausted condition of one that has been drawn up just before death from the bottom of a well occupied by foul gases; and, of course, hours before he had reached that perilous point of depression, he had lost all power of distinguishing, understanding, or connecting. I, for my part, without needing to think of the unamiable arrogance involved in such a habit, simply on principles of deadliest selfishness, should have avoided thus incapacitating my hearer from doing any justice to the rhetoric or the argument with which I might address him.

Some great advantages I had for colloquial purposes, and for engaging the attention of people wiser than myself. Ignorant I was in a degree past all imagination of daily life – even as it exists in England. But, on the other hand, having the advantage of a prodigious memory, and the far greater advantage of a logical instinct for feeling in a moment the secret analogies or parallelisms that connected things else apparently remote, I enjoyed these two peculiar gifts for conversation: first, an inexhaustible fertility of topics, and therefore of resources for illustrating or for varying any subject that chance or purpose suggested; secondly, a prematurely awakened sense of *art* applied to conversation. I had learned the use of vigilance in evading with civility the approach of wearisome discussions, and in impressing, quietly and oftentimes imperceptibly, a new movement upon dialogues that loitered painfully, or see-sawed unprofitably. That it was one function of art to hide and mask itself (*artis est artem celare*), this I well knew. Neither was there much art required. The chief demand was for new facts or new views, or for views newly-coloured impressing novelty upon old facts. To throw in a little of the mysterious every now and then was useful, even with those that by temperament were averse to the mysterious; pointed epigrammatic sayings and jests – even somewhat worn – were useful; a seasonable quotation in verse was always effective; and illustrative anecdotes diffused a grace over the whole movement of the dialogue. It would have been coxcombry to practise any elaborate or any conspicuous art: few and simple were any artifices that I ever employed; but, being hidden and seasonable, they were often effective. And the whole result was, that I became exceedingly popular within my narrow circle of friends. This circle was necessarily a fluctuating one, since it was mainly composed of tourists that happened to linger for a few weeks in or near Snowdonia, making their headquarters at Bethgellert or Carnarvon, or at the utmost roaming no farther than the foot of Cader Idris. Amongst these fugitive members of our society, I recollect with especial pleasure Mr De Haren, an accomplished young German, who held, or *had* held, the commission of lieutenant in our British navy, but now, in an interval of peace, was seeking to extend his knowledge of England, and also of the English language; though in *that*, as regarded the fullest command of it colloquially, he had little, indeed, to learn. From him it was that I obtained my first lessons in German, and my first acquaintance with German literature. Paul Richter I then first heard of.[165] ... But the most stationary members of this semi-literary circle were Welshmen; two of them lawyers, one a clergyman. This last had been regularly educated at Oxford – as a member of Jesus (the Welsh college) – and was a man of extensive information. The lawyers had not enjoyed the same advantages, but they had read diligently, and were interesting companions. Wales, as is pretty well known, breeds a population somewhat litigious. I do not think the worse of them for *that*. ... This temper, widely spread amongst the lower classes of the Welsh, made it a necessity that the lawyers should itinerate on market-days through all the principal towns in their districts. In those towns continually I met them; and continually we renewed our literary friendship.

Meantime alternately I sailed upon the high-priced and the low-priced tack. So exceedingly cheap were provisions at that period, when the war taxation of Mr Pitt was partially intermitting, that it was easy beyond measure upon any three weeks' expenditure, by living with cottagers, to save two guineas out of the three. Mr De Haren assured me even in an inn, and not in a poor man's cottage (but an unpretending rustic inn, where the mistress of the house took upon herself the functions of every possible servant in turn – cook, waiter, chambermaid, boots, ostler), he had passed a day or two; and for what he considered a really elegant dinner, as regarded everything except the table equipage (that being rude and coarse), he had paid only sixpence. This very inn, about ten or twelve miles south of Dolgelly, I myself visited some time later; and I found Mr De Haren's account in all points confirmed: the sole drawback upon the comfort of the visitor being that the fuel was chiefly of green wood, and with a chimney that smoked. I suffered so much under this kind of smoke, which irritates and inflames the eyes more than any other, that on the following day reluctantly I took leave of that obliging pluralist the landlady, and really felt myself blushing on settling the bill, until I bethought me of the green wood, which, upon the whole, seemed to balance the account. I could not then, nor can I now, account for these preposterously low prices; which same prices, strange to say, ruled (as Wordsworth and his sister often assured me) among the same kind of scenery – *i.e.*, amongst the English lakes – at the very same time. To account for it, as people often do, by alleging the want of markets for agricultural produce, is crazy political economy; since the remedy for paucity of markets, and consequent failure of competition, is, certainly not to sell at losing rates, but to forbear producing, and consequently not to sell at all.*

---

* Thirteen years later – viz., in the year of Waterloo – happening to walk through the whole Principality from south to north, beginning at Cardiff, and ending at Bangor, I turned aside about twenty-five miles to inquire after the health of my excellent hostess, that determined pluralist and intense antipole of all possible sinecurists. I found her cleaning a pair of boots and spurs, and purposing (I rather think) to enter next upon the elegant office of greasing a horse's heels. In that design, however, she was thwarted for the present by myself and another tourist, who claimed her services in three or four other characters previously. I inquired after the chimney – was it still smoking? She seemed surprised that it had ever been suspected of anything criminal; so, as it was not a season for fires, I said no more. But I saw plenty of green wood, and but a small proportion of peats. I fear, therefore, that this, the state-room of the whole concern, still poisons the peace of the unhappy tourists. One personal indemni-

So cheap in fact were all provisions, which one had any chance of meeting with in a labouring man's house, that I found it difficult under such a roof to spend sixpence-a-day. Tea or coffee there was none : and I did not at that period very much care for either. Milk, with bread (coarse, but more agreeable by much than the insipid *whity-grey* bread of towns), potatoes if one wished, and also a little goat's, or kid's, flesh – these composed the cottager's choice of viands; not luxurious, but palatable enough to a person who took much exercise. And, if one wished, fresh-water fish could be had cheap enough; especially trout of the very finest quality. In these circumstances, I never found it easy to spend even five shillings (no, not three shillings, unless whortleberries or fish had been bought) in one week. And thus it was easy enough to create funds for my periodical transmigrations back into the character of gentleman-tourist. Even the half of five shillings I could not always find means to spend : for in some families, raised above dependence upon daily wages, when I performed any services in the way of letter-writing, I found it impossible at times to force any money at all upon them.

---

fication, meantime, I must mention which this little guilty room made to me on that same night for all the tears it had caused me to shed. It happened that there was a public dance held at this inn on this very night. I therefore retired early to my bedroom, having had so long a walk, and not wishing to annoy the company, or the excellent landlady, who had, I dare say, to play the fiddle to the dancers. The noise and uproar were almost insupportable; so that I could not sleep at all. At three o'clock all became silent, the company having departed in a body. Suddenly from the little parlour, separated from my bedroom overhead by the slightest and most pervious of ceilings, arose with the rising dawn the very sweetest of female voices perhaps that ever I had heard, although for many years an *habitué* of the opera. She was a stranger; a visitor from some distance; and (I was told in the morning) a Methodist. What she sang, or at least sang last, were the beautiful verses of Shirley, ending –

> 'Only the actions of the just
> Smell sweet, and blossom in the dust.'

This incident caused me to forget and forgive the wicked little chimney.

[*When De Quincey decided to go to London to raise money on his inheritance, he walked as far as Shrewsbury where he spent the evening at an inn waiting for the night mail coach to London.*]

[xv] About this time – just when it was becoming daily more difficult to eke out the weekly funds for high-priced inns by the bivouacking system – as if some over-mastering fiend, some instinct of migration, sorrowful but irresistible, were driving me forth to wander like the unhappy Io of the Grecian mythus, some oestrum of hidden persecution that bade me fly when no man pursued,[166] not in false hope – for my hopes whispered but a doubtful chance, not in reasonable fear – for all was sweet pastoral quiet and autumnal beauty around me, suddenly I took a fierce resolution to sacrifice my weekly allowance, to slip my anchor, and to throw myself in desperation upon London. ...

The day on which I left Oswestry (convoyed for nearly five miles by my warm-hearted friend) was a day of golden sunshine amongst the closing days of November. As truly as Jessica's moonlight (*Merchant of Venice*), this golden sunshine might be said to *sleep* upon the woods and the fields; so awful was the universal silence, so profound the death-like stillness. It was a day belonging to a brief and pathetic season of farewell summer resurrection, which, under one name or other, is known almost everywhere. In North America it is called the 'Indian Summer.' In North Germany and Midland Germany it is called the 'Old Wives' Summer,' and more rarely the 'Girls' Summer.' It is that last brief resurrection of summer in its most brilliant memorials, a resurrection that has no root in the past, nor steady hold in the future, like the lambent and fitful gleams from an expiring lamp, mimicking what is called the 'lightning before death' in sick patients, when close upon their end. There is the feeling of a conflict that has been going on between the lingering powers of summer and the strengthening powers of winter, not unlike that which moves by antagonist forces in some deadly inflammation hurrying forwards through fierce struggles into the final repose of mortification. For a time the equilibrium has been maintained between the hostile forces; but at last the antagonism is overthrown; the victory is accomplished for the powers that fight on the side of death; simultaneously with the conflict, the pain of conflict has departed: and thenceforward the gentle process of collapsing life, no longer fretted by counter-movements, slips away with holy peace into the noiseless deeps of the Infinite. So sweet, so ghostly, in its soft, golden smiles, silent as a dream, and quiet as the dying trance of a saint, faded through all its stages this departing day, along the whole length of which I bade farewell for many a year to Wales, and farewell to summer. In the very aspect and the sepulchral stillness of the motionless day, as solemnly it wore away through morning, noontide, afternoon, to meet the darkness that was hurrying to swallow up its beauty, I had a fantastic feeling as though I read the very language of resignation when bending before some irresistible agency. And at intervals I heard – in how different a key! – the raving, the everlasting uproar of that dreadful metropolis, which at every step was coming nearer, and beckoning (as it seemed) to myself for purposes as dim, for issues as incalculable, as the path of cannon-shots fired at random and in darkness.

It was not late, but it was at least two hours after nightfall, when I reached Shrewsbury. ... I announced myself as a passenger 'booked' for that night's mail. This character at once installed me as rightfully a guest of the inn, however profligate a life I might have previously led as a pedestrian. Accordingly I was received with special courtesy; and it so happened that I was received with something even like pomp. Four wax-lights carried before me by obedient mutes, these were but ordinary honours, meant (as old experience had instructed me) for the first engineering step towards effecting a lodgment upon the stranger's purse. In fact the wax-lights are used by innkeepers, both abroad and at home, to 'try the range of their guns.' If the stranger submits quietly, as a good anti-pedestrian ought surely to do, and fires no counter gun by way of protest, then he is recognised at once as passively within range, and amenable to orders. ... I stepped into the sumptuous room allotted to me. It was a ball-room* of

---

*'It was a ball-room': – The explanation of the case was simply, that the hotel was under some extensive process of purification, adorn-

noble proportions – lighted, if I chose to issue orders, by three gorgeous chandeliers, not basely wrapped up in paper, but sparkling through all their thickets of crystal branches, and flashing back the soft rays of my tall waxen lights. There were, moreover, two orchestras,[167] which money would have filled within thirty minutes. And, upon the whole, one thing only was wanting – viz., a throne – for the completion of my *apotheosis*.

It might be seven p.m. when first I entered upon my kingdom. About three hours later I rose from my chair, and with considerable interest looked out into the night. For nearly two hours I had heard fierce winds arising; and the whole atmosphere had, by this time, become one vast laboratory of hostile movements in all directions. Such a chaos, such a distracting wilderness of dim sights, and of those awful 'sounds that live in darkness' (Wordsworth's *Excursion*), never had I consciously witnessed. Rightly, and by a true instinct, had I made my farewell adieus to summer. All through the day, Wales and her grand mountain ranges – Penmaenmawr, Snowdon, Cader Idris – had divided my thoughts with London. But now rose London – sole, dark, infinite – brooding over the whole capacities of my heart. Other object – other thought – I could not admit. Long before midnight, the whole household (with the exception of a solitary waiter) had retired to rest. Two hours, at least, were left to me, after twelve o'clock had struck, for heart-shaking reflections. More than ever I stood upon the brink of a precipice; and the local circumstances around me deepened and intensified these reflections, impressed upon them solemnity and terror, sometimes even horror. It is all but inconceivable to men of unyielding and callous sensibilities, how profoundly others find their reveries modified and overruled by the external characters of the immediate scene around them. Many a suicide that hung dubiously in the balances has been ratified, and carried into summary effect, through the forlorn, soul-revolting aspect of a crazy, dilapidated home. Oftentimes, without extravagance, the whole difference between a mind that spurns life and

---

ment, and, I believe, extension: and, under the accident of being myself on that particular night the sole visitor of the house, I slipped unavoidably into the honours of a semi-regal reception.

the same mind reconciled to life, turns upon the outside features of that particular domestic scenery which hourly besieges the eyes. I, in this Shrewsbury hotel, naturally contemplated a group of objects tending to far different results. And yet in some respects they agreed.

The unusual dimensions of the rooms, especially their towering height, brought up continually and obstinately, through natural links of associated feelings or images, the mighty vision of London waiting for me afar off. An altitude of nineteen or twenty feet showed itself unavoidably upon an exaggerated scale in some of the smaller side-rooms – meant probably for cards or for refreshments. This single feature of the rooms – their unusual altitude, and the echoing hollowness which had become the exponent of that altitude – this one terrific feature (for terrific it was in the effect), together with crowding and evanescent images of the flying feet that so often had spread gladness through these halls on the wings of youth and hope at seasons when every room rang with music – all this, rising in tumultuous vision, whilst the dead hours of night were stealing along, all around me – household and town – sleeping, and whilst against the windows more and more the storm outside was raving, and to all appearance endlessly growing, threw me into the deadliest condition of nervous emotion under contradictory forces, high over which predominated horror recoiling from that unfathomed abyss in London into which I was now so wilfully precipitating myself. Often I looked out and examined the night. Wild it was beyond all description, and dark as 'the inside of a wolf's throat.' But at intervals, when the wind, shifting continually, swept in such a direction as to clear away the vast curtain of vapour, the stars shone out, though with a light unusually dim and distant. Still, as I turned inwards to the echoing chambers, or outwards to the wild, wild night, I saw London expanding her visionary gates to receive me, like some dreadful mouth of Acheron (*Acherontis avari*). Thou also, Whispering Gallery! once again in those moments of conscious and wilful desolation didst to my ear utter monitorial sighs. For once again I was preparing to utter an irrevocable word, to enter upon one of those fatally tortuous paths of which the windings can never be unlinked.

Such thoughts, and visions without number corresponding to them, were moving across the *camera obscura* of my fermenting fancy, when suddenly I heard a sound of wheels; which, however, soon died off into some remote quarter. I guessed at the truth – viz., that it was the Holyhead Mail wheeling off on its primary duty of delivering its bags at the post-office. In a few minutes it was announced as having changed horses; and off I was to London.

[In 1856 De Quincey was able to name the attorney Brunell in whose house he lodged in London, and give a fuller description of him, which he could not do in 1821 when Brunell was still alive.]

[1856] I lost no time in opening the business which had brought me to London. By ten a.m., an hour when all men of business are presumed to be at their posts, personally or by proxy, I presented myself at the money-lender's office. My name was already known there: for I had, by letters from Wales, containing very plain and very accurate statements of my position in life and my pecuniary expectations (some of which statements it afterwards appeared that he had personally investigated and verified), endeavoured to win his favourable attention. The money-lender, as it turned out, had one fixed rule of action. He never granted a personal interview to any man; no, not to the most beloved of his clients. One and all – myself, therefore, among the crowd – he referred for information, and for the means of prosecuting any kind of negotiation, to an attorney, who called himself, on most days of the week, by the name of Brunell, but occasionally (might it perhaps be on *red-letter* days?) by the more common name of Brown. Mr Brunell-Brown, or Brown-Brunel, had located his hearth (if ever he had possessed one), and his household goods (when they were not in the custody of the sheriff), in Greek Street, Soho. The house was not in itself, supposing that its face had been washed now and then, at all disrespectable. But it wore an unhappy countenance of gloom and unsocial fretfulness, due in reality to the long neglect of painting, cleansing, and in some instances of repairing. There were, however, no fractured panes of glass in the windows; and the deep silence which invested the house, not only from the absence of all visitors, but also of those common household functionaries, bakers, butchers, beer-carriers, sufficiently accounted for the desolation, by suggesting an excuse not strictly true – viz., that it might be tenantless. The house already had tenants through the day, though of a noiseless order, and was destined soon to increase them. Mr Brown-Brunell, after reconnoitring me through a narrow side-window (such as is often attached to front-doors in London), admitted me cheerfully, and conducted me, as an honoured guest, to his private *officina diplomatum*[168] at the back of the house. From the expression of his face, but much more from the contradictory and self-counteracting play of his features, you gathered in a moment that he was a man who had much to conceal, and much, perhaps, that he would gladly forget. His eye expressed wariness against surprise, and passed in a moment into irrepressible glances of suspicion and alarm. No smile that ever his face naturally assumed, but was pulled short up by some freezing counteraction, or was chased by some close-following expression of sadness. One feature there was of relenting goodness and nobleness in Mr Brunell's character, to which it was that subsequently I myself was most profoundly indebted for an asylum that saved my life. He had the deepest, the most liberal, and unaffected love of knowledge, but, above all, of that specific knowledge which we call literature. His own stormy (and no doubt oftentimes disgraceful) career in life, that had entangled him in perpetual feuds with his fellow-men, he ascribed, with bitter imprecations, to the sudden interruption of his studies consequent upon his father's violent death, and to the necessity which threw him, at a boyish age, upon a professional life in the lower branches of law – threw him, therefore, upon daily temptations, by surrounding him with opportunities for taking advantages not strictly honourable, before he had formed any fixed principles at all. From the very first, Mr Brunell had entered zealously into such conversations with myself as either gave openings for reviving his own delightful remembrances of classic authors, or brought up sometimes doubts for solution, sometimes perplexities and cases of intricate construction for illustration and disentanglement. Hunger-bitten as the house and the household genius seemed, wearing the legend of *Famine* upon every mantelpiece or 'coigne of vantage,' and vehemently protesting, as it must have done through all its echoes, against the introduction of supernumerary mouths, nevertheless there was (and, I suppose, of necessity) a clerk, who bore the name of Pyment, or Pyemont, then first of all, then last of all, made known to me as a possible surname. Mr Pyment had no *alias* – or not to my knowledge – except, indeed, in the vituperative vocabulary of Mr Brunell, in which most variegated nomenclature he bore many scores of opprobrious names, having no reference whatever to any real habits of the man, good or bad. At two rooms' distance, Mr Brunell always assumed a minute and circumstantial knowledge of what Pyment was doing then, and what he was going to do next. All which Pyment gave himself little trouble to answer, unless it happened (as now and then it did) that he could do so with ludicrous effect. What made the necessity for Pyment was the continual call for 'an appearance' to be put in at some of the subordinate courts in Westminster – courts of conscience, sheriff courts, &c. But it happens often that he who is most indispensable, and gets through most work at one hour, becomes a useless burden at another; as the hardest-working reaper seems, in the eyes of an ignoramus, on a wet, wintry day, to be a luxurious idler. Of these ups and downs in Pyment's working life, Mr Brunell made a most cynical use; making out that Pyment not only did nothing, but also that he created much work for the afflicted Brunell. However, it happened occasionally that the truth vindicated itself, by making a call upon Pyment's physics – aggressive or defensive – that needed an instant attention. 'Pyment, I say; this way, Pyment – you're wanted, Pyment.' In fact, both were big, hulking men, and had need to be so; for sometimes, whether with good reason or none, clients at the end of a losing suit, or of a suit nominally gained, but unexpectedly laden with heavy expenses, became refractory, showed fight, and gave Pyment reason for saying that at least on this day he had earned his salary by serving an ejectment on a client whom on any other plan it might have been hard to settle with. ...

[*De Quincey amplified his account of the first part of his time in London, and added a pathetic apostrophe on the sufferings of the old and poor from cold. He spoke from much experience; opium addicts suffer greatly from cold in their periods of abstinence from the drug.*]

[XVII] I continued for seven or eight weeks to live most parsimoniously in lodgings. These lodgings, though barely decent in my eyes, ran away with at the least two-thirds of my remaining guineas. At length, whilst it was yet possible to reserve a solitary half-guinea towards the more urgent interest of finding daily food, I gave up my rooms; and, stating exactly the circumstances in which I stood, requested permission of Mr Brunell to make use of his large house as a nightly asylum from the open air. Parliament had not then made it a crime, next door to a felony, for a man to sleep out-of-doors (as some twenty years later was done by our benign legislators); as yet *that* was no crime. By the law I came to know sin; and looking back to the Cambrian hills from distant years, discovered to my surprise what a parliamentary wretch I had been in elder days, when I slept amongst cows on the open hillsides. Lawful as yet this was; but not, therefore, less full of misery. Naturally, then, I was delighted when Mr Brunell not only most readily assented to my request, but begged of me to come that very night, and turn the house to account as fully as I possibly could. The cheerfulness of such a concession brought with it one drawback. I now regretted that I had not, at a much earlier period, applied for this liberty; since I might thus have saved a considerable fund of guineas, applicable, of course, to all urgent necessities, but at this particular moment to one of clamorous urgency – viz., the purchase of blankets. O ancient women, daughters of toil and suffering, amongst all the hardships and bitter inheritances of flesh that ye are called upon to face, not one – not even hunger – seems in my eyes comparable to that of nightly cold. To seek a refuge from cold in bed, and then, from the thin, gauzy texture of the miserable, worn-out blankets, 'not to sleep a wink,' as Wordsworth records of poor old women in Dorsetshire, where coals, from local causes, were at the very dearest – what a terrific enemy was *that* for poor old grandmothers to face in fight ! How feelingly I learned at this time, as heretofore I had learned on the wild hillsides in Wales, what an unspeakable blessing is that of warmth! A more killing curse there does not exist for man or woman, than that bitter combat between the weariness that prompts sleep, and the keen, searching cold that forces you from the first access of sleep to start up horror-stricken, and to seek warmth vainly in renewed exercise, though long since fainting under fatigue. However, even without blankets, it was a fine thing to have an asylum from the open air; and to be assured of this asylum as long as I was likely to want it.

[De Quincey's description of the rhythms of sleep anticipated by a century the recent discoveries of the undulations, between deep repose and the shallower sleep when dreams come, in which we pass our night's rest.]

[XVIII] Too generally the very attainment of any deep repose seemed as if mechanically linked to some fatal necessity of self-interruption. It was as though a cup were gradually filled by the sleepy overflow of some natural fountain, the fulness of the cup expressing symbolically the completeness of the rest: but then, in the next stage of the process, it seemed as though the rush and torrent-like babbling of the redundant waters, when running over from every part of the cup, interrupted the slumber which in their earlier stage of silent gathering they had so naturally produced. Such and so regular in its swell and its collapse – in its tardy growth and its violent dispersion – did this endless alternation of stealthy sleep and stormy awaking travel through stages as natural as the increments of twilight, or the kindlings of the dawn: no rest that was not a prologue to terror; no sweet tremulous pulses of restoration that did not suddenly explode through rolling clamours of fiery disruption.

[In 1856 De Quincey gave the case-history of the surgeon, Dr Abernethy, whom he had briefly mentioned in 1821 as talking nonsense when under the influence of opium. He also described contemporary methods of preparing and measuring opium doses.]

[XIX] He was a surgeon, and had himself taken opium largely for a most miserable affection (past all hope of cure) seated in one particular organ. This affection was a subtle inflammation, not acute, but chronic; and with this he fought for more (I believe) than twenty years; fought victoriously, if victory it were, to make life supportable for himself, and during all that time to maintain in respectability a wife and a family of children altogether dependent on him.*

[*De Quincey expanded his reminiscence of Grassini's unforgettable voice in a characteristic passage of classical learning brought to life.*]

[xx] Thrilling was the pleasure with which almost always I heard this angelic Grassini. Shivering with expectation I sat,

---

*This surgeon it was who first made me aware of the dangerous variability in opium as to strength under the shifting proportions of its combination with alien impurities. Naturally, as a man professionally alive to the danger of creating any artificial need of opium beyond what the anguish of his malady at any rate demanded, trembling every hour on behalf of his poor children, lest, by any indiscretion of his own, he should precipitate the crisis of his disorder, he saw the necessity of reducing the daily dose to a *minimum*. But to do this he must first obtain the means of measuring the quantities of opium; not the apparent quantities as determined by weighing, but the *virtual* quantities after allowing for the alloy or varying amounts of impurity. This, however, was a visionary problem. To allow for it was simply impossible. The problem, therefore, changed its character. Not to measure the impurities was the object; for, whilst entangled with the operative and efficient parts of the opium, they could not be measured. To separate and eliminate the impure (or inert) parts, this was now the object. And this was effected finally by a particular mode of boiling the opium. That done, the residuum became equable in strength; and the daily doses could be nicely adjusted. About 18 grains formed his daily ration for many years. This, upon the common hospital equation, expresses 18 times 25 drops of laudanum. But, since 25 is$=\frac{100}{4}$, therefore 18 times one quarter of a hundred is$=$one quarter of 1800, and that, I suppose, is 450. So much this surgeon averaged upon each day for about twenty years. Then suddenly began a fiercer stage of the anguish from his disease. But then, also, the fight was finished, and the victory was won. All duties were fulfilled: his children prosperously launched in life; and death, which to himself was becoming daily more necessary as a relief from torment, now fell injuriously upon nobody.

when the time drew near for her golden epiphany; shivering I rose from my seat, incapable of rest, when that heavenly and harp-like voice sang its own victorious welcome in its prelusive *threttánelo – threttánelo* * ($\theta\varrho\varepsilon\tau\tau\acute{a}\nu\varepsilon\lambda\omega - \theta\varrho\varepsilon\tau\tau\acute{a}\nu\varepsilon\lambda\omega$).

[*In 1856 De Quincey added a footnote, lamenting the spoliation of Grasmere by the building of an unnecessary road – a lament which sounds very topical today.*]

[XXI] The cottage and the valley concerned in this description were not imaginary: the valley was the lovely one, *in those days*, of Grasmere; and the cottage was occupied for more than twenty years by myself, as immediate successor, in the year 1809, to Wordsworth. Looking to the limitation here laid down – viz., *in those days* – the reader will inquire in what way Time can have affected the beauty of Grasmere. Do the Westmoreland valleys turn grey-headed? O reader! this is a painful memento of some of us! Thirty years ago, a gang of Vandals (nameless, I thank heaven, to me), for the sake of building a mail-coach road that never would be wanted, carried, at a cost of £3000 to the defrauded parish, a horrid causeway of sheer granite masonry, for three-quarters-of-a-mile, right through the loveliest succession of secret forest dells and shy recesses of the lake, margined by unrivalled ferns, amongst which was the *Osmunda regalis*. This sequestered angle of Grasmere is described by Wordsworth, as it unveiled itself on a September morning, in the exquisite poems on the 'Naming of Places.' From this also – viz., this spot of ground, and this magnificent crest (the Osmunda) – was suggested

---

* *'Threttánelo – threttánelo'*: – The beautiful representative echo by which Aristophanes expresses the sound of the Grecian *phorminx*, or of some other instrument, which conjecturally has been shown most to resemble our modern European harp. In the case of ancient Hebrew instruments used in the temple service, random and idle must be all the guesses through the Greek Septuagint or the Latin Vulgate to identify any one of them. But as to Grecian instruments the case is different; always there is the remote chance of digging up some marble sculpture of orchestral appurtenances and properties.

that unique line – the finest independent line through all the records of verse,

> 'Or lady of the lake,
> Sole-sitting by the shores of old romance.'

Rightly, therefore, did I introduce this limitation. The Grasmere before and after this outrage were two different vales.

[*In place of the three points with which he opened the original 'Pains of Opium' section, De Quincey substituted a detailed analysis of the connection between childhood experiences and the dreams induced by opium; and of the progress of addiction, and methods of withdrawal from it. A further digression – on opium as a cure for nervous irritation and tuberculosis, and on the unreasonableness of insurance offices in refusing life insurance to opium eaters – is not quoted below.*]

[XXII] 1. You are already aware, I hope – else you must have a low opinion of my logic – that the opium miseries, which are now on the point of pressing forward to the front of this narrative, connect themselves with my early hardships in London (and therefore more remotely with those in Wales) by natural links of affiliation – that is, the early series of sufferings was the parent of the later. Otherwise, these Confessions would break up into two disconnected sections – first, a record of boyish calamities; secondly, a record (totally independent) of sufferings consequent upon excesses in opium. And the two sections would have no link whatever to connect them, except the slight one of having both happened to the same person. But a little attention will show the strictness of the inter-connection. The boyish sufferings, whether in Wales or London, pressing upon an organ peculiarly weak in my bodily system – viz., the stomach – caused that subsequent distress and irritability of the stomach which drove me to the use of opium as the sole remedy potent enough to control it. Here already there is exposed a sufficient *casual* connection between the two several sections of my experience. The opium would probably never have been promoted into the dignity of a daily and a life-long resource, had it not proved itself to be the one sole agent equal to the task of tranquillising the miseries left behind by the youthful privations. Thus far the *nexus*, as between cause and effect, is sufficiently established between the one experience and the other – between the boyish records and the records of mature life. There needed no other *nexus* to justify the unity of the entire Confessions. But, though not wanted, nevertheless it happens that there *is* another and a distinct link connecting the two separate records. The main phenomenon by which opium expressed itself permanently, and the sole phenomenon that was communicable, lay in the dreams (and in the peculiar dream-scenery) which followed the opium excesses. But naturally these dreams, and this dream-scenery, drew their outlines and materials – their great lights and shadows – from those profound revelations which had been ploughed so deeply into the heart, from those *encaustic records* which in the mighty furnaces of London life had been burnt into the undying memory by the fierce action of misery. And thus in reality the early experiences of erring childhood not only led to the secondary experiences of opium, but also determined the particular form and pressure of the chief phenomena in those secondary experiences. Here is the briefest possible abstract of the total case: – The final object of the whole record lay in the dreams. For the sake of those the entire narrative arose. But what caused the dreams? Opium used in unexampled excess. But what caused this excess in the use of opium? Simply the early sufferings; these, and these only, through the derangements which they left behind in the animal economy. On this mode of viewing the case, moving regressively from the end to the beginning, it will be seen that there is one uninterrupted bond of unity running through the entire succession of experiences – first and last: the dreams were an inheritance from the opium; the opium was an inheritance from the boyish follies.

2. You will think, perhaps, that I am too confidential and communicative of my own private history. It may be so. But my way of writing is rather to think aloud, and follow my own humours, than much to inquire who is listening to me; for, if once I stop to consider what is proper to be said, I shall soon come to doubt whether any part at all is proper. The fact is, I imagine myself writing at a distance of twenty – thirty – fifty years ahead of this present moment, either for the satisfaction of the

few who may then retain any interest in myself, or of the many (a number that is sure to be continually growing) who will take an inextinguishable interest in the mysterious powers of opium. For opium *is* mysterious; mysterious to the extent, at times, of apparent self-contradiction; and *so* mysterious, that my own long experience in its use – sometimes even in its abuse – did but mislead me into conclusions ever more and more remote from what I now suppose to be the truth. Fifty-and-two years' experience of opium, as a magical resource under *all* modes of bodily suffering, I may now claim to have had – allowing only for some periods of four and six months, during which, by unexampled efforts of self-conquest, I had accomplished a determined abstinence from opium.* These parentheses being subtracted, as also, and secondly,

---

*With what final result, I have much difficulty in saying. Invariably, after such victories, I returned, upon deliberate choice (after weighing all the consequences on this side and that), to the daily use of opium. But with silent changes, many and great (worked apparently by these reiterated struggles), in the opium-eating habits. Amongst other changes was this, that the quantity required gradually fell by an enormous proportion. According to the modern slang phrase, I had in the meridian stage of my opium career used '*fabulous*' quantities. Stating the quantities – not in solid opium, but in the tincture (known to everybody as *laudanum*) – my daily ration was eight thousand drops. If you write down that amount in the ordinary way as 8000, you see at a glance that you may read it into eight quantities of a thousand, or into eight hundred quantities of ten, or lastly, into eighty quantities of one hundred. Now, a single quantity of one hundred will about fill a very old-fashioned obsolete tea-spoon, of that order which you find still lingering amongst the respectable poor. Eighty such quantities, therefore, would have filled eighty of such antediluvian spoons – that is, it would have been the common hospital dose for three hundred and twenty adult patients. But the ordinary tea-spoon of this present nineteenth century is nearly as capacious as the dessert-spoon of our ancestors. Which I have heard accounted for thus: – Throughout the eighteenth century, when first tea became known to the working population, the tea-drinkers were almost exclusively women; men, even in educated classes, very often persisting (down to the French Revolution) in treating such a beverage as an idle and effeminate in-some off-and-on fits of tentative and intermitting dalliance with opium in the opening of my career – these deductions allowed for, I may describe myself as experimentally acquainted with opium for something more than half-a-century. What, then, is my final report upon its good and evil results? In particular, upon these two capital tendencies of habitual opium-eating under the popular misconceptions; viz., its supposed necessity of continually clamouring for increasing quantities; secondly, its supposed corresponding declension in power and efficacy. Upon these ugly scandals, what is my most deliberate award? At the age of forty, the reader is aware that, under our ancestral proverb, every man is a fool or a physician. Apparently our excellent ancestors, aiming undeniably at alliteration, spelled *physician* with an *f*. And why not? A man's physic might be undeniable, although his spelling should be open to some slight improvements. But I presume that the proverb meant to exact from any man only so much medical skill as should undertake the responsibility of his own individual health. It is my duty, it seems, thus far to be a physician – to guarantee, so far as human foresight *can* guarantee, my own corporeal sanity. And this, trying the case by ordinary practical tests, I have accomplished. And I add solemnly, that without opium most certainly I could not have accomplished such a result. Thirty-five years ago, beyond all doubt, I should have been in my grave. And as to the two popular dilemmas – that either you must renounce opium, or else indefinitely augment the daily ration; and, secondly, that, even submitting to such a postulate, you must content yourself, under any scale of doses, with an effect continually decaying, in fact, that you must ultimately descend into the despairing condition of the martyr to dram-drinking – at

---

dulgence. This obstinate twist in masculine habits it was that secretly controlled the manufacture of tea-spoons. Up to Waterloo, tea-spoons were adjusted chiefly to the calibre of female mouths. Since then, greatly to the benefit of the national health, the grosser and browner sex have universally fallen into the effeminate habit of tea-drinking; and the capacity of tea-spoons has naturally conformed to the new order of cormorant mouths that have alighted by myriads upon the tea-trays of these later generations.

this point, I make a resolute stand, in blank denial of the whole doctrine. Originally, when first entering upon my opium career, I did so with great anxiety : and before my eyes floated for ever the analogies – dim, or *not* dim, according to my spirits at the moment – of the poor, perishing brandy-drinker, often on the brink of *delirium tremens!* Opium I pursued under a harsh necessity, as an unknown, shadowy power, leading I knew not whither, and a power that might suddenly change countenance upon this unknown road. Habitually I lived under such an impression of awe as we have all felt from stories of fawns, or seeming fawns, that have run before some mounted hunter for many a league, until they have tempted him far into the mazes of a boundless forest, and at that point, where all regress had become lost and impossible, either suddenly vanished, leaving the man utterly bewildered, or assumed some more fearful shape. A part of the evil which I feared actually unfolded itself; but all was due to my own ignorance, to neglect of cautionary measures, or to gross mismanagement of my health in points where I well knew the risks, but grievously underrated their urgency and pressure. I was temperate : that solitary advantage I had; but I sank under the lulling seductions of opium into total sedentariness, and *that* whilst holding firmly the belief, that powerful exercise was omnipotent against all modes of debility or obscure nervous irritations. The account of my depression, and almost of my helplessness, in the next memorandum (No. 3), is faithful as a description to the real case. But, in ascribing that case to opium, as any transcendent and overmastering agency, I was thoroughly wrong. Twenty days of exercise, twenty times twenty miles of walking, at the ordinary pace of three and a-half miles an hour, or perhaps half that amount, would have sent me up as buoyantly as a balloon into regions of natural and healthy excitement, where dejection is an impossible phenomenon. O heavens ! how man abuses or neglects his natural resources ! Yes, the thoughtful reader is disposed to say; but very possibly distinguishing between such *natural* resources and opium as a resource that is *not* natural, but highly artificial, or even absolutely unnatural. I think otherwise : upon the basis of my really vast, perhaps unequalled, experience (let me add of my *tentative* experience, varying its trials in every conceivable mode, so as to meet the question at issue under every angle), I advance these three following propositions, all of them unsuspected by the popular mind, and the last of them (as cannot much longer fail to be discovered) bearing a national value – I mean, as meeting our English hereditary complaint: –

I. With respect to the morbid growth upon the opium-eater of his peculiar habit, when once rooted in the system, and throwing out *tentacula* like a cancer, it is out of my power to deliver any such oracular judgment upon the case – *i.e.*, upon the apparent danger of such a course, and by what stages it might be expected to travel towards its final consummation – as naturally I should wish to do. Being an oracle, it is my wish to behave myself like an oracle, and not to evade any decent man's questions in the way that Apollo too often did at Delphi. But, in this particular instance before me, the accident of my own individual seamanship in presence of this storm interfered with the natural evolution of the problem in its extreme form of danger. I had become too uneasy under the consciousness of that intensely artificial condition into which I had imperceptibly lapsed through unprecedented quantities of opium; the shadows of eclipse were too dark and lurid not to rouse and alarm me into a spasmodic effort for reconquering the ground which I had lost. Such an effort I made: every step by which I had gone astray did I patiently unthread. And thus I fought off the natural and spontaneous catastrophe, whatever *that* might be, which mighty Nature would else have let loose for redressing the wrongs offered to herself. But what followed? In six or eight months more, upon fresh movements arising of insupportable nervous irritation, I fleeted back into the same opium lull. To and fro, up and down, did I tilt upon those mountainous seas, for year after year. 'See-saw, like Margery Daw, that sold her bed and lay on straw.' Even so did I, led astray, perhaps, by the classical example of Miss Daw, see-saw for year after year, out and in, of manœuvres the most intricate dances the most elaborate, receding or approaching, round my great central sun of opium. Sometimes I ran perilously close to my perihelion; sometimes I became frightened, and wheeled off into a vast cometary aphelion,[169] where for six months 'opium' was a word unknown. How nature stood all these see-sawings is quite a mystery to me: I must have led her a sad life in those days. Nervous irritation forced me, at times, upon frightful excesses; but terror from anomalous symptoms sooner or later forced me back. This terror was strengthened by the vague hypotheses current at that period about spontaneous combustion.[170] Might I not myself take leave of the literary world in that fashion? According to the popular fancy, there were two modes of this spontaneity; and really very little to choose between them. Upon one variety of this explosion, a man blew up in the dark, without match or candle near him, leaving nothing behind him but some bones, of no use to anybody, and which were supposed to be *his* only because nobody else ever applied for them. It was fancied that some volcanic agency – an unknown deposition – accumulated from some vast redundancy of brandy, furnished the self-exploding principle. But this startled the faith of most people; and a more plausible scheme suggested itself, which depended upon the concurrence of a lucifer-match. Without an incendiary, a man could not take fire. We sometimes see the hands of inveterate dram-drinkers throw off an atmosphere of intoxicating vapours, strong enough to lay flies into a state of sleep or *coma*; and on the same principle, it was supposed that the breath might be so loaded with spirituous particles, as to catch fire from a match applied to a pipe when held between the lips. If so, then what should hinder the 'devouring element' (as newspapers call fire) from spreading through the throat to the cavity of the chest: in which case, not being insured, the man would naturally become a total loss. Opium, however, it will occur to the reader, is not alcohol. That is true. But it might, for anything that was known experimentally, be ultimately worse. Coleridge, the only person known to the public as having dallied systematically and for many years with opium, could not be looked to for any candid report of its history and progress; besides that, Coleridge was under a permanent craze of having nearly accomplished his own liberation from opium; and thus he had come to have an *extra* reason for self-delusion. Finding myself, therefore, walking on a solitary path of bad repute, leading *whither* no man's experience could tell me, I became proportionably cautious;

and if nature had any plot for making an example of me, I was resolved to baulk her. Thus it was that I never followed out the seductions of opium to their final extremity. But, nevertheless, in evading that extremity, I stumbled upon as great a discovery as if I had *not* evaded it. After the first or second self-conquest in this conflict – although finding it impossible to persist through more than a few months in the abstinence from opium – I remarked, however, that the domineering tyranny of its exactions was at length steadily declining. Quantities noticeably less had now become sufficient: and after the fourth of these victories, won with continually decreasing efforts, I found that not only had the daily dose (upon relapsing) suffered a self-limitation to an enormous extent, but also that, upon any attempt obstinately to renew the old doses, there arose a new symptom – viz., an irritation on the surface of the skin – which soon became unsupportable, and tended to distraction. In about four years, without any further efforts, my daily ration had fallen *spontaneously* from a varying quantity of eight, ten, or twelve thousand drops of laudanum to about three hundred. I describe the drug as *laudanum*, because another change ran along collaterally with this supreme change – viz., that the solid opium began to require a length of time, continually increasing, to expand its effects sensibly, oftentimes not less than four hours; whereas the tincture manifested its presence instantaneously.

Thus, then, I had reached a position from which authoritatively it might be pronounced, as a result of long, anxious, and vigilant experience, that, on the assumption of earnest (even though intermitting) efforts towards recurrent abstinences on the part of the opium-eater, the practice of indulging to the very greatest excess in this narcotic tends to a natural (almost an inevitable) euthanasy.[171] Many years ago, when briefly touching on this subject, I announced (as a fact even *then* made known to me) that no instance of abstinence, though it were but of three days' continuance, ever perishes. Ten grains, deducted from a daily ration of five hundred, will tell through a series of many weeks, and will be found again modifying the final result, even at the close of the year's reckoning. At this day, after a half-century of oscillating experience, and after no efforts or trying acts of self-denial beyond those severe ones attached to the several processes (five or six in all) of reconquering my freedom from the yoke of opium, I find myself pretty nearly at the same station which I occupied at that vast distance of time. It is recorded of Lord Nelson that, even after the Nile and Copenhagen, he still paid the penalty, on the first days of resuming his naval life, which is generally exacted by nature from the youngest little middy or the rawest griffin[172] – viz., sea-sickness. And this happens to a considerable proportion of sailors: they do not recover their sea-legs till some days after getting afloat. The very same thing happens to veteran opium-eaters, when first, after long intermissions, resuming too abruptly their ancient familiarities with opium. It is a fact, which I mention as indicating the enormous revolutions passed through, that, within these five years, I have turned pale, and felt warnings, pointing towards such an uneasiness, after taking not more than twenty grains of opium. At present and for some years, I have been habitually content with five or six grains daily, instead of three hundred and twenty to four hundred grains. Let me wind up this retrospect with saying, that the powers of opium, as an anodyne, but still more as a tranquilliser of nervous and anomalous sensations, have not in the smallest degree decayed; and that, if it has casually unveiled its early power of exacting slight penalties from any trivial inattention to accurate proportions, it has more than commensurately renewed its ancient privilege of lulling irritation and of supporting preternatural calls for exertion.

My first proposition, therefore, amounts to this – that the process of weaning one's-self from the deep bondage of opium, by many people viewed with despairing eyes, is not only a possible achievement, and one which grows easier in every stage of its progress, but is favoured and promoted by nature in secret ways that could not, without some experience, have been suspected. This, however, is but a sorry commendation of any resource making great pretensions, that, by a process confessedly trying to human firmness, it can ultimately be thrown aside. Certainly little would be gained by the negative service of cancelling a drawback upon any agency whatever, until it were shown that this drawback has availed to disturb and neutralise great positive blessings lying within the gift of that agency. What are the advantages connected with opium that can merit any such name as blessings?

*[The little girl who is described as having, on the verge of drowning, recalled the whole of her past life, was almost certainly De Quincey's mother. In 1856 he elaborated this incident in a footnote.]*

[XXIII] The heroine of this remarkable case was a girl of about nine years old; and there can be little doubt that she looked down as far within the *crater* of death – that awful volcano – as any human being ever *can* have done that has lived to draw back and to report her experience. Not less than ninety years did she survive this memorable escape; and I may describe her as in all respects a woman of remarkable and interesting qualities. She enjoyed throughout her long life, as the reader will readily infer, serene and cloudless health; had a masculine understanding; reverenced truth not less than did the Evangelists; and led a life of saintly devotion, such as might have glorified '*Hilarion or Paul.*' – (The words in italic are Ariosto's.) – I mention these traits as characterising her in a memorable extent, that the reader may not suppose himself relying upon a dealer in exaggerations, upon a credulous enthusiast, or upon a careless wielder of language. Forty-five years had intervened between the first time and the last time of her telling me this anecdote, and not one iota had shifted its ground amongst the incidents, nor had any the most trivial of the circumstantiations suffered change. The scene of the accident was the least of valleys, what the Greeks of old would have called an ἄγκος, and we English should properly call a dell. Human tenant it had none: even at noonday it was a solitude; and would oftentimes have been a silent solitude but for the brawling of a brook – not broad, but occasionally deep – which ran along the base of the little hills. Into this brook, probably into one of its dangerous pools, the child fell: and, according to the ordinary chances she could have had but a slender prospect indeed of any deliverance; for, although a dwelling-house was close by, it was shut out from view by the undulations of the ground. How long the child lay in the water was probably never inquired earnestly until the answer had become irrecoverable; for a servant, to whose care the child was then confided, had a natural interest in suppressing the whole case. From the child's own account, it should seem that *asphyxia* must have announced its commencement. A process of struggle and deadly suffocation was passed through half consciously. This process terminated by a sudden blow apparently *on* or *in* the brain, after which there was no pain or conflict; but in an instant succeeded a dazzling rush of light; immediately after which came the solemn apocalypse of the entire past life. Meantime, the child's disappearance in the water had happily been witnessed by a farmer who rented some fields in this little solitude, and by a rare accident was riding through them at the moment. Not being very well mounted, he was retarded by the hedges and other fences in making his way down to the water; some time was thus lost; but once at the spot, he leaped in, booted and spurred, and succeeded in delivering one that must have been as nearly counted amongst the populations of the grave as perhaps the laws of the shadowy world can suffer to return.

[*After the reference to* The Excursion *De Quincey inserted a foot-note again claiming priority as a recogniser of Wordsworth's genius when he was still scorned by the general public (see also note 153).*]

[XXIV] '*From a great modern poet*': – What poet? It was Wordsworth; and why did I not formerly name him? This throws a light backwards upon the strange history of Wordsworth's reputation. The year in which I wrote and published these Confessions was 1821; and at that time the name of Wordsworth, though beginning to emerge from the dark cloud of scorn and contumely which had hitherto overshadowed it, was yet most imperfectly established. Not until ten years later was his greatness cheerfully and generally acknowledged. I, therefore, as the very earliest (without one exception) of all who came forward, in the beginning of his career, to honour and welcome him, shrank with disgust from making any sentence of mine the occasion for an explosion of vulgar malice against him. But the grandeur of the passage here cited inevitably spoke for itself; and he that would have been most scornful on hearing the name of the poet coupled with this epithet of 'great' could not but find his malice intercepted, and himself cheated into cordial admiration, by the splendour of the verses.

[*The original Confessions recorded, after the climax of the opium visions, that De Quincey had successfully reduced his opium dosage. In 1856, after thirty-five more years of fluctuating addiction, De Quincey inserted a passage qualifying this claim.*]

[XXV] Now, at last, I had become awestruck at the approach of sleep, under the conditions of visions so afflicting, and so intensely life-like as those which persecuted my phantom-haunted brain. More and more also I felt violent palpitations in some internal region, such as are commonly, but erroneously, called palpitations of the heart – being, as I suppose, referable exclusively to derangements in the stomach. These were evidently increasing rapidly in frequency and in strength. Naturally, therefore, on considering how important my life had become to others besides myself, I became alarmed; and I paused seasonably; but with a difficulty that is past all description. Either way it seemed as though death had, in military language, 'thrown himself astride of my path.' Nothing short of mortal anguish, in a physical sense, it seemed, to wean myself from opium; yet, on the other hand, death from overwhelming nervous terrors – death by brain fever or by lunacy – seemed too certainly to besiege the alternative course. Fortunately I had still so much of firmness left as to face that choice, which, with most of instant suffering, showed in the far distance a possibility of final escape.

This possibility was realised: I *did* accomplish my escape. And the issue of that particular stage in my opium experiences (for such it was – simply a provisional stage, that paved the way subsequently for many milder stages, to which gradually my constitutional system accommodated itself) was, pretty nearly in the following words, communicated to my readers in the earliest edition of these Confessions.

# Notes

1 (p. 29). *demi-reps*. Demi-reputable women, women of doubtful virtue.

2 (p. 29). *French literature*. The reference is clearly to Rousseau's *Confessions*.

3 (p. 30). *one celebrated man*. Samuel Taylor Coleridge.

4 (p. 31). The names thus left blank in the 1821 version of the *Confessions* were, except for one, filled in by De Quincey in the 1856 version. The names were William Wilberforce (1759–1833, leader of the movement for the abolition of slavery); Isaac Milner (1750–1820, Dean of Carlisle and President of Queen's College, Cambridge; a confirmed addict who took 8½ grains of opium every six hours); Thomas first Lord Erskine (1750–1823, Lord Chancellor; not an opium eater – De Quincey was misinformed about him); Henry Addington (1790–1870, diplomatist and eventually Permanent Under-Secretary for Foreign Affairs); and Samuel Taylor Coleridge. For De Quincey's account of Coleridge's opium addiction, see Appendix A and B.III. By 1856 De Quincey had forgotten whom he had meant to indicate in 1821 by 'Mr ——, the philosopher'. It is possible that this was James Mackintosh, an eminent lawyer and writer on philosophical and literary topics, who was an opium eater; though as he was knighted in 1803, it would be odd for De Quincey to refer to him as 'Mr ——' when writing in 1821.

5 (p. 31). *one, two, or three grains*. 25 drops of laudanum equalled one grain of opium. De Quincey usually quoted his dosage in drops.

6 (p. 32). *Mead*. Dr Richard Mead (1673–1754). Physician at St Thomas's Hospital. His patients included George I and Isaac Newton.

7 (p. 32). φωνάντα συνετοισι=speaking to the wise.

8 (p. 32). *the Turks*. Eighteenth-century travellers' tales such as the Baron de Tott's *Memoirs of the Turks and the Tartars* had represented Constantinople as the world capital of opium-eating.

9 (p. 32). In 1856 De Quincey changed this to 'I do not at all concur'.

10 (p. 33). *day-dreams or night-dreams*. De Quincey uses the word 'dreams' to cover not only dreams of sleep but also the semi-conscious reveries which opium induces, specially in the early stages of addiction.

11 (p. 33). *Humani nihil à se alienum putat*=he deems nothing that is human foreign to him.

## Notes

12 (p. 34). *David Ricardo.* 1772–1823, economist, author of *Principles of Political Economy and Taxation.*

13 (p. 34). *A third exception.* Probably William Hazlitt (1778–1830), essayist and literary and art critic, who was privately educated and whose works included a philosophical study, *The Principles of Human Action.* He and De Quincey were acquainted.

14 (p. 34). *only one.* John Wilson (1785–1854), poet and critic, contributor to *Blackwood's* under the name of Christopher North, elected Professor of Moral Philosophy, Edinburgh, in 1820. A lifelong friend of De Quincey's.

15 (p. 35). *one of my masters.* Dr Morgan, Headmaster of Bath Grammar School, where De Quincey was sent when he was eleven.

16 (p. 36). *a blockhead.* The Rev. Edward Spencer, Rector of Winkfield and headmaster of a private school there.

17 (p. 36). *a respectable scholar.* Charles Lawson, Headmaster of Manchester Grammar School. His appointment was in the gift of Brasenose College, Oxford.

18 (p. 36). *Archididascalus*=Headmaster.

19 (p. 37). *a woman of high rank.* Lady Carbery, a friend of De Quincey's family.

20 (p. 37). *when I came to leave* ——. Manchester Grammar School.

21 (p. 38). *the ancient towers of* ——. The fifteenth-century Church of St Mary, Manchester, founded for a college of canons, did not become a cathedral until 1848. The 'ancient towers' which De Quincey saw in 1802 have since been reconstructed.

22 (p. 39). *a picture of the lovely* ——. A copy of a Van Dyck portrait of a woman, reported to have been a benefactress of Manchester Grammar School or of Brasenose College.

23 (p. 40). *contretems.* Obsolete spelling of *contretemps*=unexpected mishap.

24 (p. 40). *the Seven Sleepers.* A legend of seven Early Christians who took refuge in a mountain cave from the persecution of the Emperor Decius, and slept for three hundred years.

25 (p. 40). *étourderie*=giddiness.

26 (p. 40). *on other personal accounts.* That is, to make the acquaintance of Wordsworth (see Appendix B.VIII).

27 (p. 40). *a small neat house in B*—. Bangor.

28 (p. 41). *noli me tangere*=touch me not. οι πολλοι=the many, the common people.

29 (p. 41). *the Bishop of* ——. Dr Cleaver, Bishop of Bangor and Principal of Brasenose College, Oxford.

30 (p. 44). *prize-money.* At this time, and up to the First World

217

War, all members of the crew of a war-ship received a proportionate share of the value of a captured enemy ship.

31 (p. 44). This anecdote may be an unconscious plagiarism of a well-known reminiscence by the novelist Samuel Richardson, describing how as a boy he used to write love-letters for young girls, rather than an actual experience of De Quincey's. See Mrs Barbauld's *Life of Richardson*, vol. i, pp. 39–40.

32 (p. 45). *Sapphics or Alcaics*. Metres in Greek poetry, associated with Sappho of Lesbos and Alcaeus of Mytilene.

33 (p. 45). *Mr Shelley*. Perhaps a reference to Shelley's *Revolt of Islam*, which had been sent to De Quincey for review three years earlier.

34 (p. 47). *Mr* ——. The attorney Brunell (see Appendix B.XVI).

35 (p. 49). *My partner in wretchedness*. De Quincey's description of this child is believed to have inspired Dickens's character 'The Marchioness' in his novel *The Old Curiosity Shop*.

36 (p. 49). *Sine Cerere*. 'Sine Cerere et Libero friget Venus'=Without bread and wine lust grows cold.

37 (p. 50). *more Socratico*=in the Socratic manner.

38 (p. 54). *a Jew named D*——. In the revised *Confessions* De Quincey gave this man's name as Dell and said that 'like all the other Jews with whom I have had negotiations, he was frank and honourable in his mode of conducting business. What he promised, he performed; and if his terms were high, as naturally they could not but be, to cover his risks, he avowed them from the first.' De Quincey always sympathized with Jews, as a persecuted people, some of the 'pariahs' to whom he felt so psychologically akin.

39 (p. 55). *the second son of* ——. Thomas Quincey.

40 (p. 55). *the Earl of* ——. Lord Altamont, a schoolfellow of De Quincey's at Bath, with whom he spent a summer in Ireland in 1800. Altamont's father, the Marquess of Sligo, owned much landed property in the counties of Mayo and Sligo.

41 (p. 58). *the Gloucester coffee-house*. A regular stop for the mail-coaches from London to the West Country.

42 (p. 60). *Lord* ——. Altamont.

43 (p. 61). *Pote's*. A bookseller in Eton High Street.

44 (p. 61). *the University of* ——. Jesus College, Cambridge.

45 (p. 61). *Ibi omnis effusus labor*=Here was all my labour wasted!

46 (p. 61). *the Earl of D*——. The second Earl of Desart. De Quincey had met him with Lord Altamont, whose cousin he was. At the time of De Quincey's visit to Eton he was still Viscount Castle Cuffe; he succeeded to the Earldom in 1804.

## Notes

47 (p. 62). *the story about Otway.* Thomas Otway (1652–85), author of *Venice Preserved* and other plays. There is a questionable legend that, when hiding from his creditors in an inn on Tower Hill, he was actually starving when a stranger's alms enabled him to buy a roll of bread, but he was choked to death by the first mouthful that he took.

48 (p. 63). *those of ——.* Of Altamont, heir to £70,000 a year.

49 (p. 68). *the road to the north, and therefore to ——.* To Grasmere, where Wordsworth then lived.

50 (p. 68). *beloved M.* His wife, Margaret.

51 (p. 69). *I am again in London.* De Quincey refers to the moment in 1821 when he was actually writing this passage.

52 (p. 69). *mistress of that very house.* When the Wordsworths left Dove Cottage, De Quincey became its tenant.

53 (p. 70). *the stately Pantheon.* An elaborately decorated building with several halls where public balls were given. The quotation is from Wordsworth's poem *Power of Music.*

54 (p. 71). *the tincture of opium.* De Quincey almost always took his opium in the form of laudanum, tincture of opium in alcohol, as did most addicts in the early nineteenth century.

55 (p. 72). φαρμακον νήπνθες =soothing drug.

56 (p. 72). *antimercurial.* De Quincey is punning on the double meaning of 'mercurial', which could mean both a sprightly volatile temperament and a purgative medicine such as calomel. 'Antimercurial' in this passage therefore means grave, or solemn, but also, like opium, constipating in its effects.

57 (p. 72). *on Tuesday and Saturday.* The days on which the official *Gazette* was published, in which lists of those who had gone bankrupt were announced.

58 (p. 73). *meo periculo*=at my risk.

59 (p. 74). *ponderibus librata suis*=balanced by its own equilibrium.

60 (p. 75). *the only member.* In 1856 De Quincey altered this to read 'of which I acknowledge myself to be the Pope'. By then there were all too many other 'members'.

61 (p. 75). *a surgeon.* Probably Dr Abernethy, who was himself an opium eater, and who treated both Coleridge and De Quincey (see Appendix B.XIX).

62 (p. 77). *The late Duke of ——.* Charles eleventh Duke of Norfolk (1746–1815).

63 (p. 78). *Grassini.* Giuseppina Grassini (1773–1850), operatic contralto, who performed in London in 1804–6. She was beautiful and a good actress as well as a fine singer, and had a peculiar quality of

voice which some people disliked but others found thrilling. She was rumoured to have been the mistress of both Napoleon and Wellington.

64 (p. 78). *Twelfth Night*. 'If music be the food of love . . .' (I.i.i–7); perhaps also II. iv.

65 (p. 78). *Religio Medici*. De Quincey was a great admirer of Sir Thomas Browne and was much influenced by his style. The passage here referred to is the one on harmony in Part II of *Religio Medici*.

66 (p. 79). *Weld the traveller*. Isaac Weld (1774–1856), writer and illustrator of travel books, notably *Travels through the States of North America and the Provinces of Upper and Lower Canada During the Years 1795, 1796 and 1797*.

67 (p. 79). *Marinus in his life of Proclus*. Proclus (412–485), a Neo-Platonist philosopher. Marinus, a disciple of Proclus, whose biography he wrote.

68 (p. 82). *Trophonius*. A legendary architect of Ancient Greece, who was swallowed up by the earth.

69 (p. 82). *the great town of L—*. Liverpool. De Quincey often spent holidays in lodgings at Everton, near Liverpool.

70 (p. 82). *Behmenism, quietism, &c.* Types of mysticism practised by Jakob Boehme (1575–1624), a German visionary, and the Quietists, who included Miguel de Molinos (1627–96), Madame de Guyon (1648–1717), Fénelon (1651–1715) and others in France, Italy and Holland in the seventeenth century.

71 (p. 82). *Sir H. Vane*. Sir Henry Vane the Younger (1613–62), statesman and author, executed as a regicide after the Restoration of Charles II. Author of *The Retired Man's Meditations, Of Love of God and Union with God* and other contemplative works.

72 (p. 83). *Oh! just, subtle, and mighty opium!* De Quincey borrowed this phrase from Sir Walter Ralegh's apostrophe 'O eloquent, just and mightie Death !' in his *History of the World*, chapter X, 'Of the Fall of Empires'.

73 (p. 83). *Hekatómpylos*=the hundred-gated. Used of Egyptian Thebes, as opposed to the seven-gated Grecian Thebes. Egyptian Thebes was one of the sources of opium, which was sometimes called thebaicum.

74 (p. 85). *Kant, Fichte, Schelling, &c.* Immanuel Kant (1724–1804), J. G. Fichte (1762–1814), F. W. J. Schelling (1775–1854), the leading German philosophers of the eighteenth and early nineteenth centuries. De Quincey's studies up to the time that he wrote the *Confessions* were mainly in German philosophy; he intended to write

a master-work on philosophy himself. One of his best-known later articles was 'The Last Days of Immanuel Kant'.

75 (p. 85). *honi soit qui mal y pense*=Shame be on him that thinks evil. The motto of the Most Noble Order of the Garter, founded by Edward III in the middle of the fourteenth century.

76 (p. 85). X.Y.Z. The signature which De Quincey used for the *Confessions* and other early anonymous articles.

77 (p. 85). *Custos Rotulorum*=Keeper of the Rolls.

78 (p. 85). *ladies in the straw*. In childbed.

79 (p. 86). *Anastasius*. See De Quincey's note on page 75. *Anastasius* was a novel by Thomas Hope (1774–1851).

80 (p. 86). *Dr Buchan*. See De Quincey's note on page 73.

81 (p. 86). *a very melancholy event*. The death of the Wordsworths' daughter Kate, a child of whom De Quincey was passionately fond.

82 (p. 87). *à force d'ennuyer*=by being a bore. *pandiculation*=yawning.

83 (p. 87). *Eudæmonist*=a pursuer of happiness.

84 (p. 87). *Stoic*. The philosophy of Zeno (340–260 B.C.), who taught that the will could control the passions and enable men to rise above pleasure and pain. He lectured in the Stoa (porch) at Athens, from which his followers derived their name.

85 (p. 88). *Eclectic*=choosing elements from different systems of philosophy.

86 (p. 88). *Ramadan*. Period of fasting in the ninth month of the Moslem year.

87 (p. 89). $\nu\nu\chi\theta\eta\mu\varepsilon\varrho\sigma\nu$=twenty-four hours.

88 (p. 90). *The servant*. Barbara Lewthwaite, subject of Wordsworth's poem *The Pet-Lamb*.

89 (p. 91). *Adelung*. Jean Christophe Adelung (1732–1806), German philologist, author of *Mithridate or the Universal Table of Languages, with the Lord's Prayer in 500 Dialects*.

90 (p. 92). *intercalary year*. A year in which a day has been inserted to harmonize it with the solar year. De Quincey uses the phrase here in the sense of an extra, or bonus.

91 (p. 93). *hydrophobia*. De Quincey added in 1856 that the man who inoculated himself with hydrophobia was a surgeon at Brighton, but did not give his name.

92 (p. 93). *a cottage*. Dove Cottage, Grasmere.

93 (p. 94). *Mr ——*. Thomas Clarkson, a leader of the movement for the abolition of slavery. De Quincey inserted his name in 1856.

94 (p. 94). *fee-simple*. Freehold, full ownership.

## Notes

95 (p. 94). *St Thomas's day.* 21 December, the longest night of the year.

96 (p. 94). *Dr Johnson . . . Jonas Hanway.* The *bellum internecinum* (mutually destructive war) was an exchange of published letters after Dr Johnson had reviewed unfavourably a work by Jonas Hanway (1712–86), a traveller and social reformer.

97 (p. 97). *the hands.* Those of his wife.

98 (p. 98). *My studies have now long been interrupted.* De Quincey is using the historic present; 'now' is 1817, though he probably wrote this passage in 1821. It may, however, have been one of the already written passages which he had in hand when he started writing the *Confessions* (see Introduction).

99 (p. 98). —— *reads vilely; and Mrs* ——. The actor John Philip Kemble and his sister, the actress Sarah Siddons. De Quincey filled in the names in 1856; he also added 'Neither Coleridge nor Southey is a good reader of verse. Southey is admirable in almost all things, but not in this. Both he and Coleridge read as if crying, or at least wailing lugubriously.'

100 (p. 99). *W—'s poems.* Wordsworth's; 'M.' is Margaret de Quincey; the young lady may have been Dorothy Wordsworth, but the Wordsworths had more or less broken off relations with the De Quinceys at this time.

101 (p. 99). *De Emendatione Humani Intellectus.* Baruch Spinoza (1632–77), Dutch philosopher. His unfinished work was on the correction of the human intellect.

102 (p. 100). *a friend . . . sent me Mr Ricardo's book.* David Ricardo (1772–1823), economist. His *Principles of Political Economy and Taxation* was published in 1817, and was sent by John Wilson to De Quincey for review in *Blackwood's.*

103 (p. 101). *Prolegomena*=introductory remarks. This work of De Quincey's was not completed and published till many years later.

104 (p. 102). *a state of eye.* These patterns seen when the eyes are closed are now known as hypnagogic visions.

105 (p. 105). *crimson tunic.* The signal for battle. *alalagmos.* Collective word for the Roman war-cries 'Alála, Alála!'

106 (p. 105). *Piranesi.* Giovanni Battista Piranesi (1720–78), engraver. The plates which De Quincey calls his 'Dreams' were in fact his 'Carceri d'Invenzione' (Imaginary Prisons), which show huge classical (not Gothic, as De Quincey thought) dungeons.

107 (p. 106). *a great modern poet.* Wordsworth, in *The Excursion,* Book II (see Appendix B.XXIV).

108 (p. 107). *Fuseli.* Henry Fuseli (1741–1825), historical and fan-

tastic painter, specializing in witches and apparitions. Of Swiss origin, but lived in England for much of his life.

109 (p. 107). *Shadwell*. Thomas Shadwell (1642–92), poet laureate and author of *The Squire of Alsatia*, *Epsom Wells* and other plays. A confirmed opium addict.

110 (p. 107). *the last Lord Orford*. Horace Walpole.

111 (p. 108). *some part of my London life*. In 1856 De Quincey made this more specific by inserting that it was 'the searching for Ann amongst fluctuating crowds' which caused this nightmare of watching faces.

112 (p. 108). *officina gentium*=manufactory of nations.

113 (p. 110). *cæteris paribus*=other things being equal.

114 (p. 111). *a child*. Kate Wordsworth.

115 (p. 112). *Coronation Anthem*. Composed by Handel for the Coronation of George II in 1727.

116 (p. 113). *the incestuous mother*. Sin, daughter of Satan, by whom she bore a child, Death. Milton, *Paradise Lost*, Book II, lines 787–9.

117 (p. 115). *Jeremy Taylor*. In 1856 De Quincey corrected this; the reference was to an essay on *Death* by Bacon.

Notes to Appendix A

118 (p. 118). *Sheffield Iris*. Formerly the *Sheffield Register*, an extreme reformist newspaper which modified its politics and changed its name when its editor was prosecuted and fled to America.

119 (p. 118). *Mr Montgomery*. James Montgomery (1771–1854), poet, hymn-writer, journalist, editor of the *Sheffield Iris*.

120 (p. 120). *my only companion*. His wife.

121 (p. 120). *Medical Intelligencer*. A short-lived periodical, published only from 1820–23.

122 (p. 123). *sternutation*=sneezing.

123 (p. 124). *Fox-ghyll*. The small house to which the De Quinceys moved when the family grew too large for Dove Cottage.

124 (p. 124). *Swift's Strulbrugs*. Immortals occasionally born among a normal population, whose miserable endless senility Swift describes in *Gulliver's Travels*, 'A Voyage to Laputa', chapter X.

125 (p. 129). *Amreeta*=immortal, ambrosial.

126 (p. 131). *the hulks*. Old ships used as prisons.

127 (p. 131). *causa occasionalis*=occasional cause, i.e. some circumstance preceding an effect which, without being the real cause, becomes the agent of the action of the efficient cause. *causa sine qua*

*non*=cause without which (an effect would) not (have occurred), i.e. efficient cause.

128 (p. 132). *camera obscura*. An apparatus in which images of landscapes and surrounding objects, received through a double convex glass, are projected onto a white surface in a darkened room.

129 (p. 133). *praemissis praemittendis*=having first taken into account any relevant considerations. De Quincey is making again the point that his excessive opium-taking caused him to dream only because of other pre-existing considerations.

## Notes to Appendix B

130 (p. 135). *tædium vitæ*=weariness of life.

131 (p. 141). *A letter of his*. Published by James Gillman in his *Life of S. T. Coleridge*, 1838. Coleridge claimed in this letter, as in many others, that he himself had never taken opium in search of pleasurable sensations, but only as an anodyne against pain; he added that De Quincey, in spite of warnings from Coleridge, willingly gave himself up to the pleasures of opium, and seduced others to follow his example.

132 (p. 141). *A citizen of Sybaris or Daphne*. The cities of Sybaris, near the Gulf of Taranto in Southern Italy, and Daphne, near Antioch in Syria, were classical bywords for the luxury of their inhabitants.

133 (p. 144). *more than once*. Although De Quincey was never able to renounce opium altogether, he succeeded four times (in 1816, 1820, 1822 and 1844) in greatly reducing his dosage from the enormous quantities which he had been taking in the immediately previous years.

134 (p. 144). *Irasque leonum Vincla recusantum*=the rage of lions fretting against their chains. Virgil, *Aeneid* VII. 16.

135 (p. 150). *averruncation*=pruning.

136 (p. 150). *palæstra*=wrestling-school.

137 (p. 150). *Isaac Barrow or Jeremy Taylor*. Barrow (1630–77), a Cambridge scholar who became Master of Trinity and a famous preacher. Taylor (1613–67), Bishop of Down and of Dromore, author of *Holy Living* and *Holy Dying*. De Quincey revered Taylor's style and often modelled his own on it.

138 (p. 151). *Richard Baxter*. Baxter (1615–91) a Presbyterian divine, took the Parliamentary side in the Civil War and suffered imprisonment and fines after the Restoration.

139 (p. 151). *the Whitfield of the seventeenth century – the Leuconomos of Cowper*. George Whitefield (1714–70), leader of the Cal-

vinistic Methodists, famous in England and America for his powerful preaching. The name is pronounced Whitfield, hence de Quincey's spelling. 'Leuconomos' (white pasture) was Cowper's code name for Whitefield –

> 'Leuconomos (beneath well-sounding Greek
> I slur a name a poet must not speak)'.
>
> *Hope* 11, 554–5

140 (p. 152). *Curtius.* When in 362 B.C. a chasm appeared in the Roman forum, and the soothsayers declared that it could only be filled by throwing Rome's greatest treasure into it, Mettius Curtius – declaring rather complacently that Rome had no greater treasure than a brave citizen – leapt on horseback into the gulf, which then closed over him.

141 (p. 152). *Algernon Sidney.* Sidney (1622–83) took the Parliamentary side in the Civil War and was executed for complicity in the Rye House Plot against Charles II.

142 (p. 152). *armilustrium*=a muster, or review, of military forces.

143 (p. 158). *Dr Byrom.* Byrom (1692–1763), Fellow of Trinity College, Cambridge, teacher of shorthand and a minor poet.

144 (p. 159). *impluvium*=a courtyard into which rain drains from the roof.

145 (p. 160). *plagosus Orbilius.* A Roman grammarian notorious for flogging (Horace, *Epistles* II.i.71).

146 (p. 161). *the society of accomplished women.* De Quincey had just been staying with the bookish Lady Carbery.

147 (p. 162). *Dr Cooke Taylor.* William Cooke-Taylor (1800–1849), historian, journalist and pamphleteer.

148 (p. 165). *four weeks.* In fact De Quincey had spent all May and most of June 1802 on holiday at Everton.

149 (p. 166). *an apothecary.* Medical men were then divided into physicians and surgeons, who were qualified by a hospital course, and apothecaries whose prime function was the dispensing of medicines, but who also carried out the functions of general practitioners in many places.

150 (p. 166). *calomel or blue pill.* Both preparations of mercury, widely used as purgatives in the early nineteenth century.

151 (p. 170). *Anne Radcliffe.* Mrs Radcliffe (1764–1823), author of *Observations during a Tour to the Lakes of Lancashire, Westmorland and Cumberland*, included in her *Journey through Holland and the Western Frontier of Germany* (1795). Best known for her novels *The Mysteries of Udolpho*, *The Italian* and *The Romance of the Forest.*

## Notes

152 (p. 170). *the landscape painters.* The English depicters of the Lake District best known to De Quincey were probably William Gilpin (1724–1804), in his illustrated *Tour of the Lakes*; Francis Towne (1740–1816), who did drawings of Ambleside and Grasmere; John Crome (1768–1821), whose *Slate Quarries*, inspired by a visit to the Lake District in 1802, perfectly expresses the stern simplicity and conflict described by De Quincey.

153 (p. 171). *as to me only.* De Quincey made many claims to have been the earliest recognizer of Wordsworth's genius. 'Was I then, in July 1802, really quoting from Wordsworth? Yes, reader; and I only in all Europe,' he exclaimed in the revised *Confessions*. In a diary kept in 1803, the year after his flight from school, he included Wordsworth in a list of the twelve greatest English poets, and in the same year he wrote a long admiring letter to the poet. His claim to have been a very early admirer of Wordsworth is therefore justified, though he was not as unique in his admiration as he later boasted.

154 (p. 172). *Pausanias.* Second century A.D. traveller and geographer, author of an *Itinerary of Greece.*

155 (p. 172). *Windsor.* A reference to Shakespeare's *Merry Wives of Windsor*, Act V Scene V.

156 (p. 173). *rhabdomancy*=rod-magic, i.e. water-divining, hence divination in general. De Quincey explained this in an immense footnote, here omitted.

157 (p. 175). *a friend of my own age.* Lord Westport. The visit to Saint Paul's took place in 1800.

158 (p. 177). *my petticoats.* Then, and throughout much of the nineteenth century, boys as well as girls wore skirts till they were five or six.

159 (p. 179). *my bronzed Bengal uncle.* Mrs de Quincey's brother, Colonel Thomas Penson, who often helped De Quincey with money later on.

160 (p. 181). *My next brother.* Richard de Quincey, known as 'Pink' because of his girlish good looks.

161 (p. 182). *Hercynian forest.* The wooded mountains of Central Germany.

162 (p. 185). σιντροφον ομμα=familiar eye.

163 (p. 187). *Thugs.* An Indian fraternity devoted to robbery and murder. De Quincey was fascinated all his life by accounts of the Thugs.

164 (p. 188). *cantabit vacuus coram latrone viator*=a careless traveller will sing in the face of a robber.

226

165 (p. 190). *Richter*. Johann Paul Friedrich Richter (1763–1825), generally known as Jean-Paul, German novelist and fantasist; his works include *Hesperus* and *Titan*. De Quincey later published translations of some of Richter's works and was much influenced by him.

166 (p. 193). *Io*. A Greek princess beloved of Zeus and by him changed into a heifer for fear of the jealousy of Hera, who then tormented her by a gadfly (oestros) which drove her from country to country.

167 (p. 195). *two orchestras*. Used in the original Greek sense of 'orchestra' as the platform on which the chorus stood.

168 (p. 198). *officina diplomatum*=manufactory of legal documents.

169 (p. 209). *perihelion . . . aphelion*. Points of a planet's orbit nearest to and furthest from the sun.

170 (p. 210). *spontaneous combustion*. Dickens made grisly use of this popular belief in his novel *Bleak House*, in which Krook, the rag and bottle man, meets his end in this way.

171 (p. 211). *euthanasy*. Anglicized form of euthanasia, an easy way of dying.

172 (p. 212). *Middy*=midshipman. *griffin*=young European arriving in India for the first time.

# MORE ABOUT PENGUINS
# AND PELICANS

For further information about books available from Penguins please write to Dept EP, Penguin Books Ltd, Harmondsworth, Middlesex UB7 0DA.

In the U.S.A.: For a complete list of books available from Penguins in the United States write to Dept CS, Penguin Books, 625 Madison Avenue, New York, New York 10022.

In Canada: For a complete list of books available from Penguins in Canada write to Penguin Books Canada Ltd, 2801 John Street, Markham, Ontario L3R 1B4.

In Australia: For a complete list of books available from Penguins in Australia write to the Marketing Department, Penguin Books Australia Ltd, P.O. Box 257, Ringwood, Victoria 3134.

## *Thomas De Quincey*

## RECOLLECTIONS OF THE LAKES AND THE LAKE POETS

### EDITED BY DAVID WRIGHT

Thomas De Quincey, best known perhaps as the author of *Confessions of an English Opium-Eater*, wrote most of the work in this volume for *Tait's Magazine* between 1834 and 1840. It is immensely readable and alive – an anecdotal, conversational, contemporaneous portrait and account of Grasmere, Wordsworth, Coleridge and Southey, and so near the bone that Wordsworth and his family would have nothing further to do with De Quincey after it appeared. Within this first-hand biographical/critical discussion of the lives and works of these poets, De Quincey's life of Wordsworth may still be the best we have.

This edition contains the most complete collection of De Quincey's Lake papers to appear in a single volume and the text used here is that of the original articles.

## *Daniel Defoe*

## A TOUR THROUGH THE WHOLE ISLAND OF GREAT BRITAIN

### EDITED BY PAT ROGERS

Defoe's *Tour* (1724–26) was described by G. M. Trevelyan as 'a treasure indeed' and by Dorothy George as 'far the best authority for early eighteenth-century England'. But the *Tour* is something more than an invaluable source of social and economic history: Defoe's unfailing sense of process and of the mutability of things raises the work to the level of imaginative literature. Along with his remarkable gift for observation and for the telling anecdote and his truly poetic vision, Defoe brought to the tradition of travel-writing a lifetime's experience as businessman, soldier, economic journalist and spy.

# THE PENGUIN ENGLISH LIBRARY

*A Selection*

James Boswell
THE LIFE OF JOHNSON
*Edited by Christopher Hibbert*

Robert Louis Stevenson
DR JEKYLL AND MR HYDE AND OTHER STORIES
*Edited by Jenni Calder*

George Eliot
ADAM BEDE
*Edited by Stephen Gill*

THE MILL ON THE FLOSS
*Edited by A. S. Byatt*

Anne Brontë
THE TENANT OF WILDFELL HALL
*Edited by Winifred Gérin*

Thomas Hardy
THE DISTRACTED PREACHER AND OTHER TALES
*Edited by Susan Hill*

Charlotte Brontë
VILLETTE
*Edited by Mark Lilly with an introduction by Tony Tanner*